The Turning Point for the Teaching Profession

A revolution is happening in education, with leaders and teachers now asked to focus on learning, to develop collaborative teams to impact on students, to use and raise professional standards, and to identify and esteem expertise in our profession. With new demands relating to technological advances, changing demographics, internationalism, and the inclusion of 'twenty-first-century skills,' there is pressure on schools to deliver greater and deeper success with more students.

The Turning Point aims to present the factors needed to affect real change for school systems, in classrooms, and in the teaching profession by:

- Arguing for the establishment of teaching as a true 'profession' alongside areas such as medicine or law.
- Identifying the expertise fundamental to meeting the demands of schools.
- Elaborating on evaluative thinking and clinical practice as the basis of this new profession.
- Outlining core levers of change to show how teachers can have profound impacts on educational, medical, and social dimensions of students.

This book is essential reading for teachers, school leaders, education policymakers, teacher candidates, and teacher educators. Those working in affiliated professions, such as adolescent psychologists and health workers, will also find aspects of the book relevant to their work.

Field Rickards was Dean of Melbourne Graduate School of Education for 13 years, and in that time led a revolution of its teacher education program, which moved from the traditional model to one based on clinical practice and evaluative thinking. He was also a member of the Australian Government task force in 2015 (Classroom Ready) that has led to major transformations in teacher education across Australia.

John Hattie is Laureate Professor at MGSE and has a background in measurement and research design. He wrote a series of books based on the Visible Learning® research that have now sold over a million copies and he is chair of the Australian Institute for Teaching and School Leadership, which has the major responsibility for implementing the Classroom Ready recommendations.

Catherine Reid has a long career as a teacher and teacher educator. For more than a decade, she designed and implemented programs in language and literacy education, university-school partnerships, and clinical teaching at the Melbourne Graduate School of Education.

The Turning Point for the Teaching Profession

Growing Expertise and Evaluative Thinking

Field Rickards, John Hattie and Catherine Reid

LONDON AND NEW YORK

First published 2021
by Routledge
2 Park Square, Milton Park, Abingdon, Oxon OX14 4RN

and by Routledge
52 Vanderbilt Avenue, New York, NY 10017

Routledge is an imprint of the Taylor & Francis Group, an informa business

© 2021 Field Rickards, John Hattie and Catherine Reid

The right of Field Rickards, John Hattie, and Catherine Reid to be identified as authors of this work has been asserted by them in accordance with sections 77 and 78 of the Copyright, Designs and Patents Act 1988.

All rights reserved. No part of this book may be reprinted or reproduced or utilized in any form or by any electronic, mechanical, or other means, now known or hereafter invented, including photocopying and recording, or in any information storage or retrieval system, without permission in writing from the publishers.

Trademark notice: Product or corporate names may be trademarks or registered trademarks, and are used only for identification and explanation without intent to infringe.

British Library Cataloguing-in-Publication Data
A catalogue record for this book is available from the British Library

Library of Congress Cataloging-in-Publication Data
Names: Rickards, Field, author. | Hattie, John, author. | Reid, Catherine (Catherine Frances), author.
Title: The turning point for the teaching profession : growing expertise and evaluative thinking / Field Rickards, John Hattie & Catherine Reid.
Description: Abingdon, Oxon ; New York, NY : Routledge, 2021. | Includes bibliographical references and index. |
Identifiers: LCCN 2020024493 | ISBN 9780367531850 (hardback) | ISBN 9780367531867 (paperback) | ISBN 9781003080831 (ebook)
Subjects: LCSH: Teaching. | Teachers--Professional relationships. | Teachers--In-service training. | Educational change.
Classification: LCC LB1025.3 .R537 2021 | DDC 371.102--dc23
LC record available at https://lccn.loc.gov/2020024493

ISBN: 978-0-367-53185-0 (hbk)
ISBN: 978-0-367-53186-7 (pbk)
ISBN: 978-1-003-08083-1 (ebk)

Typeset in Bembo
by SPi Global, India

Contents

Introduction vii
Acknowledgments xv

Part I   The turning point   1

1   Setting the scene   3

Part II   The nature of teacher expertise   15

2   Teacher expertise and the centrality of the student   17

3   The work and expertise of the teacher: The six key questions   31

4   The deep knowledge base of teaching   53

5   The essence of the teaching profession: Evaluative thinking   63

Part III   Implications for the profession   77

6   Evaluative thinking in the professions   79

7   Teacher education for a clinical profession   92

| 8 | A revolution of teaching and schooling | 121 |
| 9 | Conclusions | 144 |

References 154
Index 171

Introduction

The world has experienced one of the most major disruptions to schooling due to the COVID-19 pandemic. Teachers have shown their incredible creativity and versatility with the adaptions they have made to how schools operate. What a time to esteem the teaching profession. Sadly, as schools return to normal routines, we will all forget that teachers have unique and valuable expertise and we will resume debates about topics which matter less, such as tinkering with timetables, hassling about homework, and deciding whether schools should be private or public. A major aim of this book is to take a deep-dive into what it means to be a profession, how expertise and evaluative thinking are core to this notion of being a profession, and to illustrate that we already have a high percentage of teachers with these attributes and who are able to turn teaching from being seen as a craft into an esteemed profession based on expertise.

The current model of teaching and schools has been reasonably constant for 150 years, but the demands on teachers and schools over the past few decades have been increasing at a fast pace. Now, many more students are classified as requiring specific help, there is an increase in the variability of the backgrounds of the students, the content to be covered seems to be growing, accountability is everywhere, social and emotional learning has been added to the duties, and through the power of the internet, the boundaries between home and school have been blurred. The traditional career structure is cracking, with many choosing either not to come into our profession, coming into the profession at a much older age, or not wanting to move from the classroom to leadership positions. The bureaucracy, responsible for writing policy and accountability models, and pushing pet theories into schools, is growing at a faster pace and is often comprised of those with little or distant classroom experience.

We are indeed at a time where we may need to turn the profession to ask some critical questions about its purpose, its base of expertise, and its future.

Hence, the title of the book—*The Turning Point for the Teaching Profession*.

Introduction

We make the case for this turning point, beginning with introductory remarks setting the scene in Part I.

The argument is that expertise, specifically the notion of evaluative thinking, needs to be at the core of the profession. It always has been, we argue, but highlighting this depth of thinking and action—along with other core values about reciprocity, caring, respect, content knowledge, and others—is what demarcates our profession, is worth fighting for, and can be used to esteem teaching. We delve more deeply into these ideas about the nature of expertise in Part II.

When visiting schools and classrooms, it does not take long to be impressed with the excellence that is all around us. Indeed, for the three of us, this witnessing of excellence is a major motivator to continue in and be proud of being called 'a teacher.' Part III discusses some more practical illustrations of this evaluative thinking in action. We look at what it means to be part of a profession, both in teaching and in other fields, and how to translate the core notions into teacher education programs. We have 10 years of experience living and breathing daily in a teacher education program that has grappled with implementing evaluative thinking. Some have been critical of this work, most often because of terminology disputes. They do not like terms like 'clinical teaching,' which is often used as a label—and we share some of the misinterpretations this label can imply—but so often the criticism is not about what is enacted but what the critics fear is being enacted. There is no suggestion that the terms 'clinical' or 'evaluative thinking' imply cold or dispassionate practice, or disease or deficit, nor are data used without interrogation to run the class or system (not that this is what 'clinical' means in a medical setting— where compassion, values, care, and the welcoming of second opinions are dominant).

The call is for a revolution, or at least a reboot to our profession. This is an optimal time for this to occur, but we will need to take a deep breath, critically reflect about where we want to be, how we want to grow, how we want to be seen by our colleagues, how to attract new people into our profession, and how we want to be seen, valued, and resourced by parents, voters, and politicians.

The three of us have come to these views from quite different career trajectories: one from being a senior leader of teacher education; one more immersed in research; and one with her feet in the classrooms of schools and tertiary institutions. Some of the highlights of our last ten years have been coming to work every day with like-minded colleagues and critics, building a program based on evaluative thinking and developing expertise. Here is our story.

Field Rickards

In 1974, I was teaching at the University of Melbourne as the inaugural director of the university's graduate program in audiology. It was a clinical program that developed clinical thinking by linking the basic and clinical sciences with clinical practice. One of the courses was acoustics, an important basic science that underpins many dimensions in the field of audiology. As a teacher, I was passionate about the content: simple and complex tones, noise, resonance, auditory perception, speech acoustics, room acoustics, and other topics. Each is fundamental in the measurement of hearing, the fitting of hearing aids, aural rehabilitation, and education of the deaf, and taught with direct application to the field of audiology and deafness. The concepts presented in this course, along with the other basic and clinical sciences, underpinned all clinical thinking when managing people with hearing loss. The students were all graduates from a range of disciplines including science, engineering, linguistics, and psychology. The acoustics examination was straightforward and designed to assess the deep understandings of the class.

The examination results were typically bimodal. Distinction and high distinction for those who had developed a deep understanding of the topic, and a bare pass for those did not quite grasp the concepts. This is an excellent illustration of deep versus surface learning. What was wrong with my teaching? It became clear some years later that I was simply transmitting information. I was not allowing time for each student to transform the information into knowledge and understanding, or allowing enough time for me to 'diagnose' any misunderstandings of the 30 graduate students in the room. I was confusing teaching with the transmission of 'knowledge' from teacher to student. It took some years for me to understand that learning required an effort to make sense of information, which in turn may lead to the development of knowledge. The opportunity to make sense of the information and to develop the conceptual framework and thinking that underpins clinical practice happened in the clinic with patients. The job of teachers, increasingly, is to assist students in the process of sense-making. It is true that no longer the teacher, or the textbook, holds a monopoly. Instead, critically analyzing and comparing information from different sources becomes an important element in education, which in the end may lead to learning that is different from what students get from teaching through transmission.

The challenge for teachers is to deliberately move from the surface to the deep and cater for students throughout the range of development or performance. Teachers will always be confronted with considerable variation among the students in their classes. It is this reality that has produced the contemporary demand in many places for so-called 'personalized learning' to ensure that advanced students are stretched and that slower students are not routinely confronted with material that they cannot understand because they have not gained the knowledge on which it depends. Except that personalized learning methods have not been noted by their success. This is the challenge—if teachers are to meet the needs of individual learners, then they need more than the rhetoric of 'personalizing learning.' They need the skills to touch the learning lives of all students.

Teaching is a most complex and challenging profession. Teaching hearing impaired children is also a complex task, but in some sense, it is more contained than the general task of teaching in schools. Progress can be more specifically defined and monitored. Teachers' professional practice can be focused on individual students and based on clear evidence of a student's current performance and developmental need. All of this has provoked for me the questions of whether and how teaching more generally might be made evidence-based and learn from how hearing-impaired teachers use this evidence.

Over the years, I have come to know many expert teachers whose students achieved exceptional educational outcomes. One in particular was Professor Daniel Ling from Canada, an international expert on teaching deaf children spoken language. He wrote about enhancing learning in children with hearing loss. He introduced me to the notion of developmental progressions, evaluation, targeted teaching, formal and informal assessment.

I moved from the Faculty of Medicine to the Faculty of Education at the University of Melbourne in 1989 because I had become interested in how the children who were diagnosed at an early age and to whom we had granted hearing with a cochlear implant learned in their new environment. Then I became Dean of Education and had the opportunity to act on my observations of teacher education. It seemed that teacher education has increasingly been criticized for being out-of-date, out of touch with the 'real world,' and too focused on theory. A common belief that some people are just 'born to be teachers' has reinforced the idea that teacher education is an unnecessary burden on those whose natural progression into the classroom is disrupted by too much unnecessary academic work with no application in practice.

I have been challenged, as many of us have, by the assertion by Richard Elmore from Harvard that teaching is a profession without a practice. He says, by contrast, that, "Within a true profession, an individual does not have autonomy over its body of knowledge and its practice." There is a shared corpus around which initial and continuing professional development are organized. In education, it often seems to me that 'professionalism' is used to legitimate idiosyncrasy.

The introduction in 2008 of the 'Melbourne Model' (https://discover.unimelb.edu.au/about-melbourne/the-melbourne-model) moved all professional programs to graduate level, and this afforded an opportunity to rethink the our approach. The Master of Teaching degree was launched in 2008 as a creative response to a perceived need for change in teacher education. The general approach to teacher preparation has consisted of university coursework with limited, loosely connected professional experience or practice teaching. In my view, we have been recycling mediocrity for some time.

The MTeach is a paradigm shift that aims to develop a new generation of teachers, who will be interventionist practitioners, capable of using data to identify and meet the learning needs of individual learners—just like Daniel Ling. It does this through effective school partnerships and breaking away from 'forget all that stuff you heard at the university, I'll tell you all you need to know about teaching.' It is the model embraced in deaf education at the University of Melbourne for more than 30 years (more details are provided in Chapter 7), and the model which developed clinical expertise in audiology in the 1970 to 1980s. This book provides an opportunity to discuss these matters so critical to me, and in my development as audiologist and the Dean of Education.

Introduction

John Hattie

Growing up in a small provincial town in New Zealand in the 1950 to 1960s was a lesson in naivety. I never left the town till 15, there was no television to broaden horizons, and the main population and political issues were 'overseas' on another island. A major ambition was to enter a trade, and I began as a painter and paper hanger. Oh dear, there were few skills required and I did not have those, and it became clear that this was not a life destination, nor would this career allow any ventures outside the town. How to get out? I learnt that if you wanted to become a teacher, the government would pay a salary to train! So, apply, accepted, and off to Dunedin to see 'the big world.'

Every hour we had to sign the roll—every hour. At the end of the first year, I returned home for Christmas and received a letter informing me I had successfully won a scholarship to leave the teachers' college for two years and attend a university. But I do not recall having applied – it seems that I indeed did apply but thought it was the hourly roll call. Three years later, teachers' college training and a university degree behind, I taught at a middle school for a year. It was a wonderful experience, and I thoroughly enjoyed the year, hoped the students learnt something, and this experience led me to decide to stay in the business of being a teacher. But I had more scholarships to University, completed a Masters, then applied and was accepted for a PhD. My love was measurement and statistics and I was then supervised by one of the best factor analyst theorists in the world, Rod McDonald. He saw something in me I did not see in myself and he enabled me to learn so much from the best (and from his Ontario Institute for Studies in Education colleagues) such that it set my new career—teaching and researching in measurement.

Like Field, I was an outsider to teacher education. It was amazing how certain my colleagues were about how to educate new teachers and how different their answers were to this certainty. I saw micro-teaching, professional schools, depth in subject-matter knowledge, and so many variants. There was little, if any, evaluation, very few research studies on how best to educate new teachers, and strong opinions such that what seemed like a cottage industry ran schools of education. I was also, like Field, a Head of School of Education for 20-plus years in three universities and tried to bring a sense of research to teacher education, but it was a tough gig indeed.

In the late 1990s, I was appointed an advisor to the National Council for Accreditation of Teacher Education (NCATE) in the United States as it was moving from the more traditional to a standards-based approach to teacher education; at the same time I was part of the technical advisory group that was setting up the measurement of the National Board for Professional Teaching Standards (NBPTS) in the U.S. These two ventures allowed me more insight in the development of teachers, the power of research in this area, and see (based on good measurement) some stunning teacher education programs across the United States. The NBPTS was especially powerful, as it focused on the best. One of my first tasks was to analyses the hundreds of professional standards developed across the United States, and to review more than 100 videos of the best middle school English teachers—I learnt that standards without measurement were not worth the paper they were written on, and that there are few, if any, commonalities in how the best teachers teach! The latter is the main reason why I moved from trying to understand effective teaching to focusing on the thinking and decision-making made by effective teachers (Hattie, 1997).

A hobby over these years was exploring the many meta-analyses that had been published since Gene Glass introduced the notion in 1976 (and completing many meta-analyses myself). It seemed synthesizing these meta-analyses would be a quicker way to stand on the shoulders of giants—although it took me 15 to 20 years to understand what the data meant. When *Visible Learning* was published in 2009, my writings and research moved away from measurement to research synthesis, although applying good measurement and research design will remain the core of my academic self.

Being a measurement person meant regular interaction with policy and politicians. In 2014, I was appointed by the Australian Cabinet to chair the Australian Institute for School Teachers and Leaders (AITSL), and this has placed me in the middle of debates about teachers, school leaders, and teacher educators. As Chair of AITSL and along with my Visible Learning travels, I am constantly amazed at the presence of so much excellence in our schools—and the major question is, why we do not recognize this, study and understand this excellence, and upscale it? And I note that so often, it is the teachers who refuse to recognize this excellence, in themselves, or in others—preferably through diatribes like, 'we are all different,' 'we teach differently,' 'we cannot identify excellence among teachers,' 'we are all equal,' and other denigrations of our profession. The same applies to teacher education, where the mantra is more 'just give us the money and leave us alone, we know truth,' leading to the dominance of the notion of a thousand flowers blooming (and we all know what happened to Mao's application of this adage).

When asked, and it is often, what I want to achieve in my political role, the answer is easy—I want to reintroduce the notion of expertise back into teaching. Working with Field and Catherine in the Melbourne model has been an eye-opener, based on reviewing the Clinical Praxis videos from this program (more later) showing the regularity of excellence, seeing the excitement in the schools who then want to mimic the same thinking in their school, and noting that more than 90% of graduates claim they were well-prepared by the program to become teachers. This book for me is an outcome of nine years of thinking, debating, arguing, seeing, and enjoying being in Melbourne.

Catherine Reid

Sometimes I say I 'drifted' into teaching, but in reality, my career was probably always going to be in education. When I was a small child, I created a parallel world—one which included a whole school of imaginary students, their names listed as neat class groups in ledgers my Dad would bring home from work.

After finishing school, I completed an Arts degree. I then spent a couple of years doing office work and travelling before 'succumbing' to a Grad. Dip. in Education. My year of teacher training was very much the 'traditional' model of teacher education referred to and critiqued in this book. I attended university tutorials and at regular intervals during the year, I completed placements, each of which consisted of a three-week block. Like many teachers, I remember my placements vividly, much less so the coursework component. While I was placed into a course cohort focusing on gender and inclusiveness, and one of my placements was in an all girls' school, I don't recall any explicit connections between my coursework assignments and my work in schools.

As a secondary school teacher, I formed strong relationships with colleagues and students; these relationships have always been central to my work. In my early years of teaching, some of my classroom approaches were no doubt based on intuition rather than 'evidence' or 'data,' and I don't remember consciously applying theory when planning and implementing lessons. After a couple of years' experience, though, I was aware that strengths of my teaching were identifying students' existing skills and knowledge, and supporting the next stages in students' learning development. I like to think I tailored my teaching accordingly, whether that was in a whole class context, or in one-on-one sessions with Year 12 students as they planned, drafted, and polished their English writing folios. For some of those senior students, the next stage in their writing development was creating a stronger theme, or using extended metaphor, or appropriating the style of a studied author. For others, it was writing a cohesive paragraph and linking ideas, or varying and broadening vocabulary, or developing proofreading skills. It was time-consuming and sometimes challenging, especially in classes of 30 plus students. But it was enormously rewarding when a student produced outstanding and original writing that astounded me, or when a student who had struggled to write extended pieces completed something that exceeded their (and my) initial expectations. In retrospect, these successes were, in part, because I *was* using evidence to inform my teaching, evidence from work samples and other sources, but also evidence drawn from my knowledge of my students, their aspirations, their worlds outside school.

Flash forward to 2008: I had been working at the Melbourne Graduate School of Education (MGSE) for a few years when I took on coordination of the professional practice (placement) program in the first year of the Master of Teaching (Secondary). In the year leading up to the first delivery of the MTeach, I attended several presentations during which Field and others unveiled the new course structure, discussed how school placements would integrate with coursework subjects, and emphasized 'interventionist practice' and the 'clinical model'—language that I hadn't associated with teaching and learning previously. My role required me to establish and foster the 'partnerships' between MGSE and our secondary 'base schools,' and to facilitate the working relationships between university-based academic staff (Clinical Specialists), school-based mentors (Teaching Fellows), and several hundred Teacher Candidates (preservice teachers) during their school placements.

Key to these partnerships, and to the integration of theory and practice, was a shared language. We needed to use it with our Teacher Candidates, amongst our University colleagues and our school partners, and we needed to 'unpack' it and understand it in the context of our work as teachers, especially given some found the 'new' language challenged their existing notions of teaching. Another crucial factor was the design of coursework assessment tasks that relied on the Teacher Candidates' own classroom practice. A defining moment in the MTeach (and subsequently, for other programs) was the implementation of the Clinical Praxis Exam (CPE). The CPE design drew on Field's knowledge and experience of clinical exams in the medical field and was led by Dr Barbara Kameniar and a small team of core-subject coordinators. I was fortunate to be part of this team. Our weekly meetings about the rationale and requirements of the CPE generated much rich dialogue around our own definitions and conceptualizations of language such as 'clinical model,' 'interventionist,' 'evidence,' and 'praxis.' The integration of concepts, theory, and research from three coursework subjects with discipline-specific pedagogy and actual classroom experience resulted in a tangible example of the theory-practice nexus. The CPE facilitates Teacher Candidates' evaluative thinking in relation to their practice, informed by research, theory, and use of evidence, but also their knowledge of and empathy towards their students. As an oral task, it requires Teacher Candidates to articulate their practice, using language specific to a clinical model of teaching and learning. This kind of articulation of practice is fundamental to teaching as a profession. Also integral to the CPE are the close collaboration and professional dialogue between CPE assessors, comprised of school-based practitioners and university-based academic staff. One result of this has been that the CPE model has been taken up in several partner schools as a medium for practicing teachers to demonstrate their own professional development.

The design of assessment tasks and subjects across the MTeach and other MGSE courses has undergone significant development and reconceptualization over the past thirteen years, as academic staff have acknowledged and integrated key aspects of the clinical model. The experience of working on this book with Field and John has allowed me to reflect on my introduction to and immersion in the clinical model of teaching and how my own practice and 'teacher thinking' have been consolidated and transformed in the process.

Acknowledgments

Many colleagues have contributed to the development and consolidation of these ideas. Most important are the many fellow academics and the thousands of students in the Melbourne Graduate School of Education (MGSE) clinical model of teaching program, led in the early days by Collette Tayler, Barbara Kameniar, then Larissa McLean Davies. Other formative contributors were Kaye Stacey and Christine Ure, and it was a visit by this core team to Stanford University in 2007 to see the work there led by Linda Darling-Hammond that demonstrated the importance of partnerships and the focus on the impact on students. We acknowledge all course coordinators, all teaching fellows, clinical specialists, and everyone who worked so hard to understand, implement, and improve the program since these beginnings.

The program was heavily based on the thinking and research of Patrick Griffin, director of the Assessment Research Centre within MGSE. Patrick brought the notion of using interpretations, developmental-progression rubrics, targeted teaching interventions, and evidence for learning as core to the MTeach (Griffin, 2014, 2018). It is unusual to focus a teacher preparation around seeing assessment as the foundation for developing evidence-based thinking (rather than curriculum, teaching, practice, theory) but this developmental, evidence-based, interpretative focus was pivotal to the MTeach and the clinical model outlined throughout this book.

Across the University, there were many contributors to our thinking and to the program, starting with the Vice-Chancellor ('President' in United States nomenclature) Glyn Davis, who had the vision for the Melbourne Model and remains a major supporter of truly making a difference to the quality of teachers across Australia.

Lorraine Graham and Suzanne Rice provided valuable and nuanced insights into the definitions and concepts associated with 'clinical teaching' and the stages of the clinical teaching cycle discussed in Chapter 3. Case studies were provided

Acknowledgments

by Larissa McLean Davies, Lisa McKay-Brown, David Mackenzie, Susan Nikakis, Janna Wardman, June McLoughlin, Kathryn Barclay, Jeanette Breen, Jordan Goulding, Cassandra Marinopoulos and Anna Murphy. We also wish to thank Julius Colman and Ken Muir for their contributions, and Robin Evans and Richard Davis, who willingly gave their time to discuss their respective professions and the thinking, practice, and expertise fundamental to these. We are grateful for the generous philanthropic support of John and Jennifer Prescott that enabled this book to be completed.

Thanks to the team at the Australian Institute for School Teachers and Leaders (AITSL), who continue to inform, challenge, and realize so much excellence, and the Board of AITSL is an exciting place where the implementation of worthwhile policy at scale are debated and approved. The various policy people, politicians, and senior departmental leaders are enjoyable to work with, and we thank these people for their insights, commitment to making a difference, and support of our work.

Bruce Roberts at Routledge has been positive in his encouragement of this book and in his patience and understanding. We thank him and the reviewers who provided constructive feedback on earlier drafts of the manuscript.

We thank Glyn Davis, David Huggins, and Georgia Heffernan, who commented on a penultimate draft, although all errors remaining are our own. Thanks to Catriona May, who made major initiative and supportive contributions in developing Chapter 8. Janet Rivers once again shone in her editing of the final manuscript and raised the level of our prose to much higher levels.

Over the years, we have met many thousands of teachers across our conferences and workshops; indeed, tens of thousands of teachers, and there is nothing more rewarding than to hear their stories, feel their dedication, and learn from their impact. So much excellence, so much humility, so much care and commitment—this books aims to tell the story of the very best of these teachers, to understand the essence of the profession of excellence among teachers, and to challenge, cajole, and convince the profession to stand, be proud of, and deliver on the excellence that identifies our profession.

For Field and John, our biggest critics and supporters remain our partners. We thank Millie and Janet for their support, their indulgence of our regular meetings and hot debates, and their ability to laugh at our jokes! While all our 6 children are now adults and graduated from the school system (thank you, teachers), it is now our 9 grandchildren that continue to inspire us, excite us, and motivate us to want to upscale the excellence among teachers. This book is dedicated to the next generation of students: Max, Ollie, Zoe, Phoebe, Charlie, Stella, Emma, Ella, and Dianelle.

PART

The turning point

CHAPTER

Setting the scene

In many ways, schooling is the same assembly-line model that has existed for the past 150 years. This constancy in the way schools look, feel, operate, and deliver curricula has been called the "grammar of schooling" (Tyack & Cuban, 1995). Rip Van Winkle or Charles Dickens could return from the nineteenth century and recognize the rows, the age grading, the teacher up front talking, and the bells, busy work, and blackboards (or equivalent).

Since the 1880s, most western countries have introduced compulsory schooling, invested multi-trillions of dollars into these schools, hired teachers and school leaders, organized children into age groups, created policy documents, and assured parents that these teachers will educate their children. Right now across the world we spend at least US$3,376 billion each year on schools: 56% of this on salaries, 40% on structures (buildings), and 4% on education products, resources, and professional learning (Hattie & Hamilton, 2018). The evidence of the return on this investment is positive. In 1900, only 20% of the world could be considered literate and numerate, whereas in 2000 only 14% could be considered illiterate and innumerate (Figure 1.1; Roser & Ortiz-Ospina, 2016). This remarkable increase from 20% to 86% across the world surely should outclass any growth and impact from the Renaissance or the golden days of classical Greece—and this is mainly due to teachers. We have much to celebrate. We surely have richness, quality, and excellence all around us.

Of course, there are still too many students who miss out: there are too many savage inequalities in the system, and there is much to do to improve the impact on all in the schooling enterprise.

The current schooling model, adapted and tweaked over the years since its emergence from the industrial model in the 1880s, has been adapted and tweaked by so many over the past 150 years. As Tyack and Cuban (1995) noted, we have been tinkering towards Utopia. This workplace industry model has served us well, but the demands placed on today's schools and teachers are now so much broader and deeper: teachers have become responsible for developing students' social and

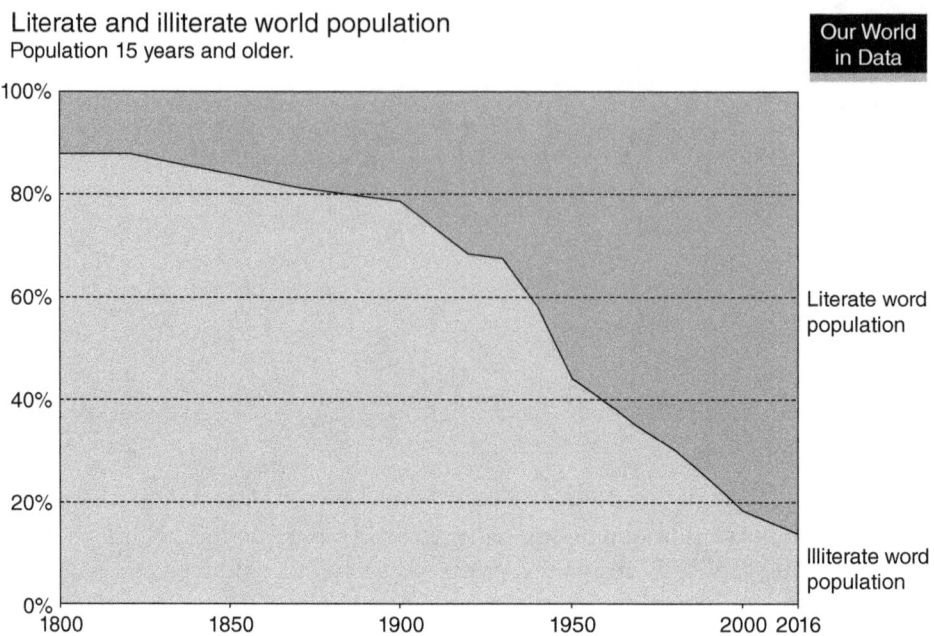

Figure 1.1 World literacy and illiteracy rates from 1800 to 2000 (from Roser & Ortiz-Ospina, 2016)

emotional well-being, teaching 'twenty-first century skills,' developing in students the respect for self and others, reducing bullying, developing cultural sensitivity, and so much more.

There is a great deal of evidence that the industrial model is cracking. Take, for example, the continual beating-up of teachers, or the tendency to see schools as the solutions for societal ills. Take the overblown emphasis on accountability, which is disrupting the day-job of teaching in often perverse ways, or the tendency to explain failures by labeling ('they are from poor families,' 'they have this condition,' 'they do not have the right motivation when they come to school'), or take the continued widening of gaps between the haves and have nots. The industrial model of schooling and the consequential demands on teachers to fit into this model are creaking at the seams. Frequently the blame for perceived failures is directed at teachers: they are poorly selected, poorly trained, and lack expertise. Proposed answers often imply teachers can simply be replaced: for example, by arguing for computers to replace teachers; by increasing the number of paraprofessionals in our schools (27% of the United Kingdom budget is now invested in these nonexperts); by seeking teacher-proof methods such as online and gaming programs; or by privileging experience more than expertise, rather than seeking both.

As will be argued throughout this book, the success of schooling relates to the expertise of the educators much more than to the structures of schools, the curriculum, the composition of the class, the assessment, and so on. Although all these structural issues play a role, they are minor compared to the expertise of teachers. We are not making a claim that 'it is all about the teacher,' as this would ignore resourcing, conditions, pay and esteem, and school leadership and quality policies. More importantly, we are not defending a claim that all teachers are equal; while there is a need to have a minimum acceptable standard for all teachers, our argument is that we need a teaching profession that is raised above this minimum standard. All teachers need to be classroom-ready, but they also need to grow in their expertise to become at least proficient, if not highly accomplished, throughout their careers. Those who are highly accomplished and demonstrate the highest levels of impact on students (and their colleagues) should be given a major role in demonstrating their expertise to the profession, community, and policymakers. Such expert teachers need to have an important say in the quality-assurance processes in schools and need to be involved in the mentoring of other teachers. It is this form of expertise which illustrates the qualities of the profession. Understanding this expertise is at the heart of any occupation claiming to be a profession. Hence, this book.

The need for a new model of schooling that privileges expertise

A major purpose of schooling is to enable opportunities for every child to be embraced and be ready for the challenges of living in, working in, and enjoying the twenty-first century world and having the skills, dispositions, and ethics to contribute to this world. And let's remember, this is not a prescription for their *future*, as it is their *now*. We are a fifth of the way into the twenty-first century, and young people starting school today will be leaders of the future, responsible for deciding on how best to prepare for the twenty-second century.

This book is about teachers: their work, the teaching profession, and their expertise. Our argument is that expert teachers are the drivers of change. Expert teachers change lives. Expert teachers see the potential in students, acknowledge and respect students' abilities and potentials, inspire students' passion for learning, and provide students with secure environments in which to set aside personal fears and any lack of confidence to allow students to see errors and not knowing as opportunities for learning. It is through expert teachers that we transmit the knowledge, the virtues, and the values necessary to understand, in some cases to preserve, and to carry forward our democratic society.

This book is also about schools. Schools need to evolve. They need to acknowledge, dependably identify, and know how to use the expertise among the teachers to raise the esteem of the profession, to create opportunities for these expert teachers to work with other teachers, and to develop structures such that expert teachers are key participants in the debates about the impact on students in and across schools.

As one example from the western world, Australia has a strong educational heritage and long history of committed educators. Since 2000, however, despite the successes and excellence previously noted for the majority of students, academic performance has declined when compared to other Organisation for Economic Co-operation and Development (OECD) countries. This suggests that Australian students and schools are not improving at the same rate as other countries, and many students across the full range of abilities are falling short of achieving their full learning potential. While this decline, both in absolute and relative terms, is heralded at the start of almost every review, there have been few policies that have stopped or reversed this trend. Perhaps the most serious problem is complacency, thinking that the schooling system has served Australians well, so all that is needed is some tinkering to make it a bit better.

There is a need to act now to raise aspirations, to reboot, to keep and esteem the effective, and to make a renewed effort to improve school education outcomes so that all students receive world-class schooling relevant to today's fast-changing and interconnected world in which students are immersed (Hattie, 2017).

Over the past 10 years, the groundwork to esteem teacher expertise has been laid. Many countries now have professional standards for teachers and school leaders. In Australia, the federal and state governments are among the few in the world to legislate national standards for teachers, school principals, and teacher educators. All teachers are classified as either graduate, proficient, highly accomplished, or lead. There is a healthy emergence of a cohort of highly accomplished and lead teachers across the nation who have formed a network and who hold annual conferences, and there is a desire to greatly expand their number and influence. But more of this later.

There is also an almost opposite issue at hand. School education in many western countries is facing challenging times. One challenge is requests for evidence for the return on the incredible investment that is made into education, and a related challenge is the claim of overeducation. Students are asked to be qualified to do jobs that do not require the skills learned in the qualification. This has led many to proclaim investment in education should be reduced, or that firms should be encouraged to undertake their own specialized training. This is an alarming proposition.

Caplan (2018) has argued that gaining a degree is a form of signaling that a credential has been acquired rather than that skills have been learned, and that students are hungry for such signals, as these are what the labor market pays for. Caplan's extreme argument posits that most education beyond the mastery of basic literacy and numeracy is a waste of time and money, and therefore governments should sharply cut back on subsidies for education and actively discourage its pursuit. Schooling is sometimes viewed as producing little valuable learning, that there is little need for the topics and content taught in most high schools or universities, and that students strive for the degree, not the content of the degree. Caplan asks the question: would you want the PhD (the credential) and not spend four years learning while you get it, or would you want the four years of learning but not get the degree? Most graduates want the former, as this is what the employers ask for; the degree is the signal, and the nature of content is almost irrelevant.

Caplan (2018, p. 23) summarized his "ubiquity of useless education" as:

> Never-ending cosmetic changes create the illusion of fluidity. Schools adopt a new history book or add Mandarin to the course catalogue. They toy with technology. Instead of playing on their phones in class while the professor lectures, college students can play on their phones in their dorm rooms while the professor streams the lectures over the Internet. Yet no matter how many cosmetic changes accumulate, the essence of school endures: students spend over a decade learning piles of dull content they won't use after graduation.

Maybe the issue is less of overeducation but rather an insufficient education of the right stuff. The reality is many of us forget what we learned in high school or college within five years. More than 50% of adults fail intermediate or proficient mastery of basic quantitative questions (an example of a task of this level is calculating the total cost of ordering specific office supplies from a catalog); and a third of science graduates do not know that atoms are bigger than electrons. While there may be overeducation for some, tell that to students who start so far behind and struggle to catch up or to those who do not have the chance to be part of the 'credentialed' and thus be eligible for employment.

Time for a reboot

There is a case for considering the role of schools and, just as importantly, the role of teachers. There are many skills such as collaboration, teamwork, and the ability to train others that are now demanded by employers—the skill set has changed, or more correctly, it has been added to, as most job advertisements still want candidates to 'know things.' But even though our school systems may not have caught up and there is a need for close scrutiny, there is hardly an argument for the reduction in investment in schooling. As Levin (1988) has shown, one of the best predictors of adult health, wealth, and happiness is not achievement at school, but the number of years of schooling, so it is important to make these years worthwhile: A major aim of schooling is to make school inviting enough to make students to want to come and invest.

There are many indicators to suggest it's time for a schooling revolution in many western countries, or at least a reboot (Hattie, 2017). We say 'many' as there are non-uniform advances and declines in some indicators within the more advanced economies. For example, the Program for International Student Assessment (PISA) is a collaborative effort among the member countries of the OECD to measure how well young adults, at age 15 and therefore approaching the end of compulsory schooling, are prepared to meet the challenges of today's knowledge societies. From 2000 to 2015, the countries with the greatest decline in PISA across reading, math, and science were the United Kingdom, Sweden, Iceland, Australia, Slovenia, New Zealand, Finland, Netherlands, and Czechoslovakia, and those with the greatest increases were Bulgaria, Latvia, Russia, Serbia, Germany, Luxembourg, Poland, Portugal, and Montenegro. There is some regression to the mean, as those countries showing an improvement typically started below the PISA mean and those showing a decline started above. There are, however, exceptions to show that the explanations for rise and decline are probably more policy-related as, for example, Germany, Russia, Singapore, Hong Kong, Denmark, and Norway all started above the mean in 2000 and continued to rise.

The past decade has seen the revival of economic growth in many developing countries, yet a stalling of growth in advanced economies (OECD, 2012). Economic transformations and shifting wealth bring challenges such as rising inequalities, and large population movements can lead to ruptures to social cohesion. The OECD has highlighted the critical need for "civic participation through an inclusive policy agenda" and "social cohesion for long-term sustainable growth" (OECD, 2012), and there are signs of social cohesion approaching a tipping point in many western countries. Increasingly diverse and pluralistic societies require policy settings and educational practices that encourage common citizenship, social cohesion, resilience, and reliance on debate and discussion as problem-solving methods. The pressure on teachers and schools is thus increased.

Too often the answer is sought in creating different names for schools (charter, trusts, academies), and ironically, many of these suggested answers revert back to more stringent, straight lines: textbook-driven, over-controlled models mirroring the factory model. With the push for more control by parents to choose schools, alternatives to state schools become more present. A key difference between the Australian school system and high-performing systems elsewhere is Australia's relatively high proportion of elementary and high schools outside the public system—about 35% of all students are enrolled in nongovernment schools (DEECD, 2013; OECD, 2015). The result of this sectorial diversity is competition rather than collaboration between schools and sectors. It leads to many unhealthy debates in the community about school choice. This, in turn, means that some parents have access to a wide range of schools, whereas others do not. Too often this choice is related to the branding claims, and most of these claims are about beautiful buildings, such as extensive sporting complexes and performance centers, and other structural claims. This choice debate is a classic example of the politics of distraction (Hattie, 2015).

McCandless (2017) analyzed school websites and found major differences in the messages to parents. In low socioeconomic government schools (SES), schools are shown as providing all that is necessary to succeed (modern classes, highly trained teachers, technology), and classes under the explicit discipline of the teacher. In low SES, the emphasis is on self-discipline and students are more serious-looking and posed by photographers for photos, but in higher SES, students look more natural and are laughing in photos. Above-average SES government schools are more likely to show students collaborating, with nary a teacher in sight, and focus on building interpersonal skills. McCandless found that elite private schools emphasize teams and how the schools will respect the students. Minority students are always shown as the center of attention, and in all cases, white students are posed to show them helping a minority student.

The experience of students

There will always be gaps between the top and bottom students, and it will never be the case that all students will be above the average, but this gap is far greater in some countries than others, pointing to equity deficiencies. This gap represents about six to eight years of achievement gain, with the largest gaps in China, Israel, Taiwan, and South Korea. While there are considerable differences in performance between schools in most developed countries, the greatest variance in student achievement is *within* schools (Lupton & Thomson, 2015), with many classes spanning learning gaps of five or six years (Masters, 2014). One must be wary, however, of the many claims to 'reduce the gap,' as this could be accomplished by lowering the scores among the top 30% to 40% of students (as is occurring in Australia). Given that there will always be a gap between the top and bottom students, we would rather enhance the learning lives of *all* students and base equity claims on ensuring every student, no matter where they start, gains at least a year's increase in learning within an academic year.

Every student has had unique learning experiences since entering the world and they form their own understandings of the world as they see and comprehend it. And yet, students in a class are treated as a homogeneous age group following the same instructions, in lock step with a curriculum that evolves over 13 years of schooling and has been designed by experts who have been through a similar process. That model does not allow for the individual differences that exist in every classroom. Within any year group, there are often massive disparities. Indeed, there could be a claim that Year 4 means there are four years spread in that year, and Year 10 means a 10-year spread. Yet most curricula are packaged according to year levels, as if all within that year group started similarly, and any student not working at that level is labeled as the problem. This leads to so much implementation of 'prefabricated knowledge' aimed at the middle of each year group (Schleicher, 2016) that is irrelevant, impossible, or too easy for the majority of students in that year.

Consider also the Jenkins curve (Figure 1.2). Lee Jenkins (2015) has tracked the changes in student enthusiasm for going to school from a high in Grade 1, where 95% of students were enthusiastic, to a low of 37% of students being enthusiastic by Year 8, with a slight increase by the end of schooling. Imagine a workplace with only 30% to 40% of staff engaged in their work and wanting to be there: production would be pitiful, staff turnover would likely be high, and

The turning point

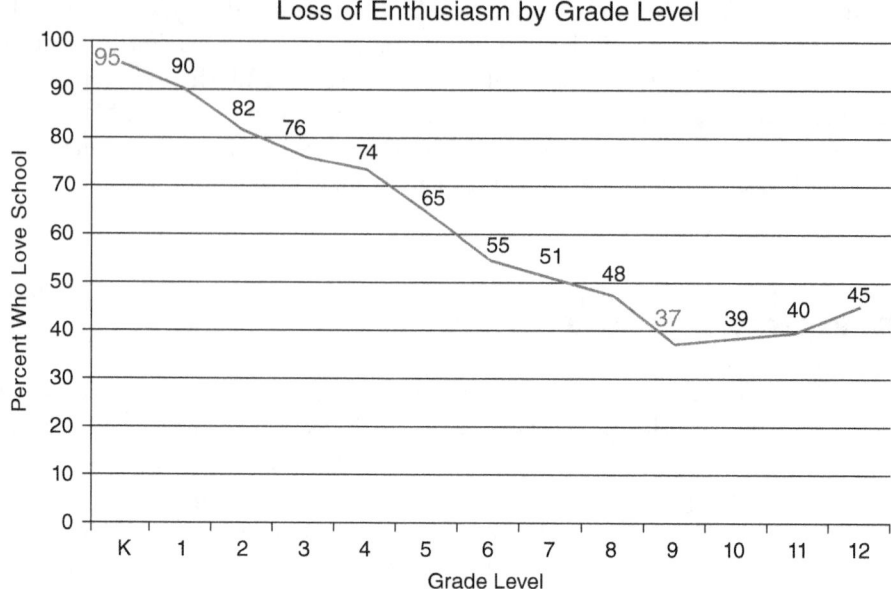

Figure 1.2 The Jenkins curve of the loss of enthusiasm for learning in schools by grade level (Jenkins, 2015)

there would be serious questions raised about the chief executive. But students have to come to school, regardless.

School engagement is central to social cohesion and student success. If students are disengaged, they are unlikely to maximize their learning opportunities at school. The aim should be to dramatically increase the percentage of students who are engaged in schooling. The focus should not be on making the student attend compulsorily (which only leads to more students at school who do not want to be there), but asking how to make schools more inviting places that will engage students in learning.

Schools achieve engagement in many ways: through curriculum innovations; through a strong culture that binds all members of the community, both within and beyond the school; and through the fostering of school as an inviting place to learn and where there is deep concern and support for every student. Schools must give students a strong sense of belonging to the school and the community. They must focus on the heart as well as the head.

We argue throughout this book is that this can be done and, in fact, is being done in many classrooms and schools right now. What is important is understanding the dynamics that make this happen and then scaling it up. It should be no surprise that a major dynamic is the passionate teacher who has high expectations that all students can grow and prosper in their classes: it is a matter of the expertise of the teachers.

The importance of teacher expertise and collaborative, evidence-based practice

Effective teachers see the potential in students, respect students' abilities, inspire passion for learning, and develop secure and enjoyable learning environments. The quality of teaching is the most important controllable factor that impacts student learning. A common theme throughout this book is that much of the success of schooling is a function of the expertise of teachers, and there are many teachers with high levels of expertise. The aim is to upscale that number and enhance the collegial involvement of these experts. There is no need to destroy a system or start with a negative set of claims about schools; instead, there is a major need to have the courage to dependably identify, esteem, and value expertise and aim to improve, but not denigrate, those who are less proficient.

Scaling up success requires collaboration. The transformation of teaching into a high-esteem profession involves a school workforce that is structured around collaborative teaching teams. These collaborative teams seem a necessary condition for an effective profession (see Chapter 6). The focus of this collaboration applies not only to curriculum and assessment planning but involves consideration of what are reasonable and high expectations, and what are the various notions of impact. Collaboration involves ensuring excellent classroom practice is implemented with fidelity and working together to evaluate of the impact of teaching on student learning.

Teacher expertise and evidence-based practice

There is a strong desire for equitable school systems that address the needs of all students, regardless of socioeconomic status, gender, location, or ability. There are varying abilities within every class. In 2016, Australia presented its first Nationally Consistent Collection of Data for School Students with Disability. This census identified 20% of students in the broad category of disability and claimed that these students require specific adjustments to their education. This is supported by a separate set of data, the Australian Early Development Census (Goldfeld, O'Connor, Sayers, Moore, & Oberklaid, 2012), which is a national measure of children's development as they enter their first year of full-time school; this census found one in five students is developmentally vulnerable in at least one area of development in a way that is likely to affect learning when they start school. Then there are those considered gifted, along with many other classifications of students. More than a fifth of students in each class have additional needs, including the need for extension, acceleration, enhancement, and specialized assistance, support, and adjustment. The challenge for teachers is to cater for all students' learning needs throughout their range of development rather than teaching to the mid-range of whole-class groups.

Children who have impaired hearing, for example, face particular challenges because, apart from a small percentage, they can hear a restricted range of sounds. The vast majority attend regular schools and can develop good levels of spoken language. A smaller number rely on sign language and have support from signing interpreters in regular schools or teachers with sign language in special schools. Hearing-impaired children can hear, but they cannot 'overhear'; that is, they cannot overhear other discussions as they need to focus on a particular speaker, typically the teacher. Moreover, these children learn because of what teachers do, not in spite of what they do. Teaching hearing-impaired children is a complex task, but in some senses, it is more contained than the general task of teaching in schools; progress can be more specifically defined and monitored. Teachers' professional practice can be focused on individual students and based on clear evidence of a student's current performance and developmental need. It is an evidence-based practice.

All of this has provoked for us the question of how teaching more generally might be made evidence-based. Over the years, we have come to know many expert teachers whose students have achieved exceptional educational outcomes. One in particular was Professor Daniel Ling (1988) from Canada, an international expert on teaching deaf children spoken language. He once wrote on enhancing learning in children with hearing loss that:

> the adults concerned must provide carefully structured situations that promote the acquisition of speech-communication skills. This means that they must plan activities – and above all, social interactions – to achieve selected and specific goals. The targeted behaviors in such activities must provide a base for the child's further development and consolidate previously learned skills. The adults must monitor the child's progress and base their future activities on what the child has achieved as a result of their efforts
>
> (p. 188).

Ling's teaching was underpinned by a firm belief that every child can learn. He set the highest expectations, his approach was developmental, he was an interventionist teacher, assessment guided his teaching, and he demanded continued growth throughout the years of schooling. Is this expert teaching the exception or the rule? It needs to be the rule.

Conclusion

Many reports, books, and articles addressing this issue often start with claims of woe that highlight the problems, the gaps, and the deficits. Usually this depressing opening is merely a justification for the following chapters that outline the latest preferred answer. In this book, we start from the opposite perspective. We acknowledge the excellence and success in teaching and learning all around us; we aim to identify the core components of this success and to esteem it, privilege it, and identify how such success can be upscaled. Great teachers and schools should be by design, not chance, and all students should get to enjoy this success.

The aim for schools and teachers is to enhance students' growth in academic achievement, increase the engagement of students, make schools inviting and safe places to come and learn, and meet the increasing demands expected from schools. Educators are responsible for every student who crosses the school gate and, at a minimum, should provide at least a year's learning for a year's input, no matter the starting point for each student. What a 'year's learning' means is an important question for all teachers and needs to be a well-debated concept.

PART

The nature of teacher expertise

CHAPTER

Teacher expertise and the centrality of the student

The claim of this book is that teachers are distinguished by their expertise—and there is much evidence of this expertise. This chapter outlines many of the domains of teacher expertise, or the breadth and depth of knowledge and skill that are demanded of teachers.

At the beginning of schooling in the early- to mid-eighteenth century, the emphasis was on the basic skills. This emphasis is still with us; however, in the past 150 years, the demands on educators have exploded, especially the exponential growth in expectations during the past two or three decades. In the meantime, the basic structure of schools has barely changed. Despite this misalignment, teachers experience much success, showing their adaptability, expertise, and leadership; however, it must be asked whether the increased expectations of teachers are reasonable as we move forward.

While there have been many claims for individualized or personalized learning, these claims have mostly failed for the obvious reason that schools are social settings in which teachers work mostly with groups. This is not undesirable, as we live in groups; we want to teach children how to live in a democracy, valuing precious knowledge as well as respect for self and others. But this too places demands on educators to have the expertise to develop each child's learning while working in and with groups of students.

Until the 1800s, most schooling was individual, often with private tutors. The increase in mass education can be traced to the Bell and Lancaster monitorial model, which compartmentalized knowledge into curricula subjects and grouped children by ability (but soon moved to grouping by age). Monitors, or more competent students, were provided with scripted lessons and students advanced when they showed mastery; hence the start of the self-paced, mastery-based, peer-learning, scripted-textbook, ability-grouped, age-streamed model of today (Dockterman, 2018).

There has always been a push for individualized instruction, and every technology innovation (blackboards, overheads, computers) has been seen as the next solution to making this individualization real. The assumption is that each child is unique; however, this belies the findings that that the most (and least) effective interventions will apply for all students (Hattie, 2009). What works best for special needs students works best for gifted students; what works best for five-year-olds works best for 15-year-olds; what works best for French students works best for American students; and so on. Hard as it may be for some to accept, it is difficult to find interaction effects between attributes of students and instructional methods (Cronbach & Snow, 1977). This is not to say students are not unique—indeed, they are, but what works best (and worst) is reasonably constant regardless of the individual attributes of most students in the western world.

Also, the most well-known notion of differentiation is commonly misinterpreted as providing different activities for different students; however, the main advocates of differentiation define it as allowing for differing paths and differing times to achieve the same success criteria (Tomlinson, 2005). This latter conceptualization results in the highest impact on student learning (Rubie-Davies, 2010).

The aim of considering that the child is central to all teaching should be to maximize the impact on each child, to ensure excellent diagnoses of what each student brings to the class and where they currently are on the trajectory of learning, to advance and accelerate learning for each child, and to ensure that each student not only meets their personal best but is taught to exceed their personal best.

Zhang, Basham and Yang (2020) reviewed 45 empirical studies that focused on the implementation of personalized learning and noted that very few of these studies had evaluated the impacts of personalized learning on student educational achievement. The nine meta-analyses on individualized instruction show the low impact. Table 2.1 shows the nine meta-analyses, the year of their study, the number of studies they included, the number of effects, and the average effect-size (d) from implementing a personalized learning approach. Comparing the effect-sizes in Table 2.1 to more than 1,600 meta-analyses incorporating over 300 influences (Hattie, 2019), these can be considered very low indeed.

In this chapter, we trace, briefly, the various phases of child development, noting the different demands that this places on teachers as students move from a world of expectations to developing literacy and numeracy skills to acquiring deeper knowledge and understanding the power of learning. These phases show the remarkable levels of knowledge and skills teachers need to develop so they can educate and work productively with students.

This all raises the question as to whether it is reasonable for any one person to have the expertise to deal with all these factors and whether one teacher in any one class may possess the skills to deal with the centrality of each student while working so often at a group level. That leads to questions about the nature of teacher expertise required to attend to the needs of each student.

TABLE 2.1 The meta-analyses, year, number of studies, number of effects, and effect-size from personalized learning studies (https://www.visiblelearningmetax.com).

	Year	No. studies	No. effects	d	
Hartley	1977	51	139	0.16	Individualization in math
Horak	1981	60	129	-0.07	Individualization in math
Willett, Yamashita, and Anderson	1983	130	131	0.17	Individualized science curriculum
Bangert, Kulik, and Kulik	1983	49	49	0.10	Individualized in high schools
Waxman, Wang, Anderson, and Walberg	1985	38	309	0.45	Adaptive methods (individual, continuous assessment, periodic evaluation)
Atash and Dawson	1986	10	30	0.09	Individualized science curriculum
Mitchell	1987	38	39	0.19	Individualized instruction in mathematics
Slavin, Lake, Davis, and Madden	2011	20	20	0.31	One-on-one tutoring in reading
Jun, Ramirez, and Cumming	2010	12	19	0.26	One-on-one tutoring in literacy
Total/Average		408	865	0.18	

Societies make schooling compulsory

Formal education is a centuries-old notion; for example, in Sparta from 800 BC, where the teacher, or pedagogue (usually a slave but later a teacher with some training), escorted the student to the school. By the early decades of the eighteenth century, attendance at private and charity schools from all sectors of society was increasing. Laws making schooling compulsory rapidly increased rates of attendance (Atkinson & Maleska, 1962; Folger & Nam, 1967). There were many reasons for this enactment of mass schooling: political parties were driven to instill certain views on the populace and these were manifested through censorship in schools; the demands of industry generated a minimum competence in foundational literacy and numeracy; new laws meant a reduction in children's hours in factories and thus allowed more time to be spent in schools; schools were financed by fees and this placed more pressure on wealthier citizens who advocated for a more even spread using taxation; and education was considered important for a more representative and democratic form of government.

In the 1870s, England, the United States, Australia, and New Zealand all accelerated the move to compulsory attendance. This led to an increased attention to the qualities of the teachers. Mann (1867) spent much time considering how to draw persons of the "highest talent and morality" to the teaching profession. He argued that the best way to do this was by increasing teachers' wages significantly and making teachers more professional. One of his arguments was economic: "The expenses incurred in punishing the smallest theft that is committed exceed the present cost of educating a child in our schools for a year." This led to the development of training methods (for example, the English monitor system noted above in which elder students taught the younger), unions, and professional associations. The expansion of student numbers meant the demand for teachers increased quickly, and standards may not have been as high as many desired. The status of teachers dropped as the standards dropped. Bureaucracy started issuing edicts about what to teach and how to teach, and standardization was introduced with the aim of maintaining a minimum set of standards for curricula and teachers. Katz (1971) outlined this process of bureaucratization as the move from a system based on paternalistic voluntarism, to one based on democratic localism and corporate voluntarism, to then a system of incipient bureaucracy.

No wonder there are pleas now for autonomy, for allowing more freedoms; however, sadly, many of these pleas can lead to the hiding of poor practice and low levels of impact on student learning. If only it was as simple as autonomy or not. Autonomy can be understood as the delegation of certain tasks from one level of governance to another, such as from school leaders to teachers in their classrooms, but there are many forms of autonomy.

There is political autonomy, where politicians elected and responsible to voters decide issues for the public good. This form of autonomy has increased, especially since the 1990s when governments started to take responsibility for driving the outcomes of schools. Before, politicians had departments with civil servants, but they have now been replaced with political advisors who ensure ministry officials enact a government minister's policy.

There is market autonomy, where consumers (parents) choose schools, can be involved in school governance, and are appealed to by school leaders (who are often funded relative to numbers in their school).

There is bureaucratic autonomy to undertake the tasks to be done for an organization to perform productively, and this form of control has been decentralized to schools since the 1980s. Central agencies used to have forms, formulae, and standard answers to distribute to all schools and this has disappeared, replaced by busy school leader bureaucrats.

There is also social autonomy, which depends on agreed-upon goals. The moves by governments to insist on vision statements, purpose, and school development plans are an attempt to exert social control. This form of control assumes that all are committed to the goals, and educators will behave as best as they can to promote these goals.

There are differing levels of curricula and program autonomy; in some countries, the curriculum is left more to the school, whereas in others it is quite prescriptive. There are countries where decisions related to resource allocation, curriculum, and assessment are local (Czechoslovakia, Netherlands, Macao); where decisions relate only to resource and not curricula and assessment (Chile, Hungary, Sweden, Bulgaria, Dubai, Shanghai); and where decisions are high relating to curriculum and assessment (Japan, Korea, New Zealand, Hong Kong, China, Thailand).

There is pedagogical autonomy whereby teachers teach as they deem appropriate. In some countries there are textbooks, scripts, and an overabundance of worksheets, while in others, this autonomy results in creative and innovative teachers. Cuban (1993), however, has demonstrated that teaching has barely changed over the past 150 years, and the 'grammar of schooling' (as he terms it) is imprinted on each new innovation—talk and practice and content-dominated lessons.

Thus, when speaking of autonomy, it is essential to specify which forms or combinations of forms are intended. It is our claim that teachers have no right to curricula, program, or pedagogical autonomy if their students fail to make at least a year's progress and if they do not share their concepts of a year's growth and have it challenged, critiqued, and defended along with their colleagues.

Broadening the outcomes of schooling

In the past, schooling allowed for the learning of facts. Mr. Gradgrind in Dickens' *Hard Times* (1854) summed this view perfectly:

> Now, what I want is, Facts. Teach these boys and girls nothing but Facts. Facts alone are wanted in life. Plant nothing else and root out everything else. You can only form the minds of reasoning animals upon Facts: nothing else will ever be of any service to them. This is the principle on which I bring up my own children, and this is the principle on which I bring up these children. Stick to Facts, sir!

Today in the age of Google, Siri, and Alexa, there are still claims that we do not teach 'the facts,' the 3Rs, or content knowledge. Such claims overlook that so much more is now demanded of schools: respect, resilience, recognition, reciprocity, reasoning, responsibility, relationships—choose any of these and you will hear them preached from lecture podiums around the western world. Teachers are expected to develop the social, collaborative, physical, and emotional, as well as cognitive, attributes of students. This 'r-creep' has come with little acknowledgment or recognition of the increased skills and demands needed of teachers, where they are expected to have the skills of Mr. Gradgrind, Mother Teresa, Dr. Phil, Edward De Bono, and many others.

There are continual debates about the content and nature of curricula. In most cases, the sheer volume of what is expected to be taught, and thus known and understood by teachers, is enormous. *The Australian Curriculum* (https://www.australiancurriculum.edu.au/), if printed, is over 2,500 pages. One commentator noted, "Today another whole series of new demands is confronting the school. Health education, education for leisure time, vocational education, home making education, consumer education, and education for life in our democratised society require that provision be made in the school" (Loomis, 1939)—and this was written in 1939!

Rarely is much retracted from the curriculum. The typical list of curriculum domains is now extensive. In the United Kingdom, for example, primary school teachers are expected to teach science; design and technology; history; geography; art and design; music; physical education; religious education; PSHE (personal, social, and health education); citizenship; one modern foreign language; and sex education. Curricula committees provide standards, rubrics, resources, lesson plans, textbooks, and so on. There are usually higher-order principles underlying curricula statements and learning progressions that allow teachers to better choose the right proportions, topics, timing, and depth.

These higher-order principles can be lofty; for example, many documents claim that "curriculum is developed to ensure that students receive integrated, coherent learning experiences that contribute towards their personal, academic and professional learning and development," and "curriculum represents an articulation of what students should know and be able to do and supports teachers in knowing how to achieve these goals." These statements and ideals are not, however, necessarily informative in relation to deciding what, how much, and to what level each domain should be covered.

Young, Lambert, Roberts, and Roberts (2014, p. 10) offer a reasonable alternative: we should choose domains to "enable all students to acquire knowledge that takes them beyond their experience"—that is, to gain that which they would not gain if they did not come to school. Schools are institutions in which children can access knowledge and knowing. Such knowledge, according to Young et al., is not only shared but has to be struggled for, and curricula need to give priority to discovering, debating, testing, and evaluating precious and powerful knowledge. Such knowledge allows children to gain access to and derive benefit from the next phases of their education—in school, in society, and in work. It is knowledge that promotes empowerment and equity, so as not to be dominated, indoctrinated, or made subservient. This view is not defending the traditional notion of a corpus of facts to be dispensed by teachers, but rather it is about making arguments, giving reasons, and, where appropriate, providing evidence (for more on purposes of schooling, see Hattie & Larsen, 2021).

Then there are the proficiencies associated with so-called 'twenty-first century' skills. In many ways, this movement is a backlash to the dominance of subject discipline and content, such as the narrow excellence measured in the PISA and PIRLS (the Progress in International Reading Literacy Study, https://www.iea.nl/studies/iea/pirls) international tests of literacy, numeracy, and science. Some have argued that with Google, Siri, and the like, we no longer need so much knowledge but more skills to process information. But there is inequity associated with this: it may deny those who do not know what to know, what to search, and what to evaluate. The outcomes of schooling should be a blend of both knowing *how* and knowing *that*. We talk of accomplished people who have this blend, and for experts it is very difficult to separate the knowing *how* from the knowing *that*—but for novices and children, we can separate these concepts. One aim of schooling is to provide the *that* and the *how* so they can then be blended. We would add that by blending the *that* and the *how*, we may be able to answer the *why*, and then we would have a more defensible sense of the purpose of schooling.

The knowing *how* was advanced in the 1940s by Gilbert Ryle (1945) as a contrast to knowing *that*. Part of the reaction against too much 'knowing that' came from an earlier critique by Whitehead (1929) who warned against 'inert ideas'; that is "ideas that are merely received into the mind without being utilized, or tested, or thrown into fresh combinations" (p. 1). Ryle wanted students to 'know that' but also wanted them to 'know how': "In other words it requires intelligence not only to discover truths, but also to apply them, and knowing how to apply truths cannot, without setting up an infinite process, be reduced to knowledge of some extra bridge-truths" (p. 6). 'Knowing how' is when you claim to know how to do something (for example, riding a bike), whereas 'knowing that' is when you claim to know that something is correct (for example, explaining the physics of how to ride a bike). You need ideas and facts before you can use, relate, and extend these ideas; or, as Ryle succinctly stated: "Rules, like birds, must live before they can be stuffed" (p. 11).

Many of these 'knowing how' methods are not expressed in the plea for twenty-first century skills. Much of the demand for these skills has come from employers looking for communication, interpersonal, and problem-solving skills. As Nickerson, Perkins, and Smith (2014) noted, the current employment world is less enamored with students knowing large amounts of information, "because the world we are educating learners for is something of a moving target, itself as much unknown as known" (p. 21). The movement to twenty-first century skills seems to claim that these are generalized traits and not embedded in some content or situational demands.

This movement also ignores the centuries-old debate about the interplay with how we think and what we think about. For example, Aristotle (384–322 BC) claimed there were at least four ways of knowing: by doing; by demonstration; by intuition; and by practical reasoning. There are many permutations of twenty-first century skills, but they typically involve creativity, critical thinking and problem solving, and communication and collaboration. The twenty-first century framework is silent on the means by which these desired skills and outcomes can or should be taught; it promotes no particular learning or teaching strategies (Claxton, 2013). In our recent work (Hattie & Donoghue, 2016), we identified over 400 different learning strategies.

Teachers are asked not only to imbue these knowledge claims, but to educate students to process, think about, use, relate, and extend these claims. We do note there is an overreliance on teaching 'facts,' or 'knowing that,' and this is compounded by a conspiracy—above average students seem to prefer high levels of teacher talk and a dominant focus on ideas and facts, and the perception among students (and many adults/employers) is that 'knowing lots' is a (more recognizable, at least) indicator of ability and success (Murphy, Barlow, & von Hippel, 2018). There is too much of a grammar of 'knowing that' in our schools.

Individualism

A major issue for teachers is that of the individual versus the group. On the one hand, schools are asked to educate each child, with their unique attributes, needs, progress, ways of learning, interests, development, families, aspirations, and much more. At the same time, students are put into groups to learn. Imagine a doctor having 30 patients in the room at one time, some with similar issues but most with different diagnoses; some responsive and some denying the teaching of the doctor; some behaving well and some loudly proclaiming priority—this is the teacher's daily lot. Dealing with groups is the core art in teaching and, as we discussed in Chapter 1, there is much evidence of remarkable success in this endeavor. However, it is an ongoing issue.

There has been a continuing search for resolving this dilemma, mostly expressed as arguments for smaller class sizes, which has not been a successful solution. The many meta-analyses of class size research show that although positive, the effects of this expensive policy are very small (Hattie, 2007; but see Blatchford and Russell, 2020). The reason that reducing class sizes has not had a major effect is because teachers often do not change how they teach when moving from larger to smaller classes. If they did change how they taught, it is likely that the effects of reducing class size would be larger. The point here is not advocacy for any particular class size, but to note that the attempts to allow for individual differences in groups have barely been affected by the number of students in the class.

Another solution has been individualized instruction: the internet, teaching machines, adaptive learning, and many other individualized plans have been promulgated and tried. Again, the effects are positive but small on achievement, self-esteem, critical thinking ability, or attitude towards the subject matter when taught through individualized programs (see Table 2.1). Teachers need to be adaptive within classrooms to accommodate individual differences and use differentiation in their teaching methods to accommodate the different progressions that students can take to meet the success criteria of the lesson.

A more recent set of claims concern personalized learning—which is in many ways a repackaging of individualized instruction—with its aim of providing instruction in which the pace of learning and the instructional approach are optimized for the needs of each learner. As noted above, the evidence is "still thin" for the effects of personalized learning (Zhang et al., 2020).

Our alternative is to speak of the 'centrality of the student,' as this does not imply each child is an island nor that each is so unique that there are not commonalities. It acknowledges that students can be taught and learn in larger groups, smaller groups, and individually. It means that the teacher needs to place each student at the center in terms of maximizing their learning but does not demand a particular teaching method or classroom configuration. It also recognizes that students are and will continue to live in social settings, learn how to learn from others, and build important social skills through working with others.

Schools are social settings

As teachers typically work with groups of students, it is important to understand that social interaction is a core factor in the success of teachers (see Blatchford, Pellegrini, & Baines, 2015; Jones & Kahn, 2017). In any one class, there can be much diversity in abilities, cultures, languages, socioeconomic backgrounds, and willingness to come to school to learn. The teacher can group students by ability, interest, or randomly, although there is still much whole-class teaching. Coe showed in the United Kingdom, 90% of the time students sit in groups and work alone. This means the teacher needs the expertise to prepare for interactions with individuals and groups of students, and interactions between students (see Blatchford, Kutnick, Baines, & Galton, 2003).

Students in western-world classes rarely sit in rows; usually they are clustered in circles. The often-claimed logic is that learning is optimized when they work individually for practice and revision tasks, in dyads to discuss and compare perspectives about incremental and new cognitive knowledge, in small groups to enrich and extend their understandings, and in large groups to respond to teacher directions and orchestrated tasks (Kutnick & Blatchford, 2014). The reality of sitting in groups is starker. In our analysis of more than 15,000 lessons, the teachers talk 89% of the time, ask 150 to 250 questions a day mostly about the facts or content, and students engage in 'doing' or completing tasks with success criteria more related to finishing on time, making their work neat and orderly, and hoping it is correct (Clinton et al., https://education.unimelb.edu.au/research/projects/ visible-classroom).

Peer-based learning and group-work is rarely used, often because of concerns about the distractions from peers, the social loafing that can occur, the worry that some may perform tasks more poorly or slower in the presence of others (social inhibition), the dominance of some, and the belief that the group could get off-task. Among the most systematic study of students in groups was that by Kutnick and Blatchford (2014), and some of their major findings included:

- There was little relationship between the size of groups and the learning tasks/interaction assigned.
- Teachers dominated the learning activity; they rarely offered opportunities for students to co-construct and further develop their own new knowledge.

- Grouping contexts were socially exclusive rather than inclusive—the composition of these groupings was dominated by homogeneous, same-sex friendships and similar attainment levels.
- Teachers, and other adults in the classroom, often worked with individuals—even within a whole-class context.
- Students were given few opportunities for interactive tasks where they could work autonomously from the teacher, yet only a few could gain the attention of the teacher when they undertook their learning tasks.
- Teacher domination of new cognitive knowledge in large groups may not allow all children in a class to participate, nor does it not allow for intensive cognitive and communicative interaction between pupils.
- Teachers rarely provided support or training for group working skills.

This, of course, does not mean this is the case for all classrooms. As Kutnick and Blatchford (2014) showed in their study, ensuring that there is a strong relational approach developed between the student and teacher and among the students can lead to major benefits from small-group work. Such "supportive relationships create a 'region of sensitivity' in which children develop trust, communication and collaborative opportunities amongst themselves that will enhance classroom learning—even when they are not working under the direct presence of the teacher" (p. 185). When supportive relationships are present:

- Students were more participative and showed more sustained engagement in group activities.
- Students showed more connectedness within their groups, focusing their attention on group members and their assigned learning tasks and group-work.
- Students were able to use symmetrical, collaborative communication to a greater extent in their problem-solving than children in control classes.
- Students showed more high-order/cognitive inferential forms of reasoning than control children.
- Teachers spent less time at the procedural level of task introduction and task focus, as student groups explained task procedures among themselves and became less dependent on the teacher.
- As the students became more task-focused in their group working, teachers became engaged more in the monitoring of pupils than in controlling them.

From the focus on building relational trust and skills with and among the students, the teacher's role evolved to cognitive-based monitoring and supporting learning within groups rather than direct teaching. Because the groups were well-tasked and based on relational and supportive principles, they were more able to move beyond the content to the deeper thinking, and it is this high level of cognitive thinking and engagement, claimed Kutnick and Blatchford (2014), that is the basis of increased school-based attainment in subjects such as reading, mathematics, and science. There was less chairing, or assigning individual tasks to group members, and more evaluation and supporting of each other, and teachers took a more guiding than directing role as they moved around the groups.

Building relational trust among teachers and with school leaders is an excellent sign of a learning organization. As Bryk and Schneider (2002, p. 144) argued, "Relational trust constitutes the connective tissue that binds ... individuals together around advancing the education and welfare of children," and placed much emphasis on the presence of skillful school leaders who actively listen to concerns of all parties and avoid arbitrary actions.

Phases of development

As children grow, major changes happen in their brain development, their social competences, and, of course, their learning around language, numeracy, and many other domains.

Bolton and Hattie (2018) traced the development of the child's brain from birth to 20 years—a period of major transformation physically and psychologically in the functioning of the brain. They found very close parallels in these changes in the brain to Piaget's model of child development. Piaget proposed a four-phased model (Piaget & Inhelder, 1969, 1973). The sensorimotor stage, from birth to two years of age, is where the child exhibits a completely egocentric approach to the world, is unable to separate thoughts from action, and is unable to recognize that the perspective of the object would differ depending on their position relative to the object. The child then moves to the preoperational stage from ages two to seven years. In this stage, object permanence is firmly established and symbolic thoughts develop.

In order to move to the next stage, referred to as the concrete operational stage (seven to 11 years), children need to be able to perform what Piaget termed 'operations': internalized actions that the individual can use to manipulate, transform, and then return an object to its original state. The child understands the principle of conservation, which states that the quantity of an object can be determined to be the same, despite a change in shape or volume of a container. The commonly used example is where the child must determine if an amount of water in two different shaped glasses is the same despite the difference in shape and size. The concrete operational stage is also marked by the child beginning to apply logic to steps and stages, assessed through the 'A not B' task in which an object is hidden from the child in one of two different locations. The final stage from 11 to 16 years, the formal operation stage, is characterized by abstract and hypothetical thought. While there is a large body of literature that supports the underlying principles of Piaget's theory, there are also a number of weaknesses in Piaget's work, such as his inability to separate memory from logic; the assumption that children exist at only one stage at a time; and the effect of cultural context.

Piaget's four phases are related to the changes in the development of executive functioning. 'Executive function' is an umbrella term for a set of higher-order, general-purpose control processes that regulate a number of different cognitive functions (such as thought and behavior) for the attainment of a specific goal (Miyake, Friedman, Emerson, Witzki, Howerter, & Wager, 2000). Executive function encompasses a wide range of cognitive processes such as working memory, cognitive flexibility, attention control, planning, concept formation, and feedback processing, each varying in complexity. There are three core components to executive functioning: inhibition of dominant or proponent responses; updating and monitoring of working memory representations; and shifting between tasks or mental sets (Miyake et al., 2000).

Executive function is also associated with emotional aspects of the child's growth and development, including, but not limited to, moral and communicative behavior and social cognition. Further, there is a large evidence base illustrating that the development of executive function is a major predictor of scholastic performance (Swanson & Alloway, 2012). In particular, a number of longitudinal studies indicate that executive function contributes to academic achievement rather than vice versa (Best, Miller, & Naglieri, 2011).

Bolton and Hattie (2018) showed that changes in brain development (for example, the changes during growth of white and grey matter) are aligned with the changes proposed by the Piagetian theory and executive functioning. What is of particular interest is the timing of the changes and their parallels with the Piagetian development trajectories. These changes highlight the remarkable changes in children that teachers need to be aware of and accommodate in their teaching. In any one class, regardless of age, there can be students across the ranges of cognitive processing and executive functioning. There is also the hint that there are some crude age guidelines in the development of both cognitive processing and executive functioning, such that what may work best at ages zero to seven could be different from ages eight to 12, and 13-plus; but the mistake is to consider these ages are in any way fixed.

From zero to eight years, child development, as the foundation for later achievement, needs to be a major focus. In the early years, the development of language, a theory of mind (a belief about how the child's world works), and ordination are critical foci. If by age eight, or by the second to third year in school, children have not achieved a reasonable competence of reading, then they are often left behind. This is commonly known as the Matthew effect from the biblical injunction: the rich get richer; the poor remain poor or become poorer. In a meta-synthesis of literature about reading, Pfost, Hattie, Dorfler, and Artelt (2014) showed much evidence that if children do not attain a reasonable competence in reading by this stage, then very few catch up later and most start the slow drift out of the schooling system. These early years are crucial, if for no other reason than few teachers teach foundational reading beyond Years 2 to 3, so opportunities to establish these foundations lessen if reading is not grasped in the early years of schooling.

In the eight to 12 age group, there is much learning about how to socialize, learn from others, and teach each other; these are teachable skills. Once teenagers, the social world becomes all-important for so many, and for others there can be loneliness, or worse, rejection from others, all of which have profound effects on school performance.

By the ages of 17 to 18, post-compulsory schooling for many involves tertiary studies of some sort (university, community college, technical school), although some systems allow students to take these paths at a much younger age. The fascination now is the new emerging years from 17 to 27 which used to be known as 'young adulthood.' With less secure employment and less defined pathways into careers these days, we might say adolescence does not finish until about 27; maybe we need a new term for this age—teen-adults.

Among the most fascinating changes in human development is the shift in social development from family to peers that starts in late primary school and accelerates in high schools. There is more peer-focused engagement and much more integration into social groups, often with complex peer relations. Adolescents want to spend more time with friends, weigh peer opinions more heavily, and aim to fit in rather than stand out in social situations (Nelson, Jarcho, & Guyer, 2016). These social interactions can have positive or sometimes intensely negative influences on behavioral, social-emotion, and academic outcomes. Adolescents have a high need for friends they can trust, who respect their feelings and beliefs and listen to them (Gray, Romaniuk, & Daraganova, 2016). Girls more than boys talk about their own difficulties and emotions, even though 75% of boys still report high levels of these forms of communication with their peers, and four out of five males and females reported that their peer groups were characterized by high levels of positive attitudes.

Carroll, Houghton, and Lynn (2013) demonstrated that during adolescence, there is a strong tendency to develop a reputation that one then strives to initiate, enhance, and maintain. A reputation is collective in that it is the product of social processes, not merely impressions that others or individuals hold of others or themselves (Emler, 1990). A key factor thence is the importance of an audience, and this could be in person or on media. Adolescents build beliefs and actions to present themselves in a particular way so that they are accredited with specific qualities of character. These reputations could be developed by the way they 'tag' or 'untag' on Facebook and who they mix with at school. Reputations could explain why gangs are attractive to some, why many adolescents undertake risky behaviors, and why others create reputations through excluding others, bullying, and delinquent behaviors. Those adolescents with a reputation to enhance can also be subjected to the devastation of loneliness (Carroll et al., 2013).

To build and maintain their reputation, many adolescents select and accomplish very specific and challenging goals—conforming or non-conforming, social or academic, collaborative or isolating, and so on. The degree of difficulty associated with the task at hand is inextricably linked to commitment, which in turn influences the reputation an individual acquires. They can go to great lengths to cultivate and protect their reputation of choice.

Conclusion

A major message of this book is that changes in students' cognitive processing, brain development, and thinking during their school years are profound, and the more teachers are aware of the development of their students, the more they are able to devise appropriate teaching methods, groupings, progressions, and ways of engaging students in learning. To improve their impact on student learning, teachers need better ways to make the experience of students more visible and more prominent in every aspect of their teaching. Teaching and learning can be improved by a closer focus and understanding of the processes of teaching and learning, much more than basing teaching and learning on the attributes of teachers or learners.

The ranges of child attributes that need to be understood to make optimal teaching decisions are clearly vast. No one person could master them all, but teachers are expected to possess a breadth of skills about how to teach as well as content knowledge related to many outcomes now desired from schooling. Teachers are required to know how to differentiate and accommodate each child's past, present, and future learning progress, to attend not only to each child but to groups of students, and to have an understanding of the developmental literature that explores the child's thinking and how to advance this thinking.

So much to do, so much to know, so much to care about. Michael Scriven (1994) made a major contribution in his paper on the duties of teachers. His list of duties shows the impressive levels of knowing, caring, and doing asked of teachers. They included: knowledge of subject matter; instructional competence; communication skills; management skills; course construction and improvement skills; evaluation of the course, teaching, materials, students, and curriculum; assessment competence; and professional competence, among others. He noted: "Those who can do these hundred difficult things can teach well; those who teach well can change the world in their lifetime; those who can't, can only do something less important" (p. 151).

CHAPTER 3

The work and expertise of the teacher
The six key questions

Teaching is multifaceted and challenging work. As discussed in Chapters 1 and 2, the demands on the twenty-first century classroom teacher are broader and more complex than ever before. The expert teacher utilizes a deep knowledge base and wide-ranging skills to ascertain students' existing skills and knowledge and their learning needs. The centrality of the student (as discussed in Chapter 2) means that these learning needs are pivotal to the teacher's decision-making about what, when, and how to teach. This chapter explores what is involved in teacher thinking, decision-making, intervention, and evaluation, while keeping student learning development central. This chapter also highlights the body of knowledge and skills that is integral to the notion of the teacher as a professional.

Expert teacher knowledge and practices

The list of attributes of the expert teacher seems daunting. Along with relationship-building and using specialist knowledge around pedagogy, the curriculum, and discipline content, we argue that the effective teacher needs to be able to identify and collect evidence about the broad range of interests, beliefs, skills, and knowledge in diverse student cohorts. The effective teacher then needs to analyze and use this evidence to make decisions about the deliberate strategies or interventions that will result in growth and cognitive change in these students. Further, teachers need the capacity and tools to evaluate the impact of these interventions both during and after implementation. Targeting teaching to the learning needs of individual and groups of students relies on teachers using their knowledge and expertise related to the different stages of cognitive, emotional, and physical development. Teachers also need to be willing and able to draw on the expertise, knowledge, and experience of others, including in research-based professional literature. The planning, implementation, and evaluation in teaching involve a collaborative process.

In discussing the multilayered work of the teacher, this chapter presents a model that addresses these attributes and practices. Importantly, this model is predicated on the notion of growth and development, not deficit, so the focus is on what the student brings to the classroom (González, Moll, & Amanti, 2006), what they can do (Griffin, 2018), and where they are ready to go to next in their learning. The model also requires the teacher to know what the student cannot do (yet) or does not know. This is a shift from some traditional and common discourses about teaching and learning.

The model

Figure 3.1 provides a graphic representation of the key stages of the model, which is what we call a 'clinical' or evidence-based teaching model that focuses on six key questions. The model is a cycle wherein each stage leads to and informs the next, and the centrality of the student (or groups of students) is clear. It should be noted, however, that there will be opportunities and necessary reasons for the teacher to revisit a stage

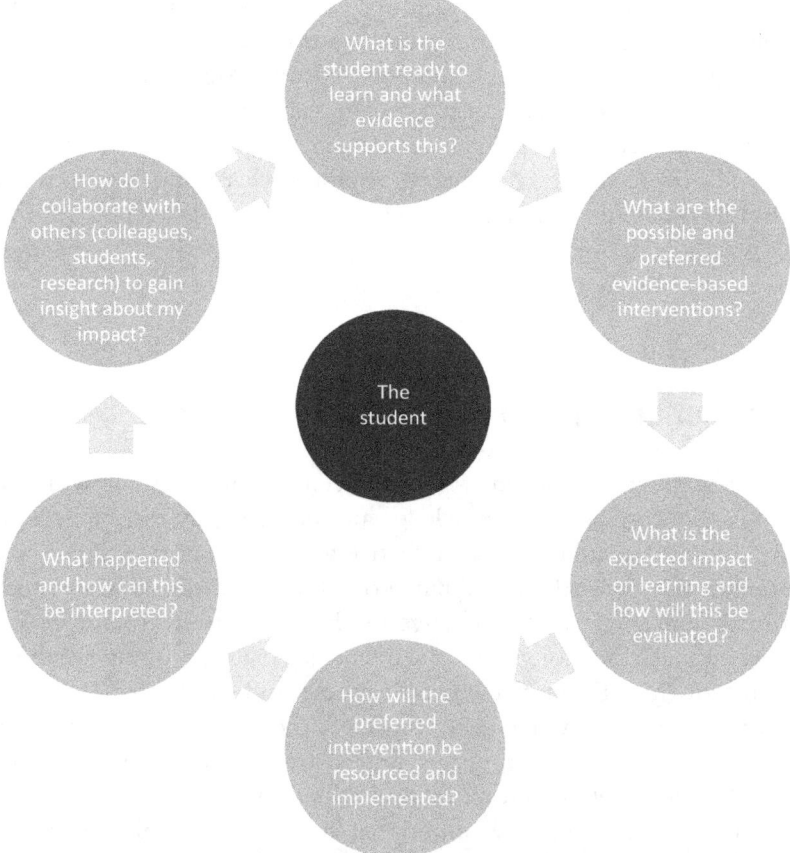

Figure 3.1 The six questions: An evidence-based teaching model

to adjust their thinking and practice as unanticipated outcomes result, new evidence is revealed, further questions are posed, and more complex decision-making is required. Key teacher knowledge and practices, including the ability to collect, analyze, and use evidence, are crucial throughout the cycle. The evaluation of the impact of the interventions on student learning informs future teaching and also enables the teacher to reflect on and evaluate their own learning throughout the cycle. While collaborative work is specifically highlighted in one of the stages, in reality, is it important to all stages.

Defining evidence

It is important to acknowledge the role of the collection and analysis of evidence at every stage of the cycle. The teacher needs to identify what constitutes evidence at each stage and how this evidence will be critiqued, considered, and interpreted collaboratively with students and colleagues. In times of regular high-stakes testing and publication of comparative tables of schools and nations, evidence is sometimes defined only in terms of statistics or numeric data, or in terms of published articles. Teachers need to have a much broader conceptualization of evidence, and this includes their experience, interpretations, and observations. Remembering that the student is at the center of the teacher's practice, teachers need to collect evidence about the whole child and their learning history. This may include understanding the student's background, interests, and social and cultural worlds, rather than or as well as their most recent test scores or school results. Useful examples of evidence that support teachers to determine what the student is ready to learn next include:

- individual or group-based interactions (both formal and informal) with the student about their existing knowledge or skill associated with the curriculum area;
- conversations with the student, both within and beyond the classroom, about their interests and recreational activities;
- information about the student's familial relationships and practical home arrangements, for example, knowing whether the student lives with both parents, one parent or caregiver, or alternates between different places of residence;
- reports (both formal and informal) of the student's general health and well being;
- classroom-based observations of the student's physical positioning in the classroom, interactions with peers, behavior, participation in activities, and completion of tasks;
- work samples and completed formative and summative assessment tasks aligned to the relevant curriculum;
- previous records of academic results, including those resulting from internally and externally organized testing;
- discussions with colleagues who teach, have taught, or otherwise interact with the student;
- research evidence in education literature and from other established professional sources;
- evidence of the teacher's own knowledge and skills (Timperley, 2010) and the impact of their practice and specific interventions implemented previously.

The nature of teacher expertise

This list is not exhaustive, but presents a range of evidence that informs, supports, and helps the teacher to justify their decision making in relation to students' learning development. In each learning context, different combinations of evidence are triangulated to increase the validity of the teacher's decisions. In this sense, the teacher is involved in ongoing interpretative research and evaluation in which evidence informs practice, practice is evaluated, and practice is modified according to further evidence collected.

Stages of the evidence-based teaching cycle

The key questions align with and encapsulate the teacher practices involved at each stage of the cycle and provide prompts about the teacher knowledge and skill-base required. In the following discussion of each of the stages of the cycle, the key teacher knowledge base, associated practices, and evidence collection and decision-making processes are highlighted.

- *What is the student ready to learn and what evidence supports this?*

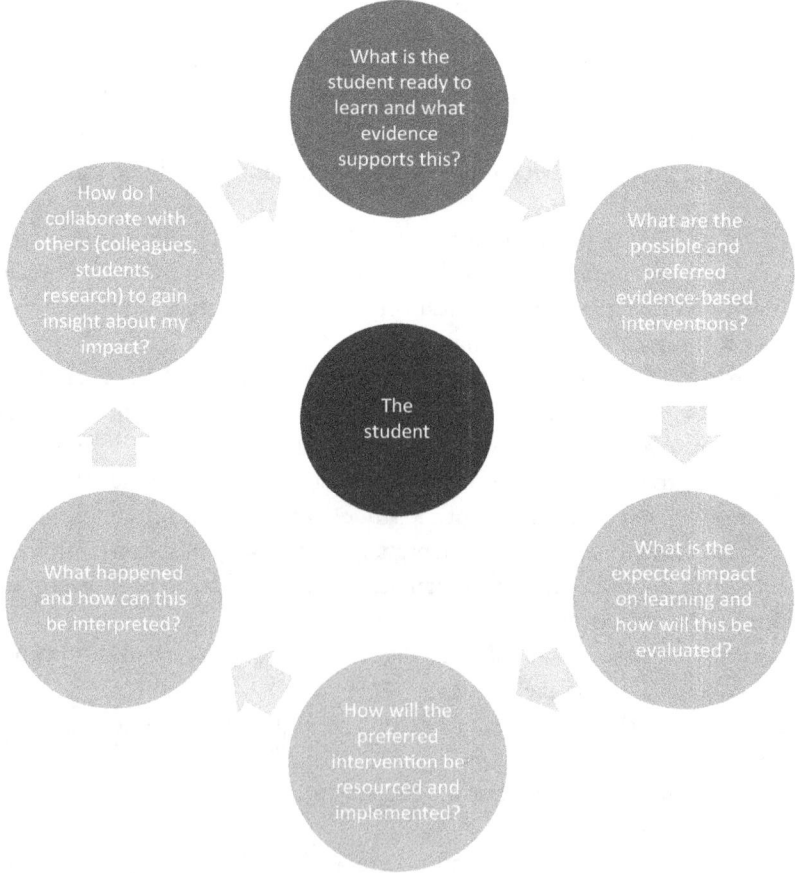

This stage of the cycle essentially deals with what the student already knows and can do, what the next step of learning development is for the student, and how the teacher ascertains this. In any learning context, each student is positioned in relation to a particular aspect of a curriculum (whether that be, for example, mandated state-run curriculum or a more individualized school-designed curriculum) or body of knowledge. With any specific student or group of students, the curriculum is a guide; it has not been developed with a specific student or cohort in mind, so the teacher's decision-making goes beyond simply adhering to the curriculum or a prescribed text. In a class of 25 students, some students may demonstrate knowledge and skills beyond the curriculum aligned to their stage of schooling; other students may need to develop further knowledge and skills to meet the demands associated with that curriculum level.

Part of the teachers' role here is to use their discipline knowledge base and understanding of the curriculum to map the developmental continuum of that particular body of knowledge or skill set with the aim of assisting the student to move along that continuum, considering what they *do* know and understand. To develop this continuum or construct, the teacher needs to be able to describe the typical skills and knowledge students demonstrate at each level of proficiency.

The teacher needs to be able to ascertain their students' content knowledge, levels of thinking (for example, their understanding at literal, inferential, and evaluative levels), and the extent to which the student can engage with the content effectively and metacognitively.

Not only is the teacher's understanding of students' prior skills and knowledge important to this stage, but also the teacher needs a deep understanding of a student's motivations, sense of confidence, willingness to invest, and many other related dispositions. It helps to know the previous experience of the student in relation to learning, how the student faces challenges to learning, and the range of strategies the student possesses to facilitate their learning, especially if one method of learning is not successful initially. This latter notion, often called self-regulation or metacognition, is part of the diagnosis relevant to this first stage of the cycle.

Each of these considerations also informs the teacher's establishment of learning intentions and success criteria associated with a task, lesson, or unit, and for the class, smaller groups, or individual students. This leads to subsequent questions more related to assessment tools, rubrics, and the choice of taxonomies that address cognitive, affective, and skills-based domains. Rubrics, as one example, allow performance to be judged in relation to well-defined success criteria (rather than globally, in comparison to other students, or just by being lengthy, neat, and handed in on-time) so that feedback focuses on improving from where the student currently is in their learning to the success criteria where they need to be.

To help inform these judgments, evidence from previous assessments and the student's own evaluation of their learning is useful. This assists the teacher to ascertain the characteristics of student work at different levels of proficiency and informs the positioning of each student in relation to the particular learning continuum. In other words, the teacher is deciding or diagnosing what the student already knows and can do in relation to that curriculum area. The teacher can then decide what the student is ready to learn and what the specific learning goals will be.

In addition to work samples, particularly those associated with the content or skill area, evidence at this stage may also include interactions with the student in one-to-one, group, and whole-class situations. The teacher's ability to pose effective questions is crucial at this stage in order to draw out the student's prior knowledge. The teacher's collection of other valuable evidence may be almost incidental; it feels instinctive, yet it is purposeful. This kind of evidence may draw on observations during the previous unit's completion or on the student's interactions and participation during classroom activities. Expert teachers collect this kind of evidence constantly, and they are able to analyze its importance both momentarily and systematically when combined with other evidence.

The following examples reveal how the collection of evidence, in an early childhood and a senior secondary setting, respectively, informs the teacher's decision-making about what the learner is ready to learn next.

Example: Early childhood teacher

I was working with a 3-year-old new to my room and I was helping her negotiate new routines, but I really wanted to know more about what she knew about 'same' and 'different.' So, my method of gathering the evidence about what she knew was to use the routine of packing away and my focused questions to encourage her to articulate and demonstrate her knowledge. In the end, I found out that she could recognize and name some shapes and placed similar shapes together. She used the terms 'longer' and 'shorter' to describe the difference between the crayon and pencil and lay one against the other to prove her point. This information allowed me to consider the mathematical and spatial knowledge and skills the child was ready to engage with next.

Knowledge of the subject was crucial. That the pencils and crayons were there was deliberate, as it was meant to provide an opportunity to have the interaction that occurred. It is one of many that have been planned by the team for just that purpose. So, although I worked one out with the child, it was planned in collaboration to gather evidence.

Example: Senior secondary teacher

The student was a Year 12 Legal Studies student completing an 'evaluation' type extended response in preparation for the end-of-year exam. The task required the student to identify and explain strengths and weaknesses of aspects of the legal system and to draw conclusions about these aspects of the legal system using evidence to support her viewpoint.

I referenced previous examples of the student's responses to this type of extended response question, and it showed that she was able to identify and explain strengths and weaknesses of different aspects of the legal system but was not making coherent links between the strength of a particular aspect and its corresponding weakness. She was listing and explaining a series of weaknesses and a series of strengths and coming to a general conclusion but not discussing a strength and its corresponding counterargument/weakness. She showed that she understood the format for responding to an 'evaluation' extended response but needed support in discussing the strengths and weaknesses of each individual aspect before coming to an overall conclusion.

The student and I analyzed her previous written responses against an exemplar of an excellent evaluation response. She was able to identify what she needed to do to improve the content and structure of her responses. The decision-making was based on the evidence, which showed that the student had mastered the basic format of an evaluation response and was ready to write more sophisticated and nuanced responses.

Collegial sharing of resources and previous work samples is also important when interpreting curriculum documentation, developing learning objectives, and designing continua and constructs relevant to the specific area of study. For the teacher to collect a range of evidence about their current students' existing skills and knowledge, consultation with colleagues is crucial.

At this stage of the cycle, the teacher's work involves intellectually complex thinking, making refined evaluative decisions, and using finely-honed skills of curriculum interpretation, goal-setting, analysis of evidence, and decision-making. The teacher's collection and interpretation of evidence inform their decisions about what the student is ready to learn and how student learning growth will be demonstrated in relation to the specific area of knowledge or skill. When this is accomplished and critiqued with other educators, a sense of triangulation is achieved and thus confidence in the diagnoses.

■ *What are the possible and preferred evidence-based interventions?*

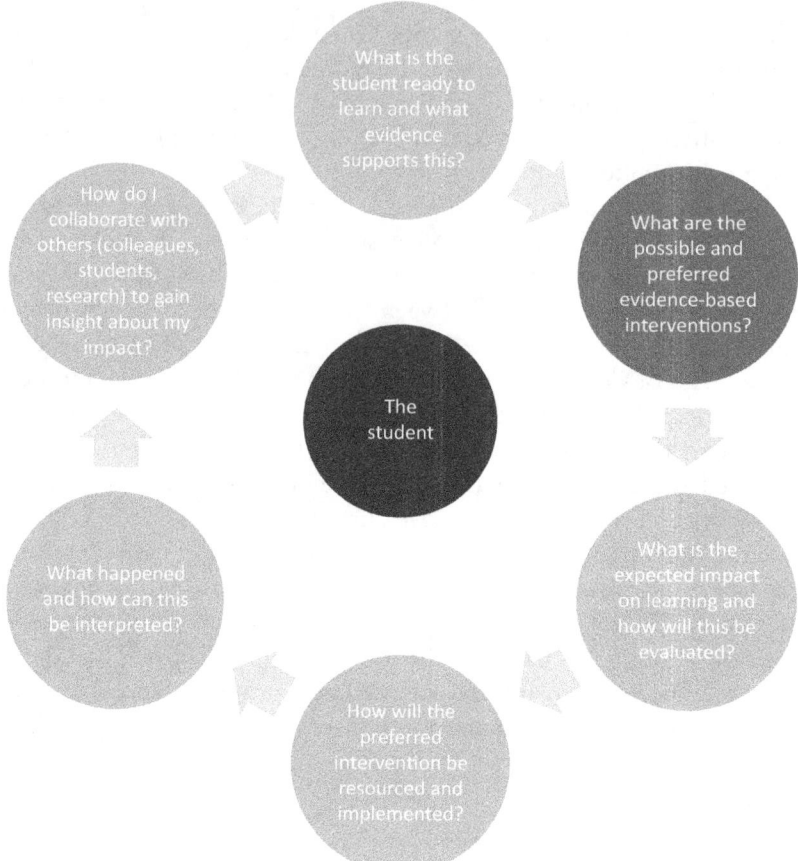

Here, the teacher needs to consider and justify their selection of interventions that is most likely to support the student to move to the next level of development within the learning focus area. This involves locating, processing, analyzing, and evaluating evidence from a range of sources. The linking of theory and practice is fundamental. The expert teacher draws on a broad repertoire of strategies and experience and considers the interventions that have worked previously in similar situations or seeks alternative strategies that have been shown to work for the diagnoses made during the first stage of the cycle. It is important that the teacher has access to relevant research literature when determining how best to advance the learning of a student or group of students. What does this research say about effective teaching practices? How relevant is the research to the teacher's student cohort and context? Does the research present evidence of impact on student learning? The teacher and colleagues need to adopt an openness to new research evidence about quality teaching and student learning, and commit to maintain and refresh their knowledge around this (Cochran-Smith & Boston College Evidence Team, 2009). This is hard to fit into the daily or weekly schedule in a school. Resourcing and time to engage in professional reading is an important professional development focus in schools.

Figure 3.2 provides the average effects of many teaching interventions, but the fidelity, dosage, adaptations, and quality of the implementation are key to success when using any of these strategies in a classroom. Further, a key issue when making these choices is that various interventions have higher probabilities of success than others, and more importantly, can work best when success criteria are more closely related to surface-level learning (content, ideas). Other interventions work best when students possess sufficient content knowledge to progress to deeper-level processing (Hattie & Donoghue, 2016). Thus, the teacher's expertise in diagnosing student learning (surface, deep, transfer) is critical when making decisions about the interventions with the highest impact. There are few interventions that deliberately teach both the content and the deep-thinking systematically—the jigsaw method, which promotes collaborative learning and peer teaching, is one of these exceptions, and it is the top of this list (see Aronson & Patnoe, 2010 for more on the Jigsaw method).

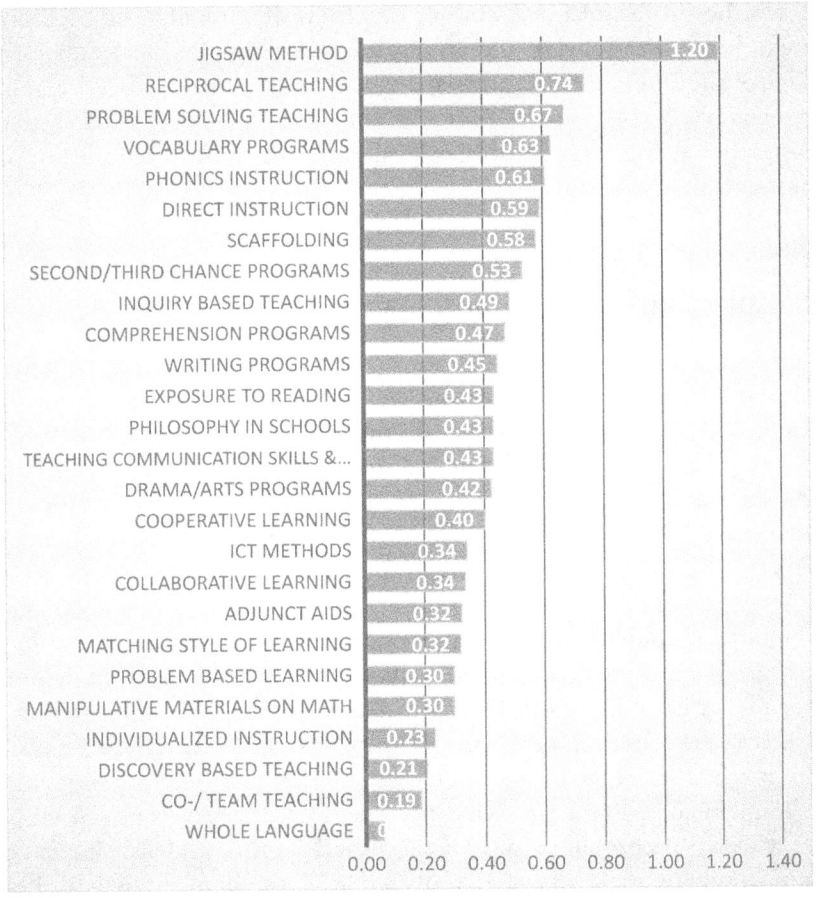

Figure 3.2 Effect-sizes for various teaching methods

Broader consideration of the student's background, well-being, and other contextual factors is also important at this stage. The teacher matches the evidence about where the student is in the learning cycle (beginning, content phase, consolidation phase, deeper-relating phase, transfer phase) with the most appropriate interventions for the learning context. The teacher's deep understanding of the ways in which cultural, social, and personal elements affect student learning also comes into play.

The teacher's ability to acknowledge, reflect on, and evaluate their own abilities and needs is important. An intervention may appear to be appropriate to the student's learning needs, but if the teacher's expertise does not align with this approach, other solutions need to be sourced or the teacher may require further professional learning to better understand and implement new interventions and seek and consider the evidence of their effectiveness. The teacher also needs to be able to reconcile other factors such as school and classroom resources, school and personal philosophies, and policy aspects with the approach to intervention.

Tentativeness is part of this decision-making. The teacher's knowledge, experience, and use of a broad range of evidence cannot guarantee that an intervention will be successful for a student or group of students in a specific learning context; hence, the importance of continually being open to feedback about the impact of the intervention and being ready to adapt or discard the approach for an alternative.

A teacher at the high school level illustrates many of these notions of clinical thinking.

Example: Junior secondary teacher

After collecting and analyzing evidence from a pre-test, I sought information from the student's Year 7 teacher and reports accessed from the school's intranet. I also was able to draw evidence from the student's Year 7 NAPLAN results for numeracy. These different evidence sources indicated that the student's progress in Maths was aligned to Level 6 of *The Victorian Curriculum* in relation to most mathematic concepts and skills. The student's previous Maths teacher and other teachers who had taught her indicated that she was a cooperative and willing learner who appeared particularly enthusiastic about activities involving digital technology. A couple of my colleagues also indicated that the student seemed to enjoy group work, particularly when allocated to a group with students of similar or higher capabilities in Maths. I had also noticed that during earlier group-work activities, the student appeared more willing to participate in discussions than in whole-class situations when a few students tended to dominate.

I implemented a group activity in which the student was placed with a close peer who was progressing at a similar level and another student who was demonstrating a slightly more advanced proficiency. Throughout the activity, I observed that the student mostly worked independently rather than collaboratively, but regularly shared information. The student appeared to note how her group members were progressing and used this as a way to gauge whether she was on task.

During a whole-class discussion towards the end of the same lesson, the student was keen to contribute to questions on the board. However, some dominant students in the class were vocal and this acted as a deterrent for not only the student but for some other students as well. Despite calling upon her to answer a question, she chose not to. If not for my observations of her working within her group previously, I believe that I would have missed an opportunity to gain valuable evidence. This prompted me to set the classroom up differently for future classroom activities.

Using my clinical reasoning, in conjunction with collegial input, I was able to conclude that the evidence suggested that the student was an independent student who worked cooperatively rather than collaboratively in small groups. This was not a learning need that I was originally looking to address but one that was important to my future teaching and her learning. This learning need was to be a focal point along with her mathematical one.

Observing the student within a small group and whole-class context supported and confirmed that I had correctly assessed her existing skills and had targeted teaching at the 'right' place. Furthermore, observation gave me the opportunity to continually track her progress throughout the completion of formative tasks. This allowed me to continually reflect on whether the tasks were beneficial throughout the unit of work.

When considering the possible interventions and deciding which of these will support the student's development, the teacher draws on the evidence about the student's existing skills and knowledge (collected during the first stage), but also considers broader evidence bases such as the student's general behaviors, interests, and contextual factors that may impact on learning. Informal and formal interactions with the student may provide rich evidence, as may observations about the student's positioning (physical and social) within the classroom and their participation in activities beyond the classroom. Colleagues and parents may also provide valuable insights into the student as a learner. It is also important that the teacher notices any discernible changes in the student's engagement with learning and takes steps to identify why these changes have occurred.

Acknowledged research literature is a key source of evidence at this stage of the cycle. This may involve seeking information from syntheses of quantitative and qualitative research, including classroom-based action research. It is important, however, to focus on the evidence of interventions on students (whatever the evidence source) and not on whether the intervention aligns with favored approaches. The teacher's engagement with and capacity to critique research literature about the effectiveness of teaching strategies must be ongoing so that informed decisions about teaching can be made (Cochran-Smith et al., 2009).

It seems there is a major lack of resources that show the impact on students of various instructional lesson plans. One is EdReports (www.edreports.org), which provides quality-assured lessons in a similar manner to Consumer or Choice reviews. Teams of four to five reviewers use well-developed and published rubrics, review tools, evidence guides, and key documents to evaluate the lessons. The resources are listed by curricula domain and age ranges. The process moves the resources through various gateways, which pertain to their alignment with standards and (in the United States) common core curricula, whether the standards are treated with the appropriate depth and quality required to support student learning, and whether the materials are user-friendly for students and teachers. The review team shares its evidence, comes to a consensus, and shares the evaluations on the website. It would be a magnificent breakthrough if evidence could be provided of actual impact on students, based on measures of fidelity (how close is the implementation to the intended design), dosage (how much training is needed to successfully implement), and adaptation of implementation.

The teacher decides which evidence-based approaches and interventions will support the students' development in the specific learning context. To justify their thinking and decision-making, the teacher needs, all the while, to be consulting acknowledged research and evidence gained from colleagues, reflecting on the effect of their past practices on learning, and using evidence collected about the student's existing skills. The teacher, in reflecting on their own practice, needs to be aware of the impact of particular classroom strategies and structures on the student's learning and consider how they might consolidate or modify these to enhance learning. Here, the teacher draws on evidence from their own teaching experience; in other words, they reflect on the strategies that have worked in similar situations previously.

In summary, valid evidence to support the teacher's decision-making at this stage may and should include a combination of acknowledged and robust research evidence, teacher evidence drawn from experience and knowledge, and student-based evidence. Understanding and using other's ways of thinking and doing are critically important when making decisions about interventions. It is crucial that the teacher acknowledges that they may need to seek information from colleagues, school leaders, and parents to gain a broad picture of the student as a learner across disciplines and learn of previous approaches that have been successful in similar learning contexts. The establishment of professional learning and research teams within and beyond the school may facilitate the locating, disseminating, and discussing of current research and professional literature pertinent to the school's learners and their stages of learning development and discipline-specific pedagogy. Sometimes these collegial teams are formed organically; ideally, they should be fundamental components of a school's structure and be supported and resourced accordingly. There is also an increasing number of online communities that source, question, and debate the merits of various interventions (Education Endowment Fund, Social Ventures Australia, What Works Clearinghouse). On a broader level, school partnerships and networks can promote collaboration at the inter-school and institution level so that experts and researchers are able to exchange ideas and approaches.

Analyzing and critiquing a range of evidence, matching evidence-based interventions to the student's learning needs, and justifying decision-making are key at this stage of the cycle.

- *What is the expected impact on learning and how will this be evaluated?*

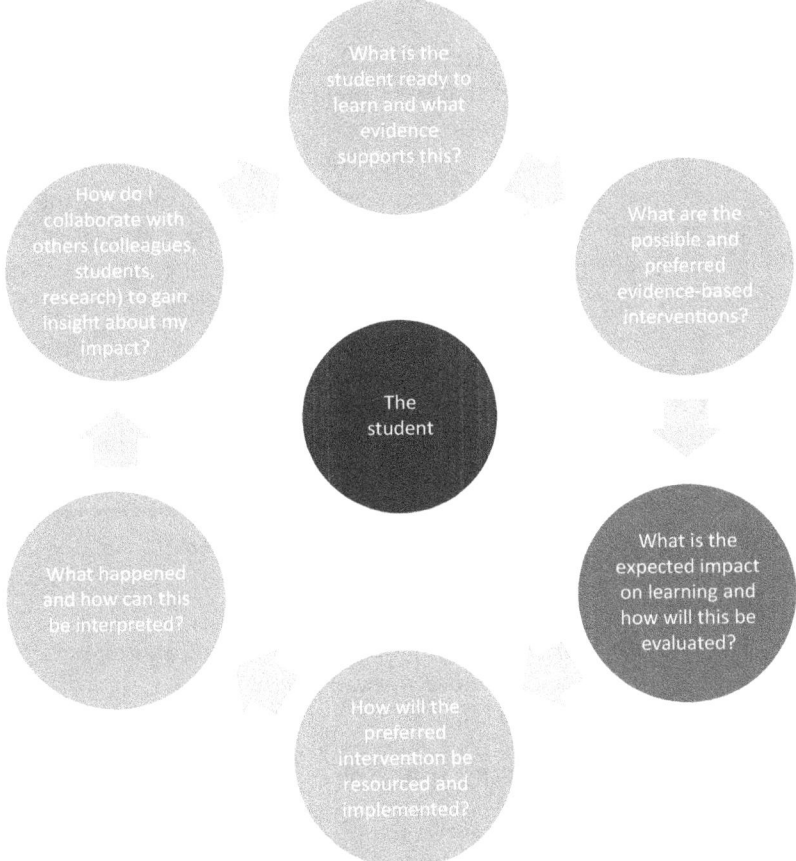

Here the teacher hypothesizes about the likely impact of the selected interventions and designs tools and processes that will measure this impact. The teacher has decided on the most appropriate interventions to support student growth in the specific learning context. Part of this reasoning involves revisiting the learning objectives and developing success criteria for the lesson or series of lessons. These success criteria can relate to the content and extension of ideas. Hattie and Clarke (2019) recommend codeveloping and certainly sharing the success criteria with students and undertaking continuous reviews of the progress the students are making from their starting point towards reaching the criteria of success. The art is not to over-assess but to involve the students in evaluating progress. This means teachers need to continually form hypotheses—what impact are the selected interventions having on the student's learning progression towards these objectives?

The teacher needs to plan for the collection of evidence in relation to the success criteria so that development can be measured. How will the evidence from previous learning episodes be compared with new evidence? The teacher decides which work samples associated with the learning intervention will be monitored or assessed formally and how this will be done. Valuable evidence also comes from observations, so the teacher may arrange for a colleague to collect evidence of classroom interactions between teacher and student, and student and student. Another important source is evidence from students about how they are learning as the interventions proceed. Where will opportunities for metacognitive response and reflection occur?

In planning for the collection of evidence, the teacher needs to revisit the purpose of the intervention, how particular types of evidence will measure learning, and how the evidence will be collected and analyzed during and after the interventions.

It is important that teachers working in the same learning environment have common or collective thinking about what constitutes progress and success in relation to the area of learning or task. The development of a shared language for teachers to articulate practice and progress is needed. Collaboration involves the shared designing of developmental continua or constructs and assessment tools, including rubrics. The designing of these can be extremely time-consuming and intellectually demanding, so working in teams is essential. In addition to this, and as noted earlier, teachers need to see that drawing on the expertise and experience of others is essential to effective teaching. The teacher who has taught this curriculum area in a range of classroom contexts will have a rich understanding of how students respond to the associated content and skills and how to articulate and recognize levels of proficiency.

A teacher, working with her junior colleague, illustrates her thoughts about impact and how to seek evidence to evaluate this impact.

Example: Early primary teacher

My colleague Jo, a first-year teacher, wanted advice about working with Tian, a young girl in her Year 1 class. From looking at work samples over the course of the term, Jo had concluded that Tian's writing development had stalled. Jo and I looked closely at Tian's writing samples and the feedback that Jo had given. We looked at writing elements at whole text, sentence, and word level in order to identify and isolate the aspects of the genre (which was informative), syntax, vocabulary, and spelling Tian appeared to have under control and those she was ready to learn. The evidence from the work samples indicated that Tian's spelling of familiar words was mostly accurate, but that the writing could have contained further vocabulary relevant to the content area (in the latest instance, information about a particular species of animal). Tian continued to write in simple sentences with few words. While her writing contained some relevant information, the organization and structuring of ideas were areas that Jo and I felt Tian could develop.

The work and expertise of the teacher

Jo and I discussed models of writing that assist students to understand and implement the key features of particular genres at text, sentence, and word levels. The Gradual Release of Responsibility Model, first developed by Pearson and Gallagher (1993), and the Teaching-Learning Cycle, adapted from the work of Christie and Derewianka (2010), each comprise stages such as building the content area, explicit modeling and deconstruction of the features and structures of specific text types, guided or joint construction of texts, and independent construction. While Jo had provided models of simple informative texts for her class, she reflected that Tian (and other students) would have benefitted from more attention to the organization of ideas. I suggested to Jo that she also implement a strategy that focused on using connectives to transform simple sentences to compound sentences.

■ *How will the preferred intervention be resourced and implemented?*

This is when the action and practical implementation of the selected intervention occurs. It is the stage when the teacher's hypotheses are tested and further evidence from within the intervention is collected. The teacher's (immediate or considered) analysis of this type of evidence may result in modification of the intervention or rethinking the approach. The expert classroom practitioner is the ultimate multitasker—one who is able to foster relationships, manage behaviors, identify isolated or disengaged students, try to address isolation and disengagement, and keep on top of practical issues such as time management, unforeseen interruptions, and technology issues. All this is in conjunction with implementing the planned intervention to support the students' cognitive development.

The teacher needs to define the learning objectives associated with the task and make these transparent to students. The teacher implements the planned interventions and the most appropriate pedagogy in relation to aspects such as content delivery, setting up group work, selecting resources, and giving students opportunities to demonstrate their learning—the teacher has selected these approaches to explicitly address the learning objectives and to maximize the opportunities for the students to achieve the objectives. The teacher is transparent in their pedagogy, making their choice of strategies clear and explicit to the students and linking these strategies back to the learning intentions.

In implementing researched and acknowledged interventions, it is important to ensure that the intervention is implemented as intended, but all the while the teacher is mindful of and responsive to the contextual factors that demand adjustments to the approach (Figure 3.3).

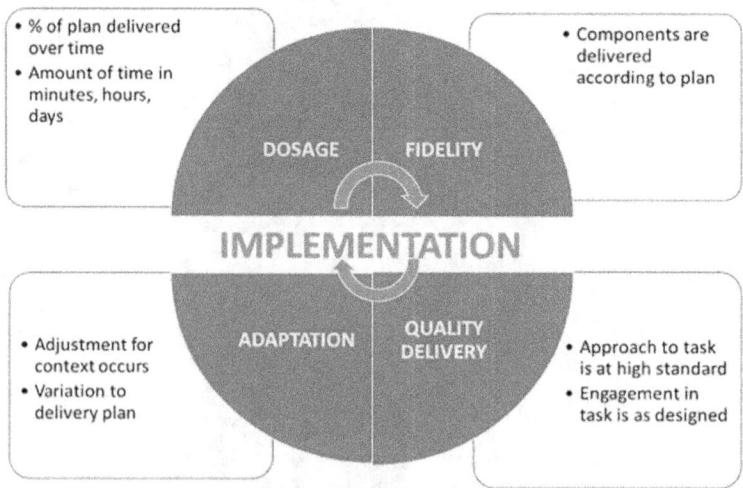

Figure 3.3 Monitoring and measuring an implementation (Clinton, 2014)

The expert teacher is strategic about collecting evidence during and after the implementation of the interventions. The teacher is aware that the evidence needs to enable the measurement of the impact of the interventions on student learning. This involves formative and possibly summative assessment strategies. Ongoing formative assessment based on development approaches enables the teacher to identify the next steps in the student's learning progression. These processes and tools require careful design so that the evidence collected can be compared with that obtained earlier.

The teacher is also alert to unanticipated evidence that may present itself as the interventions proceed. The teacher notices students' attitudes to and levels of engagement with the area of learning. They interact with the students, informally and formally, to gauge their interest and general well-being. They pay attention to the positioning of the students in the classroom space and how this is consistent or inconsistent with previous lessons. The evidence collection is continuous and requires the teacher to use their expert knowledge to understand how the student or students are responding to different intervention approaches.

Example: Upper primary teacher

At the start of the year, my assessment and evaluations of Danny's learning were pretty general and more focused on his behaviors and interactions in the classroom rather than specific areas of learning across the curriculum. I was drawn to looking at Danny's approaches to a task rather than the learning itself. I attempted to encourage Danny's engagement by using positive reinforcement and feedback, aspects our staff had explored during the first professional development day for the year.

I needed to carefully consider the way I discussed and gave instructions about the task and allowed opportunities for student questions and clarifications. By considering the questions the students (including Danny) asked, I was able to analyze how I had delivered the content and presented tasks. I began to look specifically at the overarching learning intentions for each task and the success criteria that would assist Danny and others to reach their goals.

With my colleague, I had devised a continuum of mathematical reasoning strategies. I focused on observing Danny's reasoning strategies in relation to problem-solving. Armed with the learning intention and success criteria, which I shared with all the students at the beginning of the lesson, I observed what Danny would do and say in relation to specific problem-solving tasks.

The problem involved students sharing eight apples with an unknown number of people, where everyone would receive ¾ of an apple. Danny asked his working partner questions about the task. *'How will we solve it?' 'Can we draw the apples and people?'* He then proceeded with a visual solution, while his partner worked on an equation. I asked Danny to share his strategy and listen to his partner. A discussion occurred, and I asked Danny if he could explain the other strategy in his own words. He replied, *'I'm not sure, can you say it again?'* Danny's partner showed him how to connect the equation to Danny's drawing. I asked Danny if he could apply this strategy to a new problem with more apples, and he replied, *"Can I draw it?"*

This 'fine-grained' examination of Danny's maths reasoning skills helped me gain a more specific understanding of where he was on the continuum of reasoning. Visual aids assisted Danny to conceptualize his understanding, but he was not yet able to apply a quantity to a related equation when solving a problem.

Danny was comfortable working collaboratively and may find peer tutoring a reliable way to learn new strategies and apply them when working independently. Research in other settings where maths reasoning is taught successfully show that students are more likely to learn and use a strategy with continued practice (Askew, 2009). This helps me to determine the next type of task that will assist Danny to where he needs to go next in his learning and helps to define my next interventions.

Some interventions require the participation and collaboration of expert colleagues, not only in the planning and evaluation stages of the cycle, but at the classroom implementation stage. Historically and still too often, teachers operate in isolation at the implementation stage. This is sometimes the fault of rigid timetabling and lack of resourcing (time, space, people), but is often also due to teachers feeling pressure to be adept at all strategies and not feeling confident to seek or accept assistance from others. Resourcing the intervention means drawing on and utilizing the collective expertise of colleagues, not only by selecting the most appropriate materials. This type of collaboration is becoming more common, but mostly, there is still a reliance on the solo teacher to implement interventions that an expert colleague could model or contribute to in the classroom context. Schools need to encourage the identification of the individual teacher's expertise in specific pedagogical approaches and the forming of teams that utilize this expertise effectively.

Collegial observation may facilitate collaborative analysis of evidence and planning at the implementation stage. Descriptive observation involves the recording of the students' and teachers' actions and the analysis of how these impact learning (City, Elmore, Fiarman, & Teitel, 2009). This type of collaboration requires trust and an open dialogue between colleagues with a focus on improving practice to enhance student learning. Colleagues discuss what the focus of the observation will be before the lesson. This will be linked to the specific learning intentions and intervention and may focus on observing particular students' learning and engagement. During the lesson, the observer records aspects such as the language of teacher–student interactions and student–student talk and the actual demonstration of student learning through what they have written, said, made, and done (Griffin, 2018). Importantly, the observations are descriptions, not judgments. After the observation, the colleagues discuss what has been observed, why the lesson played out as it did, what evidence of student learning resulted and why, and how this analysis is significant to future planning and implementation. The use of descriptive observation for the recording and analysis of classroom evidence has been found to foster collaborative dialogue (Kriewaldt, Nash, Windsor, Thornton, & Reid, 2018).

The teacher seeks advice from colleagues and revisits research and theory to validate decision-making. This decision-making must place the student's needs at the center (Burn & Mutton, 2013; Kriewaldt, McLean Davies, Rice, Rickards, & Acquaro, 2017).

■ *What happened and how can this be interpreted?*

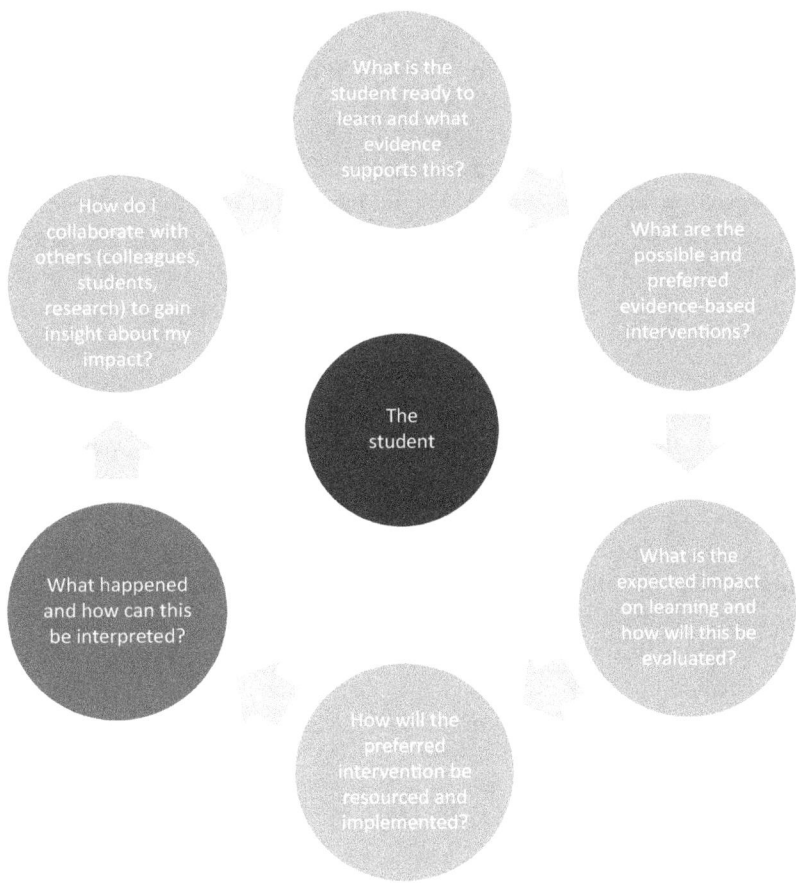

After the implementation of the intervention, teachers analyze the impact on student learning to try to gain insight about the significance of this for future planning and teaching. The key consideration is evaluation of the impact of the interventions on learning development. Again, the use of and interpretation of evidence are crucial, as is collaboration between colleagues to analyze the findings and inform future practice. This stage also allows teachers to question what they need to learn to address learning outcomes effectively, and to identify new ideas about theory, pedagogy, and curriculum that may be adapted within their learning contexts. The teachers' evaluative thinking at this stage goes beyond reflection to critical questioning and problem-solving, leading to contextualized judgments.

Example: English language-center teacher

In order to critically reflect on my teaching of Laura and her learning, I commenced with evidence from the results of her FCE (English proficiency) exam. Two months after my teaching of Laura had concluded, I was informed that she had achieved very good results in all parts of the exam apart from the speaking component. She had attained only a borderline pass for this component, which surprised me. The evidence I had collected during my work with Laura had led me to conclude that her speaking in English was quite advanced. On reflection, I considered the actual examination process and context, and how this may have impacted on Laura on the day of the exam. I concluded that perhaps I had not discussed or simulated the exam conditions fully during classes, and that I probably needed to structure the lead-up to the exam more precisely in order to prepare students, not only for the possible content of the exam, but the process.

As a means to appraise my practice, I also had a conversation with a relative of Laura who happened to be a colleague. I hoped to gauge an honest critique of my work with Laura. I felt quite vulnerable about this but realized that in order to fully evaluate my teaching, this vulnerability and openness were necessary. This 'opening up' process was generally positive; however, it did cause me to reflect on and further appraise my practice. Laura's aunt recounted that her niece had sometimes commented on my 'fast' speaking, especially when giving instructions or discussing a concept particularly important to me. I also learned that my relatively strong Australian accent (and particularly some of my vowel sounds) may have caused some confusion and uncertainty with some of the students, including Laura. I am now conscious of my pace when speaking, and check with individual students to ensure that my speech is clear. I have also tried to modulate my pronunciation of some sounds, and I use other methods (including visuals and audio resources) to consolidate some of the concepts I introduce to my EALD students.

- *How do I collaborate with others (colleagues, students, research) to gain insight about my impact?*

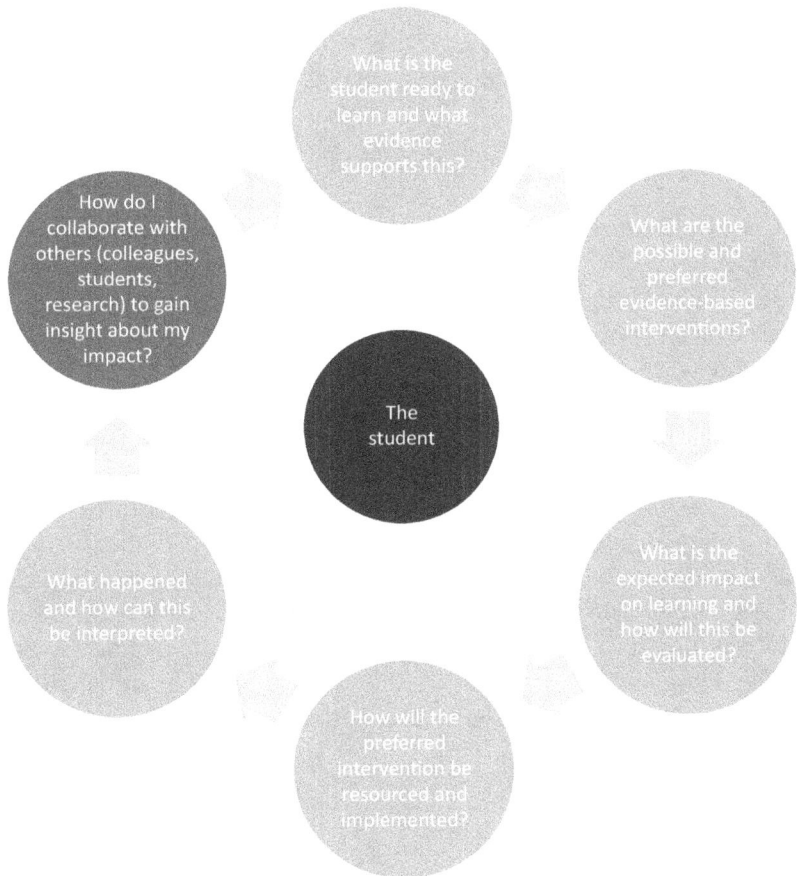

To gain insight into the impact of the interventions, the teacher collaborates with others, (colleagues, students, and evidence-based research) to reach judgments of value. These judgments will influence whether specific interventionist approaches are continued or require modification. Collaboration between colleagues and with students, as well as revisiting evidence and research literature, leads to questions and decisions about the fidelity and duration of the implementation of certain interventions. All through the cycle, and particularly at this stage when impact is measured and evaluated, expert teachers need to support their colleagues to interpret and use evidence to plan for improved future practice. These lead teachers also need to use similar kinds of evidence to inform and develop their own leadership practice (Timperley, 2010).

Teacher collaboration, as well as collaboration between teachers and students, also has a cross-disciplinary focus. Rather than being in subject-specific silos, teachers encourage each other and students to consider and evaluate how concepts are introduced, revisited, and consolidated through interventions in different classroom contexts.

Conclusion

The six questions and the associated teacher knowledge, skills, and reasoning constitute what we call 'clinical practice.' The *teachers for a new era* initiative proposed that teaching should be an "academically taught clinical practice profession" (Carnegie Corporation, 2001, p. 12). In essence, this is about meeting the needs of the individual student (Alter & Coggshall, 2009; Kriewaldt, McLean Davies, Rice, Rickards, & Acquaro, 2017), just as other clinical professions such as medicine have their client or patient needs and well-being at the center of their practice. In the case of teaching, the role of the professional is not to 'cure' but to enhance learning and to move the student along a developmental learning trajectory. Also fundamental to teaching as clinical practice are specialized teacher knowledge and skills and the use of evidence and judgments through diagnosis and intervention. As emphasized in this chapter, understanding and utilizing evidence-based research to design interventions are important characteristics of clinical teaching, as is collaboration with colleagues and students in the implementation and evaluation of these interventions. These aspects of the clinical teacher will be explored further in Chapters 4 and 5.

CHAPTER

The deep knowledge base of teaching

Often confused with experience (indeed, the Latin root *experiri* is a derivative of the word for experience), expertise is characterized by fluency of skill in a given domain. The pioneering research on expertise was by De Groot (1946), who used the 'think aloud' method with expert and novice chess players as they decided strategies and the series of moves. When asking chess players how they played, he initially found few if any differences in the thought processes employed by novices and experts. But when he showed a chess board with pieces set out after the twentieth move for five seconds, then removed it, he discovered that experts could reproduce the content of the board nearly perfectly, while novices struggled to accurately reproduce more than three or four pieces. This led to the notion that experts thought in 'chunks,' or had stores of memories of overlearned scripts to bring out when needed. This overlearning releases the working memory to be more strategic, to react and adapt with more fluency, and enables more efficient pattern recognition leading to optimal decision-making.

Chase and Simon (1973) tested this idea by showing experts chessboards with meaningless configurations of pieces: their performance was markedly impaired. But they also found that experts had many thousands (if not tens of thousands) of patterns stored in memory, and this was the case not only in chess, but in other areas like sports, music, and across the sciences. Indeed, to build these patterns requires much experience; however, experience is not enough. In teaching, for example, some can teach for years but do not build up patterns or use the information from patterns to optimize decisions.

One of the additional traits of experts is that they more commonly 'work backwards'—experts consider a solution plan as part of their initial consideration of the problem, whereas novices apply a set of rules to work forward to a solution (Larkin, McDermott, Simon, & Simon, 1980). Another is the proficiency to see a problem from multiple perspectives—in a sense, to see it from the other side. Experts seem to do this more effortlessly, or as Csikszentmihalyi (1998) argued, there is more flow of spontaneous creativity and enjoyment in the process (that is, they are in the zone, have a heightened sense of experience, and enjoy the challenge of the unfamiliar).

Note the core elements in these comments about expertise: a large corpus of knowledge, a proficiency to build and use patterns, and a willingness to see challenges as opportunities to use this knowledge and pattern recognition. It is thus not surprising that experts typically excel only in their own domain—expert doctors are capable diagnosticians of diseases, expert taxi drivers can generate secondary routes while driving, and expert teachers can diagnose misconceptions and readily provide alternative teaching strategies when the first did not work—but excellent doctors may be poor taxi drivers or teachers. Imagine a doctor with 30 patients in the consulting room at once, all asking for help, all with different issues, and you can see that the skills of teachers and doctors are unique; or imagine the teacher's life if they were able to deal with one student at a time. It is this ability to chunk or see patterns within a domain that is a defining difference between the experts and the experienced and novices. This chunking allows experts to be faster (although they can spend more time than novices in the diagnosis phase before deciding on actions), but it can also mean that they are less aware of how they think, and often act seemingly automatically (which sometimes makes them less capable of being teacher educators—anyone who says teaching is common sense is unlikely to be a good teacher of others; see Gage, 1978).

Not only does expertise require more than common sense; it is more than mere practice, practice, practice. Practice can lead to experience but not necessarily expertise. Ericsson (2014) invokes the notion of deliberate practice to separate those who do the same thing endlessly from those who learn and change from the repeated practice. Deliberate practice refers to practice that is continually checked, leading to overlearning of skills and forming higher-order patterns of behavior. Imagine teaching the square cut in cricket. It invokes four skills: (1) identifying the right ball to execute this shot—a short and wide delivery outside off stump; (2) moving the back foot towards the stump and across the line of the ball; (3) turning the front shoulder to the offside as the bat is taken back, bringing the bat down and across, making contact with the arm at full extension; and (4) following through, leaving the weight on the back foot and the bat finishing over the front foot and behind the head. These skills are often taught with a ball machine, repeating the skills, linking them into one action (one chunk) over and over with tweaks, feedback, and corrections so that in a game, there is no four-step thinking, but one thought—this ball is perfect for the square cut—and the pattern of the four steps is swung into action. It is the deliberate practice of the components leading to overlearning such that the various parts become one, and thus the working memory in the game is not overloaded with detail. The cut can then look beautiful, one flowing action executed with panache, but which is the consequence of remarkable overlearning, with input from expert coaches to provide feedback, and deliberate practice.

But it is more than chunking, pattern recognition, working backwards or from the other side, continually learning, being adaptive, not rushing to solutions, or being in the flow. There are ways of thinking that further discriminate the expert from the experienced, and in this book, we term this 'evaluative thinking.' The claim is that evaluative thinking is also an overlearned behavior for many teachers (overlearned, as discussed at the start of the chapter), with expert teachers having higher-level representations, 'chunks,' or world-views that guide them. They have greater pattern recognition, are more adept at checking biases and constraints, are more able to monitor errors of judgment, and are more likely to seek alternative actions. Experts are slower to come to problem representations and conclusions. Experts try to see the world through others' eyes, and they check back with the problem statement more regularly. They overlearn the skills and views from evaluating situations to better integrate these skills to make more immediate and automatic selection.

With regard to the chess players and their thinking processes, Chi, Feltovich, and Glaser (1981) found that experts showed a greater degree of monitoring skills when they made errors, when they failed to comprehend, and when they needed to triangulate their solutions. They needed more time to detect patterns in scenarios and to understand what was happening, and they learnt from their experiences; they did not merely choose from a repertoire of solutions and apply this solution without adaptation. Ericsson (2014, p. 306) claimed experts "generate a complex representing of the encountered situation, where information about the contact is integrated with knowledge to allow selection of actions as well as evaluation, checking and reasoning about alternative actions." Experts' skills are highly adaptive representations that lead to optimal planning, prediction, and evaluation. These skills are not just overlearned but overlearned for a purpose of immediate or automatic selection. This then relates to the quality as well as quantity of deliberate practice, to the inherent enjoyment in the activity of deliberate practice, and serves as an instrumental means to higher performance: a mission to improve performance. There is a process of planning, prediction, and decision-making. This is the core of evaluative thinking that demarcates experts from experienced practitioners and novices.

Expertise in teaching

Berliner and his team (1992, 2004) asked novice teachers and expert teachers to observe many scenarios. For example, both groups of teachers were shown a series of slides (drawn from two 55-minute secondary class sessions) for about one to three seconds and were then asked to write what they saw (Carter, Cushing, Sabers, Stein, & Berliner, 1988). A novice saw "a blond-haired boy at the table, looking at papers. Girl to his left reaching in front of him for something" whereas an expert saw "a group of students may be doing small group discussion on a project as the seats are not in rows." One response is descriptive, the other interpretative. Blond hair is just not important. Novices were more focused on the static features of the class whereas experts were more likely to comment on the work being done, and the atypical. The novices were less able to distinguish "what was important from what was not in the booming, buzzing confusion of life in classrooms" (p. 21). The experts were more cautious in their explanations and wanted to check their explanations by interacting with the students, ignoring many less critical details, and engaging in more hypothesis-making cognitive claims. Novices used more descriptive explanations, were less likely to see patterns across the lesson, and were more focused on the content. Both groups saw the same classroom, but the evaluative interpretations were quite different.

In another Berliner study, experts and novices were asked about what students might do when answering a series of test items (the teachers were shown these items). The experts had richer and deeper knowledge about the way students could respond; they focused on errors as much as right strategies and answers and were better able to predict wrong answers and think through wrong answers more proficiently. Novices rarely discussed wrong answers or misconceptions but were more focused on describing the content of the items.

From Berliner's work (1994, 2004), it can be concluded that experts 'see' classrooms differently. They are more likely to see classrooms as classrooms 'ideally ought to be,' are more likely to note atypical events and situations earlier, and are more critical of their teaching—sometimes deeply critical of their teaching.

> Berliner (2004, pp. 200–201) concluded that "Expert teachers often develop automaticity and routinization for the repetitive operations that are needed to accomplish their goals; expert teachers are more sensitive to the task demands and social situation when solving pedagogical problems; expert teachers are more opportunistic and flexible in their teaching than are novices; expert teachers represent problems in qualitatively different ways than do novices; expert teachers have fast and accurate pattern-recognition capabilities, whereas novices cannot always make sense of what they experience; expert teachers perceive meaningful patterns in the domain in which they are experienced; and although expert teachers may begin to solve problems slower, they bring richer and more personal sources of information to bear on the problem that they are trying to solve."

It is also important to note that the process of becoming an expert takes time, deliberate practice, continual learning, and an openness to alternatives. Expertise is not gained by repeating the same lessons but rather by adapting and learning from the impact of each lesson. Expertise is not changing the peripherals or the superficial aspects of teaching but going to the core of whether you are maximizing the impact on student learning. It is not reflecting on what happened but using resources to analyze the lesson and trying to understand a problem from multiple viewpoints before attempting to implement a solution. Expertise is not rushing to solutions (see Hill & Ridley, 2001) but considering and evaluating many viable possibilities and continuing to ask 'what if' but discarding the 'not possible' from the 'possible' reasonably quickly. It is being adaptive more than routine in thinking and decision-making: not seeing problems as familiar, but seeing them as new, worth exploring, and needing understanding (Holyoak, 1991). Expertise is knowing the limits of what you know and being able to seek help, continually learning and collaborating with others in diagnoses, problem-solving, considering 'what ifs', and evaluating the impact of the chosen solutions.

Berliner noted that it took seven years for most teachers to develop expert dispositions—though, of course, not all become experts after seven (or even many more) years. In this regard, teaching is not too different from other occupations. For example, expert radiologists were estimated to have looked at 100,000 x-rays, and chess experts had spent 10,000 to 20,000 hours looking at and thinking about chess positions. One golf expert hit an estimated 4 million golf balls as he strove to master and then maintain his golf ball driving ability (Berliner, 2004, p. 201). Berliner also noted that in teachers' first seven years of teaching, the scores of their students were higher every year, but the scores stopped improving in about the seventh year and remained at the same level until they showed a small decline (Lopez, 1995). Across the initial seven years, to attain this expertise, is about 10,000 to 12,000 hours.

This corresponds with the claims extensively documented by Anders Ericsson and his colleagues. For example, they monitored the hours of practice logged by violinists undergoing training at the Music Academy of West Berlin. Although all were excellent musicians, large differences in their prior training were disclosed through studio training records. The most expert violinists had spent around 10,000 hours practicing, whereas the least accomplished performers had logged around 5,000 hours. The records for the most accomplished students were found to match those of a group of professional symphony musicians. Such findings gave support to the concept of deliberate practice, or the type of practice consciously devoted to the improvement of a skill as distinct from the exercise of that skill. Such practice is usually highly structured, involves a teacher or coach, includes participations in tasks initially outside of current performance levels, but which can be mastered within hours by focusing on critical aspects and refining technique though repetition and feedback.

Most of Berliner's research compared experts with novices, but a tighter test by Smith, Baker, Hattie, and Bond (2008) compared expert teachers with experienced teachers. Smith et al.'s (2008) research compared a group of expert teachers who had passed National Board assessment with a group of similarly experienced teachers who also sat the assessment but did not pass. The experts excelled on all criteria (with effect-sizes from .25 to 1.13). Figure 4.1 shows that on all dimensions, the experts outperformed the experienced peers. Most critically, there were crucial differences in what the teachers were teaching and how the students were thinking in the experienced and expert teachers' classrooms. By analyzing transcripts of the lessons and coding artifacts of student work from the lessons, Smith et al. (2008) found that 74% of the work samples of students in the classes of expert teachers were judged to reflect a level of deeper understanding and 26% reflected a level of more surface understanding (Figure 4.2). It was the opposite in the experienced but non-expert classrooms.

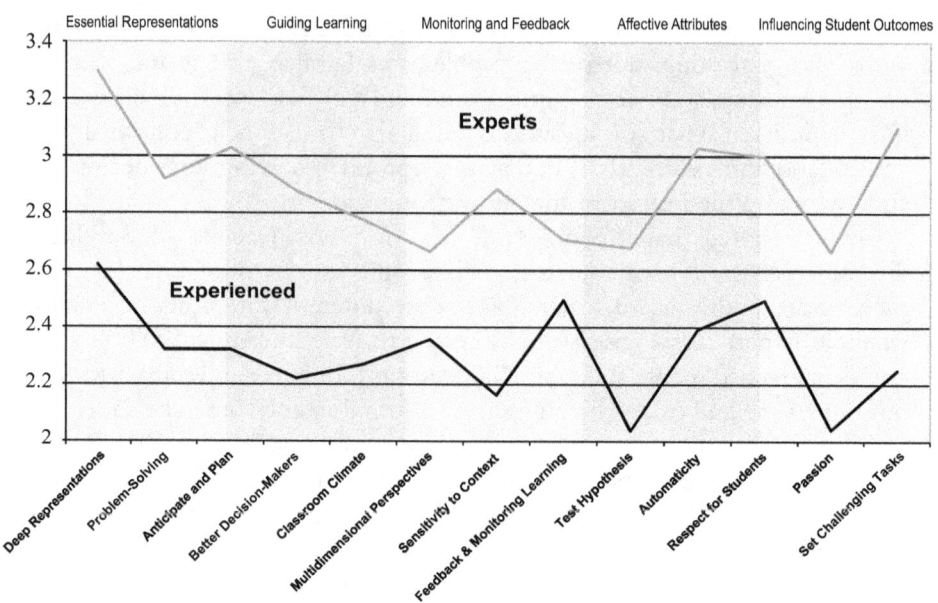

Figure 4.1 Comparison of performance between expert and experienced teachers

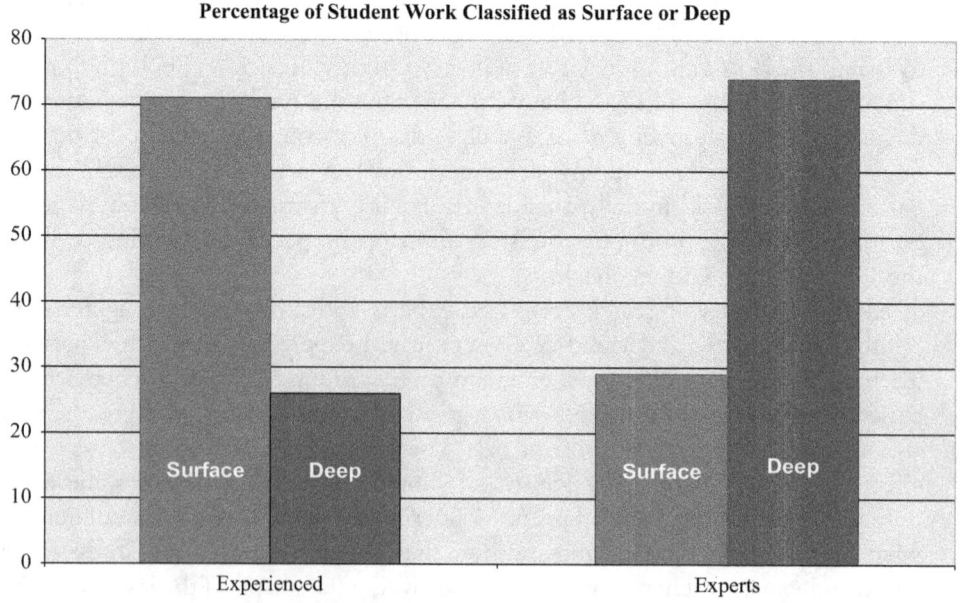

Figure 4.2 Comparison of surface to deep learning in classes of experienced teachers and expert teachers

The overwhelming inference from comparing expert teachers with experienced teachers and novices is that there are major differences in how experts think, what they value, and their passion to optimize their impact on student learning. It is less about their pedagogical or curriculum knowledge, their background, or their ways of teaching. One can watch a teacher teach, but the need is to better understand how they *think* about their teaching, problem solve, anticipate, and detect and deal with errors and atypical situations. Expert teachers are more context-dependent, sensitive to task demands, deeply know their students, and create and test hypotheses about student learning. It is understanding how experts are more opportunistic and flexible in their teaching, how they are selective in their use of information during planning and teaching, how they heighten opportunities for providing feedback to students about their progress, and how they inform students of appropriate and challenging tasks to be undertaken in future work. These attributes all relate to making judgments and to evaluative thinking.

Evidence from visible learning research

The Visible Learning research is based on a synthesis of (now) over 1,600 meta-analyses in education. It started by asking a vexed question in education—that is, why is it that we can find so many studies supporting nearly everything, such that teachers, policymakers, and parents can make claims "we should do x, because there is evidence it enhances student achievement"? In the language of meta-analysis, the aim is to find the size of magnitude of effects on student learning. If an effect (or strictly speaking, an effect-size) is greater than zero, this means that the influence (e.g., class size, expertise of teachers) is positive, and if negative, it detracts from student learning. From the quarter-billion students across the 100,000 studies in the Visible Learning research, it turns out that over 95% of influences on students have an average effect greater than zero—so in this sense, teachers and policymakers are correct to argue there is evidence for most of what they do. Clearly, we need to do better than just claiming that what we do in schools has a positive effect—almost everything does. Instead, in the Visible Learning research, it was discovered that the average effect-size was much higher than zero, at .40; and the story in this work is based on understanding the common themes underlying those influences greater than this average compared to those below this average. We need to stop asking 'What works?' and replace it with 'What works best?' (All the data from Visible Learning, including updated information, a glossary, a search function, and many other resources, is available at https://www.visiblelearningmetax.com)

The structural aspects of schooling that have the lowest impact include new forms of schools (for example, charter schools), changing classroom structures (for example, smaller class sizes, changing the architecture of classrooms), grouping the students (for example, tracking or streaming), changing curriculum (or calendars and timetables), and simply providing more money. The various forms of teaching are the most variable, with lower effects relating to deeper teaching methods (inquiry and problem-based methods) and higher effects from deliberate methods of teaching (direct instruction, mastery learning, and reciprocal teaching). A major factor, however, is a combination of surface- through deep-teaching and learning is needed, as a student needs to have the content and ideas before relating and extending these ideas. There are few methods which cross these surface and deep outcomes (however, see the Jigsaw method based on dividing the work into pieces, first relating to the essential knowledge and understanding, then using this knowledge to relate ideas and work with others to form connections and transfer to a task assigned to the group of students. The Jigsaw method has a very high effect-size [$d = 1.06$, explained in Chapter 3]). Determining the right mix of surface and deep requires the deep knowledge of the teacher as to when to focus on surface and when to move from the surface to the deeper tasks and thinking.

The greatest effects relate to teacher expertise (Table 4.1). The most powerful is when teachers have the disposition and skills to evaluate their impact on their students' learning. This way of thinking does not dictate any methods, any program of work, or any format for the class. Instead, it highlights the capacity of teachers to design effective programs, implement them with quality and fidelity, and then be able to critically determine the magnitude of the effect of their educational programs on student learning. It raises the moral purpose questions about what the teacher means by impact, how many students experience this impact, and how evaluations measure the magnitude of the impact.

The thinking of the teachers with the greatest impact on student learning relates to their expectations of growth in learning, having and sharing explicit success criteria (not too hard and not too boring), building trust with and between students so that errors can be seen as opportunities to learn, having multiple outcomes such as both surface and deep learning (and building confidence and making classrooms worthwhile places for students to want to come and learn), and seeking out of feedback on their impact such that they learn,

TABLE 4.1 The seven major themes underlying what works best for enhancing the learning lives of students.

	Theme	ES
1	Teachers and students, working together, as evaluators of their impact	.90
2	All having high expectations	.90
3	All moving towards explicit success criteria	.77
4	Using the Goldilocks principles of challenge	.74
5	Errors and trust are welcomed as opportunities to learn	.72
6	Maximize feedback to teachers about their impact	.72
7	A focus on learning: The right proportions of surface to deep	.69

adapt, modify, diagnose, and thence enhance their ongoing impact on students: again, a powerful set of thinking strategies.

The major message for teachers, then, is 'know thy impact'. That is, the teacher needs to ask about the merit, worth, and significance of the impact of their interventions on their students. The educator's role is not merely collecting data, creating reports, and teaching students, but involves interpretation of evidence of the impact of their teaching. There needs to be a culture of seeking evidence to support interpretations about impact, hypothesis-testing these interpretations, and continually questioning the meaning and pervasiveness of their impact on students. Such evaluation requires teachers to make judgments about their impact and seek alternative views (the second opinion) about the credibility of their interpretations of this impact (triangulating with test scores, reviewing with colleagues, and listening to student interpretations of their own learning).

Maximizing the truthfulness of their evaluative judgments about their impact requires teachers to have deep knowledge of their students' prior learning, an understanding of how students use learning strategies, and, near the start of a series of lessons, a method to be explicit with students about what success looks like. It requires teachers to implement programs that have the optimal proportion of emphasis on surface and deep learning, and have appropriate levels of challenge—and never accepting 'do your best.' Teachers must ensure that the success criteria are sufficiently challenging for all students (for a more detailed explanation, see Clinton & Hattie, 2014).

This emphasis on knowing impact does not dictate any methods, any program of work, or any structures for the class. Instead, it highlights the capacity of educators to design effective programs, implement them with quality, and then critically determine the magnitude of the impact of their educational programs on student learning. An emphasis on the magnitude of the change is paramount: Given that more than 95% plus of methods employed to enhance learning will lead to a positive impact on learning (Hattie, 2009), merely enhancing learning is not enough. To maximize the learning for students, teachers need to know the magnitude of their impact and evaluate whether this impact is sufficient. An evaluative way of thinking fosters improvement.

The following set of mind frames, or ways of thinking, were developed from the Visible Learning research base: I am an evaluator of my impact; I am a change agent; I explicitly inform students what successful impact looks like from the outset; I see assessment as providing feedback about my impact; I work with other teachers to develop common conceptions of progress; I engage in dialogue, not monologue; I strive for challenge and not 'doing your best'; I use the language of learning; I see errors as opportunities for learning; and I collaborate.

This Visible Learning and Mind-frames model asks educators to evaluate the quality of the evidence they can provide with reference to four major themes: (1) their strategic planning and self-review that incorporates feedback about interventions and teaching impact; (2) their proficiency in adapting their choice of teaching strategies to impact both surface and deep aspects of learning; (3) their use of student voice as important evidence of impact; and (4) their gathering and interpretation of evidence about impact.

One of the most difficult aspects is successful implementation of these four ideas. In our work, we use the acronym **DIIE** as the basis for overseeing implementation: teachers participate in **D**iagnosing the status of students as they begin lessons: they have multiple **I**nterventions that are **I**mplemented with fidelity; and they **E**valuate the students' responses to their interventions. This is closely mirrored in the key questions outlined in Chapter 3.

Conclusion

This chapter has explored the notions of *expert* and *expertise* within teaching and has differentiated between *expertise* and *experience*. Central to teacher expertise is the aim for maximum impact on student learning. To achieve this, we argue for the clinical model whereby teachers possess the skills and knowledge to ascertain each student's learning needs through evidence, plan for and implement relevant interventions to meet these needs, and evaluate the impact of these interventions. All of these aspects require evaluative thinking, hence the focus of Chapter 5.

CHAPTER 5

The essence of the teaching profession
Evaluative thinking

The previous chapter discussed the premise that expertise is a defining aspect of the teaching profession. In this chapter, we outline the core notions of expertise that relate to the six key teacher questions identified in Chapter 3, and five evaluative thinking skills. We also discuss the core knowledge components that relate to the key questions and to the evaluative thinking skills.

Table 5.1 shows the five evaluative thinking skills and the six teacher questions, with examples of roles that teachers perform shown in each cell. These roles, while not exclusive to each cell, aim to exemplify the expertise needed by teachers to address the key questions. We illustrate each of the five evaluative thinking roles by referencing the main key question it addresses.

Evaluative thinking

There are many aspects of expertise unique to teaching, and they are all based on a rich knowledge base about teaching, students, learning, and context. But to develop our argument about the nature of this knowledge, it is first necessary to outline the ways of thinking that epitomize the excellent teacher and thus be more specific about the nature of teaching expertise. The claim is that these ways of thinking cohere around the concept of evaluative thinking, and this is core to the notion of teaching as a profession.

Evaluation is a broad discipline, relating to making value statements about the merit, worth, or significance of programs, people, policies, performances, or processes. While there are major differences between various researchers and practitioners in this field, this core notion of *value* is the essence. House (2014), who has

TABLE 5.1 Evaluative thinking skills and the six key questions.

Evaluate thinking involves…	The six critical teacher questions					
	What is the learner ready to learn and what evidence supports this?	What are the possible and preferred evidence-based interventions?	What is the expected impact on learning and how will this be evaluated?	How will the preferred evidence-based teaching interventions be implemented and resourced?	What happened and how can this be interpreted?	How do I collaborate with others (peers, students, research) to gain insight about and improve my impact?
…reasoning and critical thinking in valuing evidence, leading to 'where to next' recommendations	as diagnostician as seeker of evidence				as diagnostician	
…addressing the fidelity of implementation, continually checking for unintended consequences, and allowing for adaptations to maximize the impact		as intervenor as anticipator as implementer as adapter as learning expert			as learning expert	
…a focus specific to the major decisions each profession aims to make: in the case of teachers, it is knowing impact			as change agent as evaluator		as evaluator	
…investigating potential biases and confounds that may lead to false conclusions				as problem-solver as hypothesis-tester	as problem-solver	
…understanding others' points of view leading to judgments of value or worth					as collaborator	seeking insight as collaborator

long argued for this core notion of values in evaluation, claimed that values are beliefs about the worth of something, or whether something is good or bad. Values and facts are not neatly separable, but House argued they blend together somewhere around the middle of a continuum of "brute facts" and "bare values." The differences among many evaluation theories relate more to how and who makes these value statements.

This focus on value leads directly to Scriven's (1981) distinction between evaluation and research in that the former is more about the 'so what' and the latter about the 'what is so.' Evaluation is less concerned with the causal mechanisms leading to the findings, less about psychologizing or socializing about why x or y happened, and more about the value of the effects and consequences. Scriven's argument is that research and evaluation respectively derive from a different way or emphasis in how we think. Of course, there is overlap: research relates both to the power to generalize and the power to convince, whereas many evaluations are mostly the latter. Both require dependable measures (surveys, interview, tests), and both care deeply about the quality of interpretation or validity of the arguments. Scriven (1991) argued that the core evaluative thinking skills are critical thinking, reasoning, and understanding others (how they think, reason, judge, interact). Hence, evaluation involves understanding the minds of others to then form a judgment about merit, worth, or significance. To make thesee valuative judgments, it is critical to consider the notion of reflective thinking within evaluation, or "getting people in organizations to look at themselves more critically through disciplined processes of systematic inquiry" (Preskill & Boyle, 2008, p. 148); reality checking, or "how do we know what we think we know?" (Patton, 2005, p. 10); and skeptical questioning, or "helping program people reflect on their practice, think critically, and ask questions about why the program operates as it does. They learn something of the evaluative cast of mind—the skeptical questioning point of view, the perspective of the reflective practitioner" (Weiss, 1998, p. 25). Note, it is not reflection as in looking in the mirror, it is reflection as in seeing how others see us.

While the idea of ways of thinking has been part of the evaluation literature for many years, recently it is coalesced around the notion of 'evaluative thinking'. Evaluative thinking is a particular kind of critical thinking and problem-solving that is germane to the evaluation field. It is the process by which one marshals evaluative data and evidence to construct arguments that allow one to arrive at contextualized value judgments in a transparent fashion (Vo, 2013).

Vo (2013) explored the multiple meanings of evaluative thinking by conducting a Delphi study with 28 evaluators. A Delphi study asks for meanings from various evaluators; these are summarized and redistributed for discussion and refinement, and there can be further rounds until a reasonable sense of agreement is met. Vo noted the long debate about reasoning, think-ing, and many related terms, such as critical thinking, logical thinking, and reasoning. Further, many fields claim to have a particular kind of thinking: the legal profession refers to ethical judgments that have to be made in light of the moral principles that have been laid out and set by the law (Spellman & Schauer, 2012), while the medical profession is more hypothesis-directed, involving "reasoning that generates and tests hypotheses so that potential causes of symptoms (clinical data) can be individually ruled out, a correct diagnosis can be reached, and a treatment plan can be decided upon" (Vo, 2013, p. 26). Of course, there are many debates about whether these are the 'right' forms of thinking, the roles of data and evidence to inform this thinking, disputes between induction, deduction, and abduction, and how we make decisions from this thinking.

Our argument is that there are five major evaluative thinking skills (see Table 5.1).

1. Evaluative thinking involves invoking reasoning and critical thinking in valuing evidence, leading to 'where to next' recommendations.

Teachers need to invoke critical thinking and reasoning in valuing evidence and making decisions about appropriate interventions, and have levels of critical thinking, logical thinking, and reasoning. We have noted that evidence comes in many forms (from research, from teachers' experiences), is often contested, and is always subject to interpretations. As Nietzsche (2009/1889, p. 27) commented, there is no such thing as 'immaculate perception'.

To Fisher and Scriven (1997, p. 21), "critical thinking is skilled and active interpretation and evaluation of observations and communications, information and argumentation." Scriven and Paul (1987) argued that such critical thinking skills relied on clarity, accuracy, precision, consistency, relevance, sound evidence, good reasons, depth, breadth, and fairness. They argued that critical thinking can be seen as having two components: (1) a set of information and belief-generating and processing skills, and (2) the habit, based on intellectual commitment, of using those skills to guide behavior. It is therefore more than the acquisition and retention of information alone, because it involves a particular way in which information is sought and treated, and more than the possession of a set of skills, because it involves the continual use of them.

The consequence of this reasoning and critical thinking is formative thinking, leading to making 'where to next' recommendations. It is not just description and diagnosis, but reasoning about the next best steps. This is the core to the notion of formative thinking and maximizing the power of feedback (Hattie & Clarke, 2019; Hattie & Timperley, 2007).

Each of the evaluative thinking skills is best exemplified in the various roles that teachers need to enact to achieve their goals of having an effect on the learning of every student. The first role related to the evaluative thinking skill of invoking reasoning and critical thinking in valuing evidence is the teacher as a *diagnostician*, both prior to and at the beginning, middle, and end of a series of lessons. The teacher as a diagnostician acknowledges the centrality of the student in terms of what each student already knows and can do, and thus what each student is ready to learn next, as well as knowing the anxieties and confidence levels of each student to then set the optimal next level of challenge. As a diagnostician, the teacher knows that progression in learning is not a smooth increase, and so allows for differences in the time and direction students need to take to attain the success criteria.

A good diagnostician is a problem solver and hypothesis tester, has all the attributes of clinical and evaluative thinking, and is prepared to allow others (students, parents, colleagues) to seek second opinions. This requires a strength and confidence in their beliefs, a knowledge that one cannot know everything, and an understanding that there may be alternative, more effective diagnoses and interventions.

A study that highlighted the importance of seeking second opinions was conducted by Ward and Thomas (2013). They collected overall teacher judgments about the progress and status of student learning from a stratified sample of 96 New Zealand schools, comprised of Year 1 to Year 8 students representative of the population of schools in terms of school type, school socioeconomic status, and geographic location. Ward and Thomas concluded that teacher judgments "lack dependability, which is problematic as these judgments are the basis on which schools tailor teaching support with the aim of improving achievement" (p. 3). This finding indicates the critical importance of the educators working together to develop, within and across schools, common conceptions of progress. It should not be the case that a student's progress is determined by different judgments that teachers have about the standards expected of their students.

The second role related to invoking reasoning and critical thinking in valuing evidence is the teacher as a **seeker of evidence**. This role and set of beliefs go to the heart of the expertise of the teacher—the seeking and use of evidence about what students already know and what it points to for the 'where to next' for the student. Seeking evidence is bound into the notion of assessment-capable teachers; however, this is not an overreliance on evidence gained from tests, but on evidence of student work, information from tasks and assignments, and listening to how the students are processing and dealing with challenging notions. Teachers need a willingness to seek this evidence and also to teach the students to listen, evaluate, and learn from their own learning and errors. And at all times, the teacher must seek to triangulate this evidence.

Evidence should be among the most contested notions in education. Biesta (2007) argued that what counts as 'effective' crucially depends on judgments about what is educationally desirable. These 'desirables' include social, moral, physical, cognitive, and affective outcomes, learning the love of learning, having the willingness and skills to reinvest into further learning, and having respect for self and respect for others. Evidence, however, like education, is never neutral, as its fundamental purpose is intervention or behavior change, and this is one of the fundamental moral questions in life.

It is the merging of professional judgment with evidence that is the hallmark of the teaching profession. An excellent description of this merging of interpretative judgments and evidence is illustrated in a letter Sackett, Rosenberg, Gray, Haynes, and Richardson (1996) submitted to *The British Medical Journal*. They start by noting that evidence-based medicine is the "conscientious, explicit, and judicious use of current best evidence in making decisions about the care of individual patients" (p. 71). Neither judgment nor evidence is enough. It is the balancing and integration of clinical expertise (proficiency and judgments) with the best-available external evidence from systematic research. The evidence and judgment relate to the accuracy and precision of diagnostic tests, the power of prognostic markers, and the efficacy and safety of therapeutic, rehabilitative, and preventive regimens. He argued we do not want practice "tyrannized by evidence" or captured by opinion and one's own experience alone. This same argument applies to teachers and teaching.

Cochrane (1989), the initiator of evidence-based medicine, maintained that the greatest resisters of evidence were the 'experts' who believed their experience was enough. Their belief in their own experience occurred even when some used less-effective methods that had been surpassed by new ideas and new medical discoveries, and they failed to listen to smarter evidence-based juniors. Again, the same applies in too many schools.

As noted above, evidence is not neutral. It needs interpretation and sometimes adaptation to context, and certainly one needs evidence of impact in one's own classroom. Non-neutrality is what makes teaching a moral profession, raising such fundamental issues as "Why teach this rather than that?" and "How does one teach in defensible and ethical ways?" Snook (2003) has argued that teaching involves close personal relationships: between teachers and students; between one student and another; between one teacher and another; and between teachers, parents, colleagues, and school leaders. Teaching involves a mission to change people in certain ways, and it often occurs in contexts in which there are hierarchies of control and rules to be obeyed. The power in these interactions and contests is very real. Hence, Snook claims that teaching involves ethics in its aims, its methods, and its relationships. He argued that the role of the teacher involves a respect for autonomy and a respect for reason. He cautioned that "when we hear too much of the technicist teacher, the competent teacher, the skilled teacher, we should remind ourselves that education is essentially a moral enterprise and in that enterprise the ethical teacher has a central role to play" (p. 8). As Dewey (1938) noted, evidence does not provide us with rules for action but only with hypotheses for intelligent problem-solving and for making inquiries about our ends of education.

It is a critical part of the profession that teachers and school leaders work together to decide on the nature of evidence, to seek disconfirmation as well as confirmation evidence about impact, and to ensure that the impact is maximized for all students. The Visible Learning approach shows that professional development starts with discussions and evidence about the impact of the educators in a school and then asks: "What knowledge and skills do we, as educators, need?"; "How can we deepen our professional knowledge and refine our skills to achieve this greater impact?"; and "How will we then know of the impact of our changed actions?" To achieve this in school settings, capacity for evaluation needs to be built in so that all can evaluate their impact. In empowerment evaluation, the process of evaluation is an integral part of teaching and learning that then includes organizational learning. This may require professional development in evaluation, such as capacity building, typically with the assistance of a critical friend or empowerment evaluator. The professional development programs in the education context need to be based on the evaluation of impact in the school. This, of course, may mean bringing in outside expertise to assist in the evaluation or in the provision of more effective processes (which then need also to be subjected to evaluation as to their impact).

2. **Evaluative thinking involves addressing the fidelity of implementation, continually checking for unintended consequences, and allowing for adaptations to maximize the value of the outcomes.**

Deciding on a program, innovation, or change in schools is relatively easy. Choosing the right intervention at the right time in the learning cycle, and then implementing the program with fidelity, turn out to be difficult. The evaluative thinking skills involved here relate to ensuring appropriate choice, dosage, fidelity, adaptation, and quality while continually checking for unintended consequences.

Implementing a program is akin to driving a car from point A to point B. Having a clear sense of what the destination looks like, how far it is from the starting point, deciding up-front the most efficient way to get there, being adaptable about the direction and speed during the journey in light of barriers and enablers, and ensuring continual maintenance, refueling, and care of the car are critical to the success of the voyage. Having a GPS that provides warnings, advice, suggestions, and corrections can be useful, provided you do not over-listen to these GPS messages and forget the purpose—to get safely, efficiently, and effectively to the destination. However, it could be that halfway into the trip, you discover a more appropriate and interesting destination—so in the classroom, be ready to improve your impact by also evaluating the quality of the destination.

Thinking about implementation often needs a sustainer, or critical friend, to ensure the intervention is delivering value for all students and teachers, and who works with all to hear their experiences of starting points, the journey, and their views of the worthwhileness of the destination (and remember, it is so important to share the destination, or success criteria, with the students from the outset). It is important to make sure communication is open and that issues are resolved in a timely and efficient manner and to build collectives of champions to help in the intervention. Consideration of surrounding school-wide issues is also important to the implementation of an intervention, to withstand disruptions from, for example, changing principals, the mobility of teachers, or the next fad.

This journey to the destination asks that attention be given to evidence that the intervention is resolving the issues it was intended to address and has not introduced unintended consequences. Training and delivery should be updated as needed. Ongoing monitoring should ensure the intervention is being implemented with fidelity, but should also allow for adaptations to local conditions (although sometimes the adaptations by some teachers remove the innovation from interventions).

Flexibility and willingness to adapt are well-identified factors in the success of many interventions in business, and recently have become more commonly discussed in schools. Despite the increased demands and uncertainty in schools, there is a need for teachers to become experts in design and implementation. The need is for agility—to be "responsive, quick to spot emerging problems or opportunities, and able to work in short, iterative cycles of adaptation, learning and improvement — [and this is] critical for this future focused work" (Breakspear et al., 2017, p. vii).

The notions of adaptation or differentiation are powerful influences – for better or for worse. Parsons, Vaughn, Scales, Gallagher, Parsons, Davis, Pierczynski, and Allen (2018) started with the assumption that classrooms are messy, unpredictable contexts; they include students at many different points in their learning, and thus teachers need to make adaptations. This can be an "awesome balancing act," with many research models, studies, standards, and observation tools that privilege these adaptations or modes of differentiation. Hattie (2009) concluded that teachers need to "possess pedagogical content knowledge that is more flexibly and innovatively employed in instruction; they are more able to improvise and to alter instruction in response to contextual features of the classroom situation ... they can more easily improvise when things do not run smoothly" (p. 261).

There has been a shift in the fundamental notion of adaptation, from the focus on teachers' decision-making in the 1970s and 1980s, through the focus on sociocultural and situated variables in the 1990s and the focus in the 2000s on adapting in light of outcomes, to the more recent multicultural attention to diverse students' needs and how teachers' instruction specifically addresses those needs to boost achievement. One of the hallmarks of the many interventions often imposed on schools and teachers is that teachers can become adept at adapting out the essence of the intervention with the result that they can continue to use the methods they have always used. As Larry Cuban (2003) noted, there can be a swirl and waves of reform from the top of the ocean but at the bottom of the sea, teachers can become immune and sometimes not even aware of these changes, and they are excellent at continuing teaching as they have always done. Adaptation is a double-edged sword, and this is why it is critical to question that which is being adapted, question whether the current practice can be and is improved by the adaptation, and question how teachers are thinking about their influence on the students.

Such thinking is a core element of the school as a learning organization where all are committed to continuously and cooperatively fostering a school's successful impact on all students and encouraging all employees to participate in decision-making and being a part of the evaluative mindset about the choice of improvement programs and their implementation. It helps to have collaboratively built a program logic or theory of change, and to have the courage to revisit, modify, and improve in light of actions, enablers, and barriers to implementation.

Thinking about implementation requires evaluating the actual effects of the intervention and matching it to the diagnosis of demonstrated needs that led to the intervention. Michael Scriven (1979) termed this goal-free formative evaluation.

An independent evaluator (or student) should be able to discern the nature and worthwhileness of the destination from the implementation, the artifacts of student work, and from discussing with the students, hence the goal-free claims. This method helps bring clarity to the goals (both at the outset and at critical points during implementation), and identifies and separates side effects (unanticipated necessities) from unanticipated effects from unwanted effects that may not have been considered from the outset. And the method welcomes changing direction, allows for moving faster or slower and for requests for more input (knowledge, resources, time), and helps build a team ownership of the intervention.

A core notion here is the checking for unintended consequences. As humans, teachers have cognitive biases (systematic errors in cognition), and there are more than 180 such biases that are now known (see www.visualcapitalist.com/every-single-cognitive-bias/). These biases can lead to faulty interpretations and thence to less effective interventions by the teacher, with decisions about next steps made too hastily, lowering the impact on students. As Daniel Kahneman (2011), the Nobel Laureate, noted, these biases often are a function of the 'thinking fast' part of us making decisions when the 'thinking slow' part should be given more information and time to interpret. When we think fast, we depend often on unconscious cues, have the desire for rapid and more automatic solutions and thus often rush to judgment; when we think slow, we search for alternative explanations, seek more evidence, and set up checks to see if our solution is optimal. Berliner (2004) in his research on expert teachers noted that they took longer to work through scenarios of classroom dilemmas than non-experts and novices, as they were more likely than non-experts and novices to collect more information and check their assumptions.

Some of the more powerful biases are confirmation bias (tendency to look for confirming rather than disconfirming evidence to support a diagnosis or impact), anchoring bias (tendency to overemphasize features about a student and failing to adjust when they perform better or worse than expected); and holding low expectations, which is a particularly nefarious bias (see Hattie & Hamilton, 2018, for more details). A powerful method to reduce the impact of biases is to 'think aloud' with colleagues about diagnoses, preferred interventions, and evidence of impact (through the notions of collective efficacy), and to adopt a goal-free model of evaluation. A teacher should always ask what evidence they would accept if their teaching did *not* have the impact needed, which students did *not* make the desired progress, and what about their teaching, and about what (in terms of content and understanding), was *not* successful and needed to improve (or be retaught).

The major role in this second evaluative thinking skill (i.e., addressing the fidelity of implementation, continually checking for unintended consequences, and allowing for adaptations to maximize the value of the outcomes) is the teacher as an ***intervenor***. Knowing what students can and cannot do and knowing evidence of best interventions are precursors to becoming an implementer who can intervene to enhance the speed, quality, and depth of learning. The interventionist teacher needs to know multiple interventions from which to choose the optimal one for the moment, the student, and the context. They need to be a problem-solver to evaluate when an intervention is working or not, and why, and to be able to distinguish between interventions that maximize surface learning (content, facts, ideas) and deep learning (relating ideas) and embrace the skills of transfer to new situations or problems. The interventionist teacher needs a depth of knowledge and knowing (knowing that and knowing how) to teach students to know critical ideas, to go deep in their understanding at the right time and to the right depth, to understand misconceptions and errors, to know how to listen to students to best understand how they are learning and processing, and to know about the psychology of learning to intervene appropriately to help students gain the best strategies of learning. Most critically, the interventionist teacher needs to know when to change the intervention when it is no longer working efficiently and effectively.

Another role is teacher as a *learning expert*. Teachers know much about how students learn, how errors and not-knowing can be seen as opportunities to learn, and how to construct learning intentions and success criteria that are both challenging and inviting given where the students are in their learning cycle. And teachers know how to teach students various strategies about how to learn in the context of various disciplines.

3. **The focus of evaluative thinking is specific to the major decisions each profession aims to make: For teachers, it is maximizing impact on student learning.**

The argument here is that the major attributes of evaluative thinking are focused on the major decisions each profession or discipline aims to make. The common thread is the aim of evaluative thinking within the discipline: in the case of law, consistency with the law; in the case of medicine, diagnosis and alleviating illness; in the case of evaluation, with defending decisions about value; and in the case of teaching, with understanding and maximizing impact on students' learning through to achievement. Each discipline thence requires knowledge to enact these aims.

Within law, for example, legal reasoning may require expertise in different systems of law, including civil, corporate, educational, family, juvenile, and tax, as well as knowledge of particular statutes; medical thinking requires both general and specialized clinical knowledge with the aim of ameliorating illness or maximizing healthiness; and pedagogical reasoning in mathematics requires "transferring a knowledge of basic, computational math as well as knowledge of properties, proofs, and theorems specific to subjects like algebra, trigonometry, and calculus" (see Vo, 2013, p. 29). The knowledge for teachers is outlined in the next chapter.

The meaning of impact has been discussed earlier in this book. The claim here is that a teacher needs to be able to identify and defend the notions of impact, particularly those concerning the centrality of each student. It is more than achievement, twenty-first century skills, or wellness; it is the overlapping of these many attributes that is needed in any impact statement.

4. **Evaluative thinking involves investigating potential biases and confounding factors that may lead to false conclusions.**

One's thinking can be wrong or informed by partial or misleading information. A teacher may not have full knowledge of the optimal diagnoses or interventions, and may be using the wrong lens to view each student or the class. As noted in the previous chapter, the classroom can be seen from multiple perspectives; thus, evaluative thinking for teachers requires them to be aware of possible biases and confounding factors that may lead to false conclusions.

This possibility of being biased and wrong in our interpretations of what we see in classrooms leads to seemingly disparate claims about the nature of evaluative thinking. Scriven (1967) highlighted the importance of being able to separate poorly constructed evaluative conclusions from valuable ones. Blair (1995) argued that the role is how to best corroborate conclusions that have been reached using non-deductive and deductive reasoning. House (1995) argued that evaluative thinking can be no more than acts of persuasion because contexts for judgment are dynamic, and more recently outlined the major biases that can interfere with good evaluative thinking (House, 2014). Buckley, Archibald, Hargraves, and Trochim (2015) claimed evaluative thinking is a cognitive process, motivated by inquisitiveness and a belief in the value of evidence, which involves identifying assumptions; posing thoughtful questions; pursuing deeper understanding through reflection and perspective taking; and making informed decisions in preparation for action (see Vo & Archibald, 2018).

As humans, everyone is prone to cognitive biases (systematic errors in cognition), and these can impact negatively on education decisions. More than 80 cognitive biases have been recorded by behavioral economists (see Hattie & Hamilton, 2018; https://betterhumans.coach.me/cognitive-bias-cheat-sheet-55a472476b18). Such biases, if left unchecked, can become major hurdles to improving the quality of the impact of teaching. The most common biases seem to be 'faulty synthesis' of information and confirmation bias (the tendency to look for evidence in favor of prior beliefs).

Other common teaching biases include self-fulfilling prophecy, or being convinced that one's teaching works and seeking evidence that supports this prophecy; the ostrich effect, where one avoids seeking evidence that might suggest that one's teaching is not working; anecdotal fallacy, which is using anecdotes to defend beliefs; the halo effect, or generalizing to all the students from a limited number of interactions; and the 'not invented here' effect, when teachers avoid using alternative teaching methods because they were developed somewhere else or privilege methods they've developed themselves, sometimes irrespective of the problems.

Two effective methods to reduce the negative impact of these biases is to work collectively with other educators to critique one's evidence about impact on students (hence the power of teachers' collective efficacy), and to continually seek evidence of where teaching has *not* worked, in terms of "about what," "with whom," and "to what impact." Popper (1995) argued this seeking of falsifiable evidence is the core of science, and similarly we argue is the core of evaluative thinking.

Two related roles in evaluative thinking include teacher as a **hypothesis tester** and teacher as a **problem-solver**. In a similar manner to being excellent at diagnosis, the expert teacher is also adept at forming and evaluating hypotheses. Forming hypotheses involves a subjective judgment about what has occurred, why it may have occurred, or the prediction of what may happen next. Such judgments should have high diagnostic value, and evidence sought to evaluate the correctness or veracity of the hypothesis. More powerfully, the judgments should be subjected to falsification.

Steen Larsen (see Hattie & Larsen, 2021) traced this notion of falsification to the writings of Karl Popper (1995) and the claim by German philosopher and sociologist Jürgen Habermas (1989) that every utterance, every communicative expression, every speech-act in principle could be wrong; that is, could be fallible. This position is called fallibilism. This fallibilistic approach is very important also for a teacher's standpoint. As an example, what we know right now of Big Bang Theory, the history of mankind, and the Missing Link is only the knowledge that we have now; what we know could be dramatically changed tomorrow. For example, we now know that "we have approximately 4% of Neanderthal genes in the human species; something we didn't know 40 to 50 years ago" (Holliday et al., 2014). So, it is not only the skill to form and evaluate hypotheses that is important, but also having the problem-solving techniques required to undertake this evaluation.

5. **Evaluative thinking relates to understanding others' points of view, leading to judgments of value or worth.**

A critical attribute of evaluative thinking relates to **how** one arrives at value claims. Schwandt (2018) cites a talk by Eileen Stryker who argued that

> evaluative thinking means being tuned in to value judgments people make (e.g., listening for such language as: that's good, he's doing a good job, the program is working, they're really getting better, and words like effective, quality, good, bad, better, improving, etc.), and questioning how those judgments were arrived at and what evidence may exist to substantiate the value claim.

This approach involves questioning to the claims by others, triangulation of evidence, and making sense of the contradictions that are most often present when understanding the minds and decisions of others. It is a type of critical thinking. Buckley et al. (2015, p. 378) claimed

> evaluative thinking is critical thinking applied in the context of evaluation, motivated by an attitude of inquisitiveness and a belief in the value of evidence, that involves identifying assumptions, posing thoughtful questions, pursuing deeper understanding through reflection and perspective taking, and informing decisions in preparation for action.

We have noted the moral imperative when asking the 'impact' question, and answers to the question relate to the purposes of schooling, the choices of curricula, the methods of instruction, the way we speak to students, parents and colleagues, and so much more. The fundamental principles of fairness, respect, trustworthiness, honesty, and kindness need to be ever-present in the profession, and these can be seen in every interaction with students and others. Dewey made this same comment: "everything the teacher does, as well as the way he does it, incites the child to respond in some way or other, and tends to set the child's attitude in some way or other" (Dewey & Bentley, 1960, p. 59).

Most systems have codes of ethics or moral conduct that assist, particularly newer teachers, with the learning of boundaries of what is permissible and what is not (and there can be fine boundaries indeed). Teachers are continually placed in situations where these boundaries are tested, such as pressure to give passing grades to mediocre students, accommodating parental demands for privilege, school policies which grate with a teacher's own moral agency, cultural norms of loyalty to fellows, and issues relating to controversial topics.

Understanding others' points of view demands that teachers know how to validate their own thinking, arguments, and judgments; that they know how to work collaboratively and to listen to others' perspectives, including when offering their own interpretations; and that they have high levels of self-awareness and a keenness to seek evidence, to listen, to question, and to think critically about their diagnosis, choice of interventions, implementation, and evaluation of the impact of these choices.

The role associated with this evaluative skill is the teacher as a collaborator. This entails as least three proficiencies: the skills to work with others; the confidence and interpersonal skills to listen, interact, and converse with others; and the belief that working with others can yield better solutions or gains compared to completing the task alone. Empathy is often cited as an important characteristic for developing trust and a sense of fairness in the class and is the basis of a philosophy of care (Stojiljković, Djigić, & Zlatković, 2012). Empathy requires not only listening to others' viewpoints, but also communicating that you have heard and understood these viewpoints. It is one of the major skills required to enable the development of teachers' collective efficacy (Donohoo, 2016), the enabler for the wisdom of the crowd to succeed (Rowe, 2020), and requires openness to others' experiences and viewpoints. There is much emerging evidence on how to develop this collaborative expertise (DeWitt, 2017; Donohoo, 2016; Sharrat & Planche, 2016).

Conclusion

The claim here is that evaluative thinking is a way of reasoning that needs to become an overlearned behavior. Expert teachers have higher-level representations, or 'chunks,' or worldviews that guide them, and they understand (and communicate this understanding of) others' worldviews. They have greater pattern recognition, are more adept at checking biases and constraints, are more able to monitor judgment, and are more likely to seek alternative actions. Experts are slower to come to problem representations and conclusions, try to see the world through other eyes, check back with the problem statement more regularly, and are proficient in skills and views from the evaluating literature (theoretical and practical) to better integrate them to make more immediate and automatic selection.

PART

Implications for the profession

CHAPTER

6

Evaluative thinking in the professions

In this chapter, we discuss the attributes associated with professions and ask whether teaching, in its current form, possesses these attributes. We argue that a defined, collective, and agreed-upon knowledge base and associated expertise are crucial to teaching being valued as a true profession, and, drawing on previous chapters, we present what this teacher knowledge comprises.

What is a profession?

Throughout history there have been endless debates about the core attributes of a profession, who should be the gatekeepers of entry to teaching, and whether or not it matters if teaching is regarded as a true profession. There are many lists, debates, and controversies about what makes a profession; some of the indicators include: credential and licensing levels; the presence of induction and mentoring programs for individual members; professional development support; specialization; authority over decision-making; compensation levels recognizing expertise in the profession; a set of principles and moral codes that oversee behaviors; and prestige and occupational social standing (Ingersoll & Merrill, 2011). Perhaps the most dominant claim to becoming a profession is an agreed-upon collective body of knowledge and principles that guide the actions of the profession. This is through an accumulation and sharing of knowledge: doctors have case studies and systematic reviews; lawyers have case law; and musicians have canons of interpretations. The question is: does teaching have such high-level public agreements about established practice that are accurate, verifiable, continually improving, and used in decision-making during practice?

Definitions of a *profession* most often highlight the importance of ethical standards and pledges ('do no harm'), professional standards and accreditation, the possession of specialized knowledge and skills in a recognized body of learning derived from research, education and training at an advanced level, and the importance of public recognition of these attributes. *Professional practice* in these fields is based on the understanding that practitioners use judgment and knowledge in ways that meet the standards expected by the profession itself and the community. These attributes are readily recognized in professions such as law, music, or medicine. A guiding principle of these and other recognized professions is a particular way of knowing, thinking, and doing, respective to the profession's specialized knowledge and role in society. Problem-solving and decision-making draw on this specialized knowledge base possessed by members of the profession. The formalized nature of the knowledge base of acknowledged professions allows various levels of abstraction and expertise, and subsequent promotion and recognition of status. The notion of 'abstract knowledge' arises from the interaction of the knowledge base and the practical skills or strategies; these in turn allow for the development of new strategies and knowledge (Abbott, 1988; Gamble, 2010). It is the characteristic of abstraction that best identifies a profession.

Members of a profession continuously and collectively evaluate their ways of knowing, thinking, and doing in order to improve and maximize the positive impact on the members of the community the profession serves. Professionals have a duty to maintain and update their knowledge and skills by engaging in formal training and professional reading and critique. The professional community is responsible for monitoring quality, disseminating knowledge, and creating the standards of practice. Professionals and training institutions are held accountable to these standards (Alter & Coggshall, 2009).

The professions and evaluative thinking

To illustrate the fundamental claim about expertise and evaluative thinking, it is worth considering how complex problems are solved in other professions, particularly in law, medicine, engineering, and music. We conducted interviews with colleagues in these four professions.

First, we interviewed a senior colleague in law. She argued that the legal profession is bound by an ethical framework in relation to service to clients and society, self-regulation, and agreed, conceptions about the law. There is also a duty to the court not to mislead. The corpus of knowledge is captured in what, in Australia, is referred to as 'The Priestly 11': 11 knowledge-based subjects, including ethics. There is debate in law schools about the balance between knowledge and practical experience. In the traditional approach to law education, knowledge or theory is undertaken in the degree, and practice is undertaken during 'articles.' Traditional law degrees contain substantive content subjects that include hypotheticals. Students need to identify legal issues in the hypothetical and breaches of the criminal acts and conduct legal analysis. In the program this professor has overseen, the emphasis is on the importance of evaluative thinking involving reasoning, critical thinking, and valuing evidence, leading to 'where to next' recommendations. Unlike the medical profession, lawyers have to ascertain the facts and contestations, look for weaknesses and limitations, and with skepticism, ascertain a single truth without asking leading questions. "The legal mindset is to look at one's own practice and identify the worst-case scenarios or the weakest point in the case," our colleague stated. Also, while lawyers possess autonomy, they do need others as experts, as peers, and as consultants.

In our interview with a professor of music and conductor of orchestras, this conductor also spoke about precision in thinking. In an orchestra, there are different levels of competency and musicianship. The conductor's role is to motivate the members of the orchestra to 'sound together' and blend the orchestra members into a 'whole sound.' In conducting, relationship-building and psychology, and constantly checking for fidelity of implementation as well as unintended consequences, are needed, and approaches are adapted accordingly. The conductor has the vision of the performance from the outset, before the actual performance. Conducting is anticipatory.

In interviews with a professor of engineering, the professor emphasized three major features of his profession. First, engineers need to know what the end product will be, as all the hypothesizing and testing have been done during the design specification process towards this end. By the time the production is under way, the engineer already knows his approach will work. The client doesn't see the 'trial and error.' A preliminary design involves asking what might be possible, and the engineer needs to provide evidence of this before the actual project proceeds. Second, problem-solving is highly esteemed: "We ask, 'How do we fix it?' We use evidence, hypothesize about the problem and solutions, and test the hypotheses through experiments, simulations, calculations. We need to have confidence that this is the solution and use a highly evidence-based manner to find solutions to a problem. We are essentially following the design process. The experiments are to find out what the problem is." The third area is inventing new solutions and specifications: "We observe standard processes and draw on professional knowledge to create a design solution. All the testing has happened prior to the implementation. Consulting evidence and research literature allows us more confidence and certainty that the design process will be successful." There is also a need to show evidence that the solution will be sustainable. If something needs to be fixed or a new instrument is needed, this involves a new process to test. Collaboration is integral, and engineers need to constantly consult others. Engineers are pragmatic and bring experts in to deal with specialized parts of the process: "Interdisciplinary collaboration allows us to find a possible solution. It's also a creative process."

We also interviewed a professor in medicine, who emphasized the knowledge base, the clinical trials, and the power of the "second opinion." It is a major issue if the problem is not diagnosed correctly. In complex medical cases, the problem-solving team will be headed up by the senior surgeon or physician and supported by specialists from the relevant area, registrars, nurses, and others from allied health.

Ultimately, it is the expertise of the team leader that produces the required diagnostic and intervention approach that leads to the optimal outcome. The audiologist, for example, when presented with a patient who is having a problem with hearing, will be concerned with the nature of the hearing issue, the resultant communication challenges, and the fundamental and underlying causes. Contextual factors, such as the age of the patient, are important in the diagnosis, as the auditory system presents with different aspects at different developmental stages. At this diagnosis phase, the audiologist is already thinking about possibilities for diagnosis and intervention. Ascertaining how long the patient has been aware of the issue is important—has it developed gradually, or is it a sudden onset? Has the patient been aware of it since childhood? Is the patient experiencing the hearing difficulty in one ear or both? Has there been a recent injury? Based on the patient's responses, initial testing, and the audiologist's previous experience and expertise, a decision must be made about whether emergency treatment is warranted. If not, the audiologist will do further testing to diagnose whether the issue is related to the outer, middle, or inner ear. A speech perception test may be done. All of the evidence from the testing and the interaction with the patient plus the audiologist's expertise and knowledge will provide information about the underlying cause. The audiologist can invoke consultation with other specialists and seek results from tests, and only then moves into deciding about appropriate intervention.

Teaching as a profession shares many common attributes with these other professions. The messages from the experts in law, engineering, medicine, and, although to a lesser extent, music conclude that: professions are bound by regulation as to content and knowledge base; the threat of repercussion (legal or other) is present if protocols are not followed; there is a duty to do no harm or not mislead; high degrees of deliberate practicing (hypotheticals, simulated patients, computer-aided design) are crucial; an upfront vision of what success looks like is needed; and professionals need to be able to create design solutions. There is an agreed-upon, although updating and changing, sense of established knowledge and practice, and a high level of sensitivity to the improvements to this knowledge base (it is not set in concrete upon graduation). The essential evaluative skills include problem-solving; using evidence; anticipating; seeking counterarguments and identifying weaknesses in approaches, thus privileging and welcoming "second opinions"; motivating towards the whole sound, product, or outcome; and the necessity of social sensitivity and relationship skills when working with others. Also central to these four professionals' practice is a particular way of thinking. Evaluative thinking across the professions involves the use and critique of data and evidence to make contextualized judgments of value, and the ability to investigate potential biases that may lead to false conclusions and to modify views accordingly. Like other professions, including medicine and engineering, professional teacher thinking involves ascertaining existing situations, devising solutions and strategies, testing hypotheses, making adjustments according to context-based variables, and using evidence to inform the future practice.

Within teaching, the student is central to effective and professional teacher practice. This is similar to the centrality and uniqueness of the patient or client in professions such as medicine and law. While 'diagnosis' in medicine implies a deficit or illness in a medical context, it also involves identifying the strengths, degree of resilience, and wellness aspirations of patients. For the teaching profession, the role of 'diagnostician' involves the ascertaining, from a range of evidence, what the child is ready to learn next and how this learning may best be fostered. Understanding patient or student 'history' is fundamental to medicine and teaching, respectively. Effective teaching involves differentiating and adjusting interventions according to the continual evaluation of evidence and an awareness of contextual factors and how these may affect the progress of the student, just as good medical practice involves adapting to address the needs and reasonable expectations of each patient.

Like other professions, teaching can build on incremental advances based on accumulated past knowledge and empirical data, but there are more contested claims about what is part of this base of knowledge. Teaching can still make claims to having autonomy to teach in the best way one knows, whereas lawyers, engineers, and medics are bound to follow certain protocols or deviate from them provided they produce evidence of increased likelihood of success.

The establishment and dissemination of a profession's knowledge base and ways of thinking are fundamental to its conceptions of initial education and training. Engineering education and training, for example, are based on the development of distinctive engineering skills and knowledge—the 'engineering method.' Training engineering students in the 'method' is an inculcation of a worldview that ideally begins on the first day of engineering school. The same can be said for medical and legal education. The professional community and regulatory bodies monitor this theoretical, practical, and technical knowledge and the ways in which these elements are incorporated into education and training. These bodies accredit courses based on their integration of their respective methods and practice.

It is worth considering what a 'teaching method' and 'worldview' look like and how they are integrated into initial teacher education. In Australia, teaching methods have traditionally been associated with specific discipline content and pedagogy, particularly in relation to secondary teaching. This book argues that clinical practice and evaluative thinking must be the foundations of 'what teaching is' across schools, sectors, and systems, across levels of schooling, and across subject disciplines. This evaluative thinking supersedes debates about particular ways of teaching, and indeed allows for multiple methods, judiciously used at the right time, to improve the right issue in student learning with the right feedback to the teacher of the success or otherwise of their diagnosis, choice of method, and level of impact.

Another common element is reliance on collaboration. It is integral to the practice of lawyers, conductors, engineers, and medical practitioners; they 'know what they know and know what they don't know,' and experts in one area of specialization systematically seek and use the expertise of others. The transformation of knowledge happens through collaboration to create collaborative expertise. Members of a medical team problem-solve together without any diminution or devaluing of their own expertise and responsibilities. Too often in teaching, however, the practice is private when the classroom door is shut. Many teachers still think they need to be solo operators, want to be alone with their students to indulge in their passion to teach, and are reluctant to consult expert colleagues and draw on the specialized knowledge of others in the planning, implementation, and evaluation of their practice and its impact on students' learning.

There is an urgent need to legitimatize 'seeking the second opinion.'

Teaching—a profession?

So, is teaching a profession? This question was tackled decades ago by, among others, Harry Broudy (1956). Broudy argued that the apathy around this question could be attributed to the largely female teaching workforce, whose main aim was marriage (recall, this is the 1950s), therefore rendering teaching as "an economic marking of time preliminary to some other career." In the 1990s, Berliner (1992) echoed these arguments, suggesting that the perception of teaching as 'woman's work' resulted in its devaluing compared with traditionally 'male domains' such as engineering. Also influencing the status of teaching is it being a 'mass profession.' Unlike other professions such as law or medicine, teaching has a relatively large workforce. It has been estimated that in some countries, one in 30 members of the workforce is a teacher (Dinham, 2016). These kinds of statistics can work against the status of the teacher who may be perceived as ubiquitous and less important than less-common professional practitioners. Indeed, most professions carefully guard their numbers and hold difficult entry standards to push the case of exclusivity. Professions such as medicine, music, and law maintain high status in society partly due to relatively small intakes of students into their university training programs; thus, places in these programs are generally highly sought after. The public status of these professions is also linked to the purposes of the work that is involved—work that is fundamental to the operation of society. On this latter point, surely the work of the teacher in educating our young people rests alongside medicine and law as a profession.

So how else does teaching measure up to the attributes of a profession today? The school systems considered the world's most successful value teaching as a profession (Jensen, 2012; Sahlberg, 2014) and view its members as highly trained experts who cultivate a "highly sophisticated set of skills" (Barber & Mourshed, 2007, p. 26), including the abilities to diagnose, intervene, and evaluate the impact of their approaches on student learning. Counteracting this claim is the fact that in some jurisdictions, the standards or preparation for teaching are low, and in others, teachers have varying expertise or knowledge about how or what to teach.

In Australia for example, the expertise and successes of teachers are not celebrated as much as they could and should be, and teaching has often been viewed more as a craft rather than a profession. Elmore (2006, 2008), as we noted in the introduction, has stated that teaching is a profession without a practice. He says, by contrast, that, within a true profession, an individual does not have autonomy over its body of knowledge and its practice. In professions, there is a shared corpus around which initial and continuing professional development are organized. It often seems that in teaching, 'professionalism' is used to legitimate idiosyncrasy. Elmore (2006, 2008) argues that teachers tend to think of other practitioners as either 'good' or 'bad' depending on deeply seated personal attributes. According to Elmore, this view of teaching is limited and 'anti-professional,' as it effectively precludes the possibility of improvement of instruction.

Professions historically have developed a collective autonomy over their professional training, certification of their professional competence, and more broadly, some oversight of their conditions of work. This typically does not apply to teachers. Teachers generally have been government employees, and the notion of professionalism needs to be examined in relation to the school as representing state control over teaching (Gamble, 2010; Wilkinson, 2005). On these grounds, teaching cannot be considered a profession.

Another argument is that within a profession, the remuneration is very much a function of expertise; and on this, also, teaching would largely fail. Teaching in Ireland, for example, is based on 26 annual increments, and in Australia, on 10 steps, all based on experience, after which teachers need to move into management and administration positions to increase remuneration. Currently in Australia, progression through pay scales is largely aligned with years of experience rather than demonstrated expertise (Dinham, Ingvarson, & Kleinhenz, 2008; McKenzie, Weldon, Rowley, Murphy, & McMillan, 2014; Victorian Competition and Efficiency Commission, 2013), and while teacher graduates start their careers on relatively solid wages, they increase far less significantly than in other professions. Australian teachers are also paid relatively less than their counterparts in other OECD countries such as Finland (Dinham et al., 2008; Ingvarson et al., 2007). In systems that primarily value experience, expertise is hardly relevant. This need not be confused with the debate about performance-based pay for teachers, which recurs every year or two in some contexts. Pham, Nguyen and Springer (2020) reviewed 44 studies on teachers' performance pay and found a tiny to zero effect on student test scores (0.05 standard deviations).

Our claims about teaching as a profession

Teaching would be classified as a profession on most of the above indicators, although it would fail on some major criteria. Most education systems now have codified sets of principles, moral codes, and minimum criteria for entering the profession (although there are, not surprisingly, hot debates about what these are or should be). There is also induction (to varying degrees of success), specialization, professional development, and authority over decision-making at the local level (though maybe too much). As this book argues, there are indeed deep levels of expertise involved in the profession of a teacher. So, our answer is simple: yes, teaching can be classified as a profession to the degree that we agree on the presence and nature of expertise. The discussion is moving from having a set of codified and agreed-upon evidence bases to having a deeper understanding of the ways in which teachers think evaluatively about their impact. But the profession still has a lot to do to convince many of the public and often their peers that teachers share deep levels of expertise and thus are members of a profession.

This, of course, is not claiming that every teacher has all the levels of expertise, adheres to the sets of principles, and has high moral codes. We are not claiming that everyone agrees on 'established practice.' Similarly, we would not claim all doctors, nurses, engineers, and so on meet these standards. Conversely, there are certainly many teachers who *do* possess these deep levels of expertise, who consistently achieve high standards, and have high moral codes. Perhaps, unlike many other professions, teachers are reluctant to promote, dependably recognize, and seek compensation for their expertise. There are claims that 'every teacher is equal,' and subsequently that pay should be based on experience rather than expertise in the classroom.

The alternative: Teaching is a craft

There is much that mitigates against the professional identity of teachers as a profession such that it could be classified more as a craft. Consider, for example, the rise and rise of amateurs in the classroom, namely teaching aides, who are welcomed by teachers, parents, and systems alike. In the United Kingdom, there are now more teaching assistants and resource staff in schools than teachers, and close to 30% of the salary budget to schools is spent on aides. This gives the false impression of higher teacher to student ratios (the new jargon is 'adult to student ratios'), but the evidence is compelling against the impact of aides—at best it is zero; at worst, negative. More dramatically, the main researcher in this area, Peter Blatchford, deems their effect 'toxic.' Blatchford, Russell, Bassett, Brown, and Martin (2003) have found that when observed, aides are less academically demanding than qualified teachers, place a greater emphasis on completing tasks rather than ensuring learning or understanding, are more active than proactive in directing learning, often do the work for the student, and tend to 'close down' rather than 'open up' learning talk linguistically and cognitively (Blatchford et al., 2003). If aides are assigned to the students most in need of expertise, this is not a great advertisement for the profession of teaching.

The rise of vouchers or funds for parents to use to choose a school, and a focus on creating different kinds of schools (charters, trusts, academies) result in an emphasis on parents or corporations running schools and providing key directions. Further, there are continual pleas for autonomy (often translated as 'local know-how') that are seen as more critical than building and using a corpus of expertise and knowledge to run schools. Teachers who want to privatize their classrooms may object when other teachers enter their fiefdoms, and too rarely do they talk about the act or impact of teaching with each other (preferring to talk about students, curricula, tests, and management). Further, in Australia there has been a recent debate about the low academic standards required to enter initial teacher education, with many of the defenders of these low standards being the teacher educators and deans of education (with claims that other personal attributes such as communication or liking children are much more important). In the United Kingdom, initial teacher education is now more located in schools than in higher education institutions, reifying the notion that craft begets craft knowledge. These claims do not help establish teaching as a profession.

The profession led by the profession: The rise of standards

Another argument is that the strengthening and enhancement of teaching as a profession need to be enacted by teachers themselves. Teaching must recognize and celebrate the teaching knowledge base and use research and theory in similar ways to professions such as medicine, engineering, and law. Just as these professions develop their own professional standards and self-regulatory processes and build an up-to-date research utilization, so are teachers' ownership and agency within the profession pivotal (Elmore, 2005; Hayes & Hegarty, 2002, p. 35).

Certainly, in the past decade in Australia, for example, the establishment of institutions such as the Australian Institute for Teachers and School Leaders (AITSL) and state-based regulatory bodies have promoted the professionalism of teaching and have developed codes of ethics for teaching. AITSL's stated mission is to "promot[e] excellence so that teachers and leaders have the maximum impact on learning in all Australian schools and early childhood settings" (https://www.aitsl.edu.au/about-aitsl). This suggests particular ways of knowing, thinking, and doing in order to facilitate this impact. Also implicit in this mission statement is that members of a teaching profession need to draw on an integrated body of knowledge (Timperley & Alton-Lee, 2008) and can expect rigorous and systematic preparation, induction, and progression based on professional standards in the way that law and medicine, for example, operate (Levine, 2006).

There are recognized practices for accreditation of teacher education programs and advanced certification, all elements that define a profession (Darling-Hammond & Bransford, 2012). In Australia, all teachers are initially classified as graduate, and within two to three years, are expected to apply and be granted proficient status. Many will remain at this level throughout their careers. Teachers are able to apply, through a rigorous process akin to the United States-based National Board for Professional Standards, to become highly accomplished or lead teachers (Ingvarson & Hattie, 2008).

The recent surge of growth of highly accomplished and lead teachers (HALTs) in Australia has led to a national organization, a network and annual conference, a commitment by some state governments to increase the number of HALTs to 5% to 9% of the workforce, and a welcomed recognition that such expertise can help define teaching as a profession. The presence of HALTs is also being used to counter the belief that all teachers are equal and to generate a healthy discussion about their roles in the system. On the one hand, becoming a HALT is a recognition of excellence and not expected to be an extra set of duties, but many HALTs are asking about how they can work with colleagues both within and outside their schools while remaining embedded in the classroom. One example is volunteering to react to graduate teachers' queries through an 'My Induction' AITSL-built app to give access to new teachers wherever they are located (https://www.aitsl.edu.au/teach/start-your-career/my-induction-app).

There is the perennial question of linking remuneration more to expertise than to experience only. The evidence of performance pay is not the correct answer to this linking—as noted above (cf., p. 89), the Pham et al. meta-analysis showed an almost zero effect ($d = .05$). While superior expertise (such as that possessed by HALTs) needs to be recognized through additional renumeration, the structures for such processes need to be transparent and rigorous (Ingvarson, Beavis, & Kleinhenz, 2007). In other recognized professions such as medicine and law, career pathways and stages and associated rewards are clearly defined, and school systems in some countries have adopted such structures (Mourshed, Chijioke, & Barber, 2010). Further incentives and professional development can also be part of these processes, as in Singapore, where teachers are offered funds for study or opportunities to teach in alternative contexts (Sclafani, 2008). Given the paucity of positive evidence for performance pay based on some measures of student impact, an alternative is to explore what some states in Australia are doing with HALTs.

Imagine you attain a PhD in any field. There is no guarantee that your salary will increase, but the qualification may present opportunities and allow application for positions that are associated with higher remuneration. Or, if you qualify as a surgeon, this does not mean you then automatically practice as a surgeon and receive the associated salary—instead it makes you eligible for positions that require the qualification of surgeon. Similarly, schools can offer positions and associated higher salaries that are open to highly accomplished or lead teachers (as happens in South Australia). In this way, the system can ensure that these HALTs are located at specific schools (those with need for particular specializations, or in areas of disadvantage, and so on) and can have control over the expansion of the salary budgets. HALTs, when successfully attaining these positions, then receive higher remuneration.

The knowledge base of teaching

To be recognized as these high-level experts, do teachers possess a specialized and established knowledge base? Much of the knowledge of teaching has centered on factors such those categorized by Shulman (1986): subject matter content knowledge;

pedagogical content knowledge; and curricular knowledge. Yet, according to Hayes and Hegarty (2002), knowledge about strategies that influence effectiveness in teaching has rarely been at the forefront of either what is taught, how preservice or initial teacher education is delivered, or part of the code of the teaching profession (p. 31). Unlike other professions in which there are specific ways of problem-solving and practicing, this has not been the case so much in teaching.

Teachers often claim the essence of their profession is based on their autonomy. As noted above Elmore (2006, 2008) has argued that within a true profession, an individual does not have autonomy over its own body of knowledge and its practice. Moreover Elmore (cited in Ryan, 2007) observes that educators do not exercise serious control over the terms and conditions of who gets to practice, they do not have a clear body of knowledge and they have not risen to the challenge of policing the competence of their own colleagues. Berliner has argued that teaching has been perceived as loosely structured and lacking elegant and clearly defined solutions to problems (Berliner, 1992). Often teachers have claimed that their professional learning and expertise have come from experience (Hayes & Hegarty, 2002), and while this experience is important, it is still common that even 'good' teachers rarely consult theory or the corpus of research to explain or underpin their classroom practice.

The use of research-informed theory is critical to claims to be a profession, and this essential knowledge of teaching needs to be conceptually organized, represented, and communicated in ways that encourage a shared and deep understanding of teaching and learning (Barnes, 1989; Darling-Hammond & Bransford, 2012). The *professional* practice of teaching requires the conscious and deliberate use of acknowledged theory and research to inform the planning and implementation of teaching strategies that can be adopted or adjusted according to the needs of particular students. It is also important to a teaching profession that teachers continue to be learners. Teachers needs to constantly update and enhance their knowledge and skills and to draw on the expertise and knowledge of others in collaborative practice.

In Part II, we have argued that there are particular ways of thinking—which we have called *evaluative thinking*—embedded in the notion of developing 'clinical practice,' and we have made the claim that these are hallmarks of effective teaching. We have provided arguments for these claims and contend that there is a systematic and large corpus of research evidence in support of these claims. It is this evaluative thinking that helps make the case for teaching being a profession, as it is rigorous and sophisticated, can be codified and taught, and leads to the greatest impact on the learning lives of students.

The diagnostic skills associated with evaluative thinking provide the expert with a deep knowledge of each child's understanding and misunderstanding of concepts and of the next series of conceptual advances that need to be made in the context of the overall curriculum. The competent teacher delivers the curriculum to the middle of the class, while the *expert* teacher has the ability to meet the learning needs of *every* student within the class. A more detailed account of the development of this kind of expertise has been presented elsewhere in this book; in summary, to consider each learner in a classroom as having the same learning goals and challenges ignores their individuality and potential. From the outset, it should be the goal of every teacher to strive for excellence in their learning for every child. A teachers' role is not merely to meet the needs of each student but to help students exceed what they think is their potential.

Intervention skills enable the expert teacher to design sequences of learning that impact individual students, while evaluation skills allow the expert to show evidence of their impact on student learning. As Shanteau (1992) puts it, "experts are those who have been recognized within their profession as having the necessary skills and abilities to perform at the highest level. In contrast, a naïve decision-maker has little or no skill in making decisions in a specific area … novices are intermediate in skills and knowledge" (p. 255). In Shanteau's theory of expert competence, expertise depends on five factors: domain knowledge, psychological traits, cognitive skills, decision strategies, and task characteristics (Shanteau, 1992). Student learning and behavior relate to the task characteristics and there is, to some degree, a level of predictability and agreement on what these should look like after successful intervention. When considering these domains, it is not difficult to see why some teachers will be more expert and effective than others. All need to be at least proficient in each, but the expert is advanced in most if not all these factors.

Conclusion

Our argument is that teaching must be positioned as a collaborative, clinical-practice profession in which expertise in evaluation thinking is central.

The foundation of teaching as a profession is based on common understandings that underpin professional practice across many disciplines. The professional identity of the teacher rests on a code of ethics, standards of practice, and particular ways of knowing, thinking, and doing. Central to evaluative thinking in teaching is the impact on student learning and growth. This aligns and integrates with specialized discipline knowledge and understanding of child development from the early years to post-compulsory secondary schooling. There is a purpose to this knowledge, and that is to make an impact on the learning lives of students. The essential skill to make this impact sufficiently high is the skill of evaluative thinking about a teacher's impact on every student.

A clinical teaching profession requires all practitioners to maximize student progress through the use of evidence so that students' learning needs are diagnosed, appropriate research-based interventions are implemented, and the impact on student learning is continuously evaluated. This evidence needs triangulating from the test and assignment information, based on artifacts of student work over time, and on listening to student voices about their beliefs of engagement and success in learning.

In the next decade, the (r)evolution of the schooling workforce needs to be based on these attributes, which will need to be formally acknowledged and integrated into policy, schooling structures, and teacher workforce conditions. The consolidation of teaching as a profession, with its specialized knowledge-base and practice, emphasis on collaboration, and redesigned career structure and conditions, will make teaching a more attractive and viable choice, both intellectually and practically. These factors will help to attract excellent candidates to the profession, and encourage them to stay in the workforce longer, thus honing their levels of expertise, and, in turn, their leadership capacities. The preparation for the development of new teachers is the focus of the next chapter.

CHAPTER 7

Teacher education for a clinical profession

Fundamental to the future of teaching in effective school systems are high-quality and consistent initial teacher education (ITE) programs and a continued investment in ongoing professional learning for teachers, which is linked to increased professional status and recognition. There is a long heritage of these initial teacher education programs, typically ranging from three to six years, focusing on classroom climate and management, subject matter knowledge, techniques of teaching, and becoming a professional. Preservice teachers are placed in schools for an apprenticeship-like set of experiences, and there are many modifications of this basic premise. For example, across Australia, with a population of approximately 26 million people, there are close to 400 initial teacher education programs, and until recently, there were no common assessment tasks, very little evidence of impact, and a fundamental belief that each program was unique, effective, and loved—at least by the teacher educators. Until recently, about 30% to 40% of graduates claimed their initial teacher education program was effective at preparing them for the classroom, and the usual damning indictment is that the recent graduates claimed that the classroom experience, not university, the modeling of one to two particular teachers in schools, and the memories of their own best teachers had the most impact on their form of teaching.

Darling-Hammond and Lieberman (2012) edited a series of articles relating to teacher education in the western world. In some systems, concerns about the quality of teachers seem to be as frequently met by efforts to reduce standards as by efforts to strengthen them; in others, teaching is seen as a long-term profession where people can grow into leadership positions and develop expertise over time, moving from supplying teachers to providing teachers of quality. Darling-Hammond and Lieberman identified a number of promising initiatives. These included connecting theory and practice through both the design of thoughtful coursework and the integration of high-quality clinical work in settings where good practice is supported; using professional teaching standards to focus attention on the learning and evaluation of critical knowledge, skills, and dispositions; and the creation of teacher-performance assessments based on professional standards that connect student learning to classroom teaching. Other promising initiatives were the establishment of induction models that support beginning teachers through skillful mentoring, collaborative planning, and reduced teaching loads; and developing career ladders that allow teachers to develop and share expertise in teaching, mentoring, curriculum development, and leadership.

Some examples: Leiden University replaced traditional courses with a set of modules designed to help new teachers develop six critical teaching roles that mapped on to the key competencies outlined in the Dutch teaching standards: subject teacher, classroom manager, expert in adolescent psychology, member of the school organization, colleague, and professional. Utrecht University, recognizing the typical 'reality shock' when teachers first enter their own classes, brought more practical experiences into the initial teacher education program to frame the program to reduce this experience (see Darling-Hammond & Lieberman, 2012).

Kennedy (2016) noted a traditional tension for teacher educators: should the curriculum focus more on knowledge or should it focus more on practice itself? "Teacher educators have a long history of vacillating between these two approaches to curriculum" (p. 6). The knowledge advocates have a tough time, as the bodies of knowledge relevant to teaching have become enormous, and the practice focus also demands so much of preservice teachers such that it can become overwhelming. Kennedy identified four approaches, which she calls "parsing." The first is "teachers do activities," which involves listing all the activities that teachers actually do, so the knowledge and practice of these 'to dos' is taught to novices. This list stretches into the thousands, does not distinguish between good and poor teaching and implementation, and it is thus not surprising that this parsing has had little impact (Forzani, 2014). The second is "teachers make moves" while interacting with students. This product–process modeling of the discrete moves of teaching activities was more successful. For example, Anderson, Evertson, and Brophy (1979) devised a list of 22 moves that were most associated with gains in student achievement, wrote a manual for teachers describing these moves, and asked teachers to tally these moves in their own classrooms for an entire school year. Four 'moves' illustrate this method:

1. The teacher should use a standard and predictable signal to get the children's attention.
2. The introduction to the lesson should give an overview of what is to come to mentally prepare the students for the presentation.
3. The teacher should have the children repeat new words or sounds until they are said satisfactorily.
4. To keep each member of the group alert and accountable at all times between turns, the teacher should occasionally question a child about a previous response from another child.

The third approach identified by Kennedy is the enactment of core principles, that is, identifying broader patterns of observable behavior. As an example, history teachers identified the following core practices: the selection and adaptation of historical sources; the modeling and support of historical writing; employing historical evidence; modeling and supporting historical reading skills; using historical questions; assessing student thinking about history; and engaging students in historical research, and so on. These patterns are not as small as the moves derived from process–product research, nor are they generic activities, as were generated by the 'to do' lists.

The fourth, and Kennedy's preferred method, is to parse in terms of addressing the following five challenges:

1. Portraying the curriculum in a way that makes it comprehensible to naïve minds, and deciding how that portrait will be constructed from some kind of live activity that takes place in a specific space, uses specific materials, and occurs within a specific time frame.
2. Enlisting student engagement.
3. Exposing student thinking so they know what their students understand, do not understand, or misunderstand.
4. Containing student behavior to minimize distraction.
5. Accommodating personal needs.

(Kennedy, 2016)

The claim by Kennedy is teachers need to be taught to address all five of these challenges, acknowledging that all of them are difficult and that all five are inherent to the work of teaching. This focus exposes preservice teachers to these five bodies of knowledge, attends to solutions, and highlights the naïve conceptions about what teaching practice entails that are often accompanied with a naïve confidence in one's own ability as a teacher. Indeed, Kennedy has argued new initial teacher education students should not visit classrooms too early as this can reify their prior conceptions as they still see the classroom through their eyes as ex-students of those classes and thus fail to see through the eyes of teachers.

The Evidence of Impact of Initial Teacher Education Programs

Hattie, Anderson, Clinton, and Rickards (2015) outlined the sad state of the literature on evidence of the impact of teacher education programs. The evidence showed the programs had little impact on teacher effectiveness, despite so many proclaiming that there are core knowledge, practices, and understandings that all future teachers should have. The reality is a 'wild west' where almost everything goes, with remarkable variation of quality and impact (CCSSO, 2012; Schmidt, Cogan, & Houang, 2011). Hattie et al. (2015) identified five "family resemblances":

1. The "horse and buggy" model, where the new teacher follows a mentor, trailing around the class with them, learning on the fly (in the same way new doctors travelled on the buggy with their mentor telling anecdotes, providing homilies, and dispensing folk wisdom).
2. The "years and years" model, where more time is requested to pack more in.
3. The "horses and courses" model, based on the qualifications of the teachers (horses) and the correspondence of the courses to some preset list of accreditation criteria.

These three models (horse and buggy, years and years, horses and courses) are variants of the apprenticeship model (Lortie, 2002; Widen, Mayer-Smith, & Moon, 1998) in that they are mostly accredited on the basis of the 'correct' number of years, the desired nature of courses, and the qualifications of the teacher educators (for example, Australia is moving from a one to two year Masters degree preparation without much evidence on which to base such an expensive decision).

4. The "graduating student" model (Elliott, 1996), which was based on asking providers to articulate their graduating standards and then provide evidence that all graduates were reaching these standards.
5. The "clinical practice" model, as outlined throughout this chapter and which is the basis of the University of Melbourne teaching model.

Hattie et al. (2015) noted that the problem is a lack of a systematic evidence base to support any or all of the above approaches. It is the case that accrediting bodies accumulate myriads of documents and recommendations that should provide some comfort about the minimum standard of these models. Systematic evidence is claimed but not necessarily systematically demonstrated, so often these claims are based on the impact of the teacher education institution on the teacher candidates. Rarely is there evidence of teacher education institutions having an impact on the students of their teacher candidates. This latter is a higher bar, but one that seems necessary if teacher education is to become an evidence-based profession with an impact on the schooling system.

Mayer (2006) noted that "there were almost no studies that could determine direct causal links from teacher education programs to student learning" (p. 10). Grossman (2008) was emphatic with regard to how little is known about the impact of teacher education programs or the characteristics of teacher education that make the most difference in preparing teachers to teach well (particularly in high poverty schools with students who most need the best teachers).

We reviewed the evidence from meta-analyses of the impact of teacher education on students taught by recently gradated teachers and noted how few meta-analyses there were and how few studies there are. Independently, Qu, Becker, and Kennedy (2003) and Darling-Hammond (2000) searched for these studies, and between them they found fewer than 100 studies of varying quality. There are now four meta-analyses, together summing 93 articles, with a very low .10 effect-size (234th in the ranking of 250 influences on student achievement) (Table 7.1). Teacher education seems to have very little impact on the students of graduating teacher candidates.

While not a meta-analysis, one of the rare random-controlled studies involved assigning students to 44 teachers with emergency licenses and 56 trained teachers (Glazeman, Mayer, & Decker, 2006). The study found no differences in reading and $d = 0.15$ in mathematics. At best, it was concluded that teacher education programs appear to make some difference compared to emergency licenses. So much more is needed on this topic, and certainly there is a need for more control over possible moderators such as quality of intake, faculty, program, and in-school experiences.

There are few longitudinal studies of teacher preparation, and even fewer that include a reasonable sample size. The longitudinal studies note the major difficulties in keeping contact with graduates and thence the low response rates. For example, Louden, Heldsinger, House, Humphry, and Fitzgerald (2010) aimed to follow 1,000 candidates from the beginning of their last year of preparation through to the end of their second year of teaching. But low response rates and difficulties of follow up led to the study concentrating on differences in programs (for example: four-year undergraduate; double degree; one-year graduate diploma; and two-year masters) and ceasing the follow-up part of their planned study. Cochran-Smith et al. (2009) aimed for a larger study but ended up following 15 teachers from point of entry through to three to four years into their classroom experiences. Grossman, Valencia, Evans, Thompson, Martin, and Place (2000) followed 10 students into their first

TABLE 7.1 Meta-analysis evidence of effects of teacher education programs on school students.

Authors	Year	No. studies	No. effects	d	Topic
Qu, Becker, and Kennedy	2004	24	192	0.08	Certified vs alternative-certified teachers
Qu, Becker, and Kennedy	2004	24	76	0.14	Traditional vs emergency licensed teachers
Sparks	2004	5	18	0.12	Traditional vs emergency or probationary training
Whitford, Zhang, and Katsiyannis	2017	32	118	0.03	Traditional vs alternative programs
Kelley and Camilli	2007	32	105	0.15	Teacher education in early childhood

three years of teaching and noted the importance of training programs to teach reflection, the importance of access to curriculum materials in the school, and the balance new teachers came to understand between the need for student ownership and their beliefs about how to teach.

The trajectory from the first year in the classroom through to the fifth to seventh year of teaching is steep, and certainly within a few years, the washout effect of preparation is evident. Atteberry, Loeb, and Wyckoff (2013) followed 5,000 teachers in their first to fifth year in New York City. The gains for students over the first five years of a teacher's career rise about 5 to 15% of a standard deviation, or "the average development over the first five years of teaching is from one-third to a full standard deviation in overall teacher effectiveness" (p. 14). Moreover, the majority of those teachers (62%) in their first year who had the lowest effects on students are also the same teachers with the lowest effects five years later. The majority of those (73%) who had the greatest effects in their first year are the same teachers with the highest effects five years later. The key, therefore, is to ensure that when teachers leave teacher preparation, they are optimally prepared, as the next five years seem to be based on their performance at the end of their teaching education program (see also Henry, Bastian, & Fortner, 2011).

Prospective Teachers

As we have argued in previous chapters, at the core of effective and expert teaching are evaluative thinking and evidence-based practice that maximize learning opportunities for every student. Our argument is that these principles—principles of a true clinical teaching profession—need to be integrated with more consistency across initial teacher education and professional development programs. While in relatively recent years, several institutions have aligned their initial teacher education programs with attributes of a clinical model (Conroy, Hulme, & Menter, 2013; McLean Davies, Anderson, Deans, Dinham, Griffin, Kameniar, Page, Reid, Rickards, Tayler & Tyler, 2013), a transformation of the teaching profession requires a sustained approach to teacher education within and beyond initial teacher education so that a 'clinical foundation' frames all teachers' work on a daily basis (Kriewaldt et al., 2017).

Another major trend is the move by many prospective teachers to online teacher education programs. In 2016, 25% ($n = 22,100$) of initial teacher education students across Australia studied all of their program off-campus through online sources, and this approach has doubled since 2007. The greatest increase is for students who have traditionally faced barriers to participating in initial teacher education, and thus this group has the potential to continue to increase diversity in the teaching profession.

These students were more likely to be studying part-time, female, older, from a low socioeconomic background, and from regional or remote areas, or outer metropolitan areas where access to a campus can be difficult. In some Australian states, there are now more students studying in a university program based in another state than in a program within their own state (27% of all Australian initial teacher education students complete their course online).

There is no evidence to believe that the graduating qualities from online compared to on-campus students are necessarily different (McMahon & Thompson, 2014), nor is there evidence to indicate that there are differences in the graduates' perceptions of the skills they developed through their studies, the quality of teaching they experienced, the learning resources provided by their institution, or the overall quality of their educational experience. Online students are less likely to complete their course within the standard period of time (50%) compared to on-campus students (66%).

There are some remarkable uses of technology in many of these online programs, such as immediate uploading of classroom teaching, artificial intelligence-involved analyses and prompting to human academics to intervene, more social media interaction among students sharing experiences and their evidence of impact, and greater tracking of progress over the course with commentaries by in-school and on-campus mentors.

Teacher education and clinical practice

The *teachers for a new era* report argued that teaching should be considered a clinical-practice profession (Carnegie Corporation, 2001). Almost two decades later, the concept of clinical practice in teaching remains somewhat contested, with continued conjecture and some unease about the application of terms such as 'clinical,' 'diagnosis,' and 'intervention' to teaching and learning (Burn & Mutton, 2013; Kriewaldt & Turnidge, 2013; McLean Davies, Angelico, Hadlow, Kriewaldt, Rickards, Thornton, Tuckerman & Wright, 2017; Nias, 1997). Some feel this appropriation of language 'pathologizes' students, assumes deficits, and suggests coldness and sterility. Nothing is further from the truth and this certainly misrepresents the way these terms are used in medicine and how we use them in relation to teaching. We use the term 'clinical thinking' to mean this balancing of evaluative thinking, reasoning, and critical thinking.

We noted earlier the argument by Sackett et al. (1996) describing clinical evidence-based medicine—it is the merging of professional judgment with evidence; it is the "conscientious, explicit, and judicious use of current best evidence in making decisions about the care of individual patients" (p. 71); it is neither the tyranny of evidence nor the opinions or reflections of the teacher. Neither judgment nor evidence is enough, but it is the judicious balancing and integration of clinical expertise (proficiency and judgements) with the best available external evidence from systematic research.

We appreciate that the term 'clinical practice' comes across to some as cold. Some of the reviewers of this book noted their antagonism: "The term suggests a narrow, highly defined approach to teaching which is not at all what is reflected in the content. It negates (dismisses even) the joy of teaching which is why many enter and stay in the teaching profession"; and another, "I understand that the term implies a connection with the medical profession in terms of professional expertise and evidence-based practice, as in 'clinical trials' and shared bodies of knowledge. However, to the bystander unfamiliar with the term it has connotations of cold, unfeeling and surgical precision which may put potential readers off."

Perhaps a less cold term is 'clinical reasoning,' but still the critics dismiss most phrases with the term 'clinical,' as they presume (falsely) that clinical starts with a deficit. Evaluative thinking can apply to many professions, and the centrality of the student aims to focus the deliberate intention of the teacher to enhance, change, and improve the student. We prefer the notion of evaluative thinking among teachers to maximize impact on the learning lives of students—this notion emphasizes the ways of thinking, the collective doing this collaboratively, and highlights the purpose of teaching (to have a marked positive impact on students).

Conroy, Hulme, and Menter (2013), writing from the Scottish perspective, emphasized that the appropriation of terminology and concepts derived from medical clinical practice is not intended to simply and uncritically overlay a medical model on teacher education. Instead, we can take the ideas and rename them as we have by using the notions of evaluative thinking. It should be noted, however, that there are aspects of medical education that can be usefully analogized with initial (and ongoing) teacher education, and other aspects that are more difficult. For example, in medicine the class size is usually $N = 1$, the support system around doctors is markedly different from teaching, and the esteem and thus trust and belief in medics are very high. Consider also the fundamental ethic of 'do no harm,' the power and fundamental right of second opinions, the hierarchy of GPs and specialists, the high bars to enter and remain in the profession, and that doctors can be sued for malpractice. No doctor would dream of claiming (with pride) that they learnt all they need to know in medical school, that there is no need to read current scholarly literature to keep up to date, that they could alone solve all problems that present to them by themselves, that all medics are equal, or that they have the right to practice as they deem appropriate and fit. It seems appropriate that medics refer to their work as 'practice' with the inference that deliberate practice is essential, and is the outcome of being up to date, knowledgeable, and maximizing their impact on the wellness of the patient.

Alter and Coggshall's paper, "teaching as a clinical practice profession" (2009), outlined five key characteristics of clinical teaching: the centrality of clients/students; specialized knowledge and skills; the use of evidence and judgements in practice; accountability to professional standards; and rigorous academic and practical training before registration as a teacher. These types of characteristics are fundamental to other clinical professions such as medicine. In the medical and paramedical fields (clinical psychology, speech pathology) the focus is on 'direct patient care,' just as in education, the focus is on the student, specifically their learning and well-being. The nexus between the theoretical and the practical is central, and significant periods of time are spent in clinical settings.

The clinical teaching model aims to emphasize how student well-being and contextual influences are as crucial to teaching and learning as cognitive development. Moreover, clinical practice in teaching does not equate to diagnosing deficiency in students but aims to use expertise to assess the existing skills and knowledge as well as the learning goals for every student and using intervention (deliberate strategies) to support their learning development (Dinham, 2016). Diagnoses emphasize the importance of knowing what the student brings to the learning in terms of their skills (prior understanding, culture, home), will (dispositions, attitudes to schooling), and the thrill (their motivations for learning). As Nuthall (2007) noted, students already know about 50% of what is taught in most classes—hence the importance of diagnoses. If the material is too hard, then some students will resign themselves to failure; if the material is boring, tedious, or too easy, there is unlikely to be much learning. Perhaps pre-assessment sometimes addresses these issues, but it is evidence from multiple sources that forms the basis of diagnosis and clinical reasoning. The basis of the model is that which is discussed earlier in Chapter 3.

The importance of teacher educator knowledge

It is the merging of professional judgment with evidence that should be the major aim of teacher education programs such that it has maximum effect on the learning lives of students. A lack of linking between theory and practice in teacher education programs has led some commentators to question the theoretical and practical knowledge of teacher educators themselves (Zeichner, Payne, & Brayko, 2015). Just as in medical education, teacher educators need to possess expert clinical practice capacities themselves to foster these capacities in preservice teachers. Writing from a medical education perspective, Bowen (2006) argued that clinical teachers "must simultaneously foster high-quality patient care and assess the clinical skills and reasoning of learners in order to promote their progress toward independence in the clinical setting" (p. 2217). Likewise, it is the role of the teacher educator to observe and guide preservice teachers in their gathering of evidence, discussion of student cases, drawing of conclusions, and reasoning processes. Just as school classroom practitioners ascertain young learners' existing skills and learning needs in order to implement appropriate interventions, the teacher educator needs to apply the same practices to their mentoring of preservice teachers, each of whom will have a different learning trajectory as they progress from being a novice to more proficient and expert teachers.

In both medical and teacher education, developing clinical practitioners' evaluative thinking skills is crucial. Charlin, Boshuizen, Custers, and Feltovich (2007) wrote that each clinical encounter involves a number of processes for the clinical practitioner as they ascertain the important aspects of the situation through evidence, begin to form and test hypotheses, and use their knowledge and experience to guide their decision-making about suitable interventions (p. 1178). This decision making involves critical thinking—"the process we use to make a judgements about what to believe and what to do about the symptoms a patient is presenting for diagnosis and treatment" (Facione & Facione, 2008, p. 2). While this definition comes from the medical education perspective, Facione and Facione highlight the importance of contextual factors in clinical decision-making. These descriptions apply equally to aspects of clinical teaching and evaluative thinking discussed in earlier chapters in this book if we swap 'learning needs' for 'symptoms,' 'student' for 'patient,' and 'teaching intervention' for 'treatment.'

Norman (2005), writing about effective medical education, states that "clinical reasoning, or one of its many synonyms (problem solving, decision making, judgements) should be taught and tested" (p. 418). If clinical reasoning is also considered fundamental to initial teacher education, how can preservice teachers be supported in the development of critical and evaluative thinking and decision-making? In initial teacher education, as in medical education, "training clinical judgement ... requires a careful pedagogical approach" in which "trainees need time to think" (Facione & Facione, 2008, p. 6). The linking of theory and practice is a key element in this type of pedagogy so that "theory has the potential both to inform practice and to be informed by it" (Kaufmann & Mann, 2014, p. 7).

Recent claims for reform

The policy debate about initial teacher education is alive and well, and there are many proclamations about how to improve it. Many traditional models of initial teacher training have involved provider-based coursework with two or three professional-practice blocks per year. In some cases, the relationship between these theory and practice components has been tenuous at best. Typically, as we noted at the start of this chapter, courses have included subject-matter pedagogy, smatterings of educational psychology and sociology, and curriculum and assessment offerings, with preservice teachers trying to put together these components in their teaching during practicum. There have been reforms and recommendations for more content in initial teacher education programs to include aspects such as special education, indigenous studies, well-being, and so on, for more time on specific topics, and calls for teacher education staff to have recent teaching experiences in schools. Despite these reforms, there has been little evidence of increased impact on the quality of graduates nor, in turn, on student learning.

The reform of initial teacher education is the first step in the development of a future workforce within a sustainable clinical teaching profession. To facilitate this, initial teacher education programs need to evolve and, in some cases, be redeveloped so that theory and practice components are fully integrated. The focus of all programs, and the subjects within these programs, must be evidence-based interventionist teaching, evaluative thinking, and collaborative practice that maximize learning outcomes for every child. For this to happen, accreditation processes associated with initial teacher education programs need more rigor and consistency.

Louden (2008) wrote a provocatively titled paper: "101 damnations: the persistence of criticism and the absence of evidence about teacher education in Australia". He noted there had been at least 101 government inquiries into Australian teacher education over the past 30 years with little to no impact on the nature or quality of courses, the levels of government funding, nor the esteem (or otherwise) of teacher education programs. And we note, there is hardly a reference in any of these reviews to evidence or research—although there are many opinions, claims, case studies (isolated and nearly always about the 'best' students), and surveys (for example, more than half the graduates still claim they were not adequately prepared for the classroom). Most of the reforms are about the supply side: enhance the selection processes for course entry; change the program (teach more of x, have more recent teachers as lecturers, have more time in schools); and improve the mentoring and induction.

Louden argued that part of this focus has been because teacher educators have not been able to provide robust evidence about the differential impact of good and weak teacher education programs. They have not demonstrated that well-funded programs are more effective than poorly funded programs; they have expressed a methodological preference for case studies and commentaries and a resistance to experimental designs; and they have screamed for autonomy and the right to be creative and innovative.

Mayer (2014) noted the increasingly polarized debates about teacher education in Australia, from the deregulation and marketization of teacher preparation to the demands for increased professional self-regulation and semi-autonomy. Major features of the Australian solution have been the development of national professional accreditation standards through which graduates are required to demonstrate that they are ready to teach. As was noted in Chapter 6, there are national professional standards for teachers (Australian Institute of Teaching and School Leadership, 2015), structured into three domains of teaching (professional knowledge, professional practice, and professional engagement) and comprised of descriptors of four professional career stages (graduate, proficient, highly accomplished, and lead). The graduate and proficient levels are used for teacher registration purposes in determining provisional registration after completion of an accredited teacher education program and full registration after a period on induction. There is now widespread acceptance of these standards by the regulators and governments (Clinton et al., 2015).

In Australia, the Teacher Education Ministerial Advisory Group (TEMAG) was established in 2014 with the aim of providing recommendations about the future training of teachers. Unlike the previous reports, TEMAG focused on the degree to which the 400-plus programs could provide evidence that their graduates were classroom-ready (TEMAG, 2014). As the TEMAG report noted, initial teacher education must focus on producing graduate teachers who are able to address the learning needs of diverse student cohorts through evidence-based practice. This is especially important as, unlike many other professions, graduating teachers take responsibility for whole classes, often alone, in their first year on the job.

This led to the development of initial teacher education standards, graduate teacher standards, teacher performance assessments, and building a research base of effective programs.

The AITSL standards for accreditation of initial teacher education programs in Australia are typical of many such standards. They are based on eight principles: impact; evidence-based; rigor; continuous improvement; flexibility, diversity and innovation; partnership; transparency; and research. There are two stages. Stage 1 asks for evidence that the program meets the standards, and a plan for evaluating impact. Stage 2 ask for the evidence from the impact plan (and these plans are adjudged on the comprehensiveness, quality, and nature of evidence) and the plan for improving the program in light of this evidence of impact. All programs must have an approved teaching performance assessment (TPA) that focuses on whether soon-to-be graduates can influence the learning lives of students in schools, with a minimum requirement that the evidence from the TPA is moderated by at least other tertiary providers of teacher education. In 2019, there were two consortia across Australia of 21 of the 48 providers, each consortium with a single TPA. Such consortia put much responsibility back to the profession to moderate its own standards, to ensure that the accreditation is focused on programs and program improvement, and set the desired standard of acceptability of programs.

The standards for initial teacher education providers cover: (1) program outcomes, employment, and registration data, and principal satisfaction with graduates; (2) program development, design, and delivery; (3) program entry (which must be transparent and rigorous, and entrants must be broadly equivalent to the top 30% of the population [and a compulsory literacy and numeracy test is required before registration]); (4) program structure and content; (5) professional experience; (6) program evaluation, reporting, and improvement. The standards for graduate teachers include specifications relating to knowing students and how they learn; knowing the content and how to teach it; planning for an improvement in effective teaching and learning; creating and maintaining supportive and safe learning environments; assessing, providing feedback, and reporting on student learning; engaging in professional learning; and engaging professionally with colleagues, parents/carers, and the community.

This is the context in which the initial teacher education program at the Melbourne Graduate School of Education, at the University of Melbourne, has been evolving since 2008.

Implications for the profession

The Melbourne master of teaching example

I *[FR]* graduated in 1971, with an honors degree in biophysics, and became one of the two very first research students for Professor Graeme Clark in Melbourne University's Department of Otolaryngology (ear, nose, and throat surgery). Clark's belief was that he could make deaf people hear again with a 'bionic ear,' which was ridiculed by professional colleagues and undermined opportunities for government funding in those early years (www.bionicsinstitute.org/our-history/). But with the help of Dame Elisabeth Murdoch and her family, Sir Reginald Ansett, and others, and a six-hour telethon in 1974, enough money was raised to prove the concept. Cochlear implants have now helped hundreds of thousands of people.

I could see that a bionic ear on its own would not be sufficient to provide deaf children with the regular education that we want for all children. Early diagnosis, world class audiology, and outstanding teachers of the deaf were the key. In 1973, with Murdoch family support, the University established Australia's first graduate program in audiology. I was appointed as the foundation lecturer to lead the program, which was to enroll its first students in 1974.

When the audiology program was started in 1974, audiology was, to a large extent, a craft. Audiologists were expected to know how to test hearing and how to fit hearing aids; they were not really equipped to ask the diagnostic questions on what the underlying causes of the hearing loss might be. However, the way one treats the hearing loss will depend on its cause; hearing aids might be the answer, but they might not. We would send our students into the existing clinics and they were often told, "Forget all that stuff you are learning at the university, we'll teach you everything you need to know about audiology." That approach simply leads to a recycling of current practice. To overcome this, Graeme and I set up an audiology clinic at the University. I worked in the clinic, with patients and students, for up to five half-days a week, linking theory to practice and taking practice back into the lecture theatre.

My own research interest was the early diagnosis of deafness, and my PhD study in auditory neurophysiology involved developing a system for measuring the hearing in babies at birth. My research led to the development of a 'brain wave audiometer' through detecting auditory steady-state responses from the brain, which can determine the hearing acuity of babies from birth. This complements the devices used for Universal Newborn Screening, and now the age of diagnosis is just a few weeks and the vast majority of children with hearing loss are educated in regular classrooms.

At the beginning of the 1970s, the average age of detection and diagnosis of a child born with a hearing loss was two to three years of age, the stage when a child with normal hearing is going through an explosion in the development of language and cognition, so early detection was key. But having identified babies with a hearing loss begs the question, what needs to happen next? So, while I was developing a program in audiology, I was also interested in intervention and language development. Even though my background is basic science, in physics and physiology, I believe in the transformative power of education, in teaching and learning. This was the motivation for changing from the medical to the education faculty. I am driven by wanting to improve the lives of as many young people as possible.

When I became Dean of the Faculty of Education in 2004, it was a typical four-department Education Faculty, offering the usual range of programs as well as initial teacher preparation in the traditional manner. Coming into teacher education was an eye opener, as the profession was dominated by apprenticeship and craft-type models, sending students into classes hoping they would observe the optimal behaviors of teachers and showing them what we think best teaching looks like, when many teachers said "ignore all that theory from the university, just watch me," and there was the usual groans from students about the practice-theory divide (only wanting the practice). Where was the *multidisciplinary* thinking? Why did they not learn that at critical times there is a need for undertaking excellent diagnoses before intervening? How did we teach them to be part of a research learning community and keep up-to-date in research about high-probability interventions? Where was the critique of our methods and results among peers? Where are the senior surgeons/teachers that we could consult with if we were not sure or things were not working? Where was the notion of the 'second opinion,' so critical to our protection as professional? Why was every teacher seeming to do everything with such massive duplication and personal costs to them? Why were departments, particularly in high schools, like competitive silos, and resource people like outsiders and not part of the team? Why was this occurring when the academics in the faculty were superb in their own work, many world-famous?

The students certainly were not happy with the program, and more than half claimed when they became teachers that our program had not prepared them well for the classroom! There was a lack of research focus across the faculty, too; many were claiming they could only do research once their teaching was over (and did not see it as a related and dual part of the role). The departments were inhibiting collaboration and there was unhealthy competition, and there was so much duplication of support services.

Early in 2005, we set a clear, new vision with an unambiguous target of being "recognized internationally as the No. 1 ranked Faculty of Education in Australia" (we became #2 in the QS world rankings in 2014 and remained #1 in Australia through the rest of my Deanship), aiming to be characterized by the narrative and delivery of research-informed teacher education programs regarded as the best possible route to employment for a beginning professional teacher, with *high*--quality, *high*-impact, collaborative, theme-led research, and *high*-quality, high-demand postgraduate specialist studies.

With the pending introduction of the Melbourne Model in 2008 (all professional programs across campus were only graduate programs) and with some key colleagues, we reinvented the narrative and the nature of the teacher education program. In 2007, we toured to see Linda Darling-Hammond's program at Stanford and were inspired, although its program at the time was small ($N < 100$) and we had large numbers ($N > 800$). We adopted the clinical way of thinking, and certainly some colleagues did not like the metaphor from medicine, until (as noted in the acknowledgments) they saw us specifically talk about the importance of relationships and listening to children to ensure they understood the task, the nature of success, and how they were thinking. We needed to emphasize a message of hope and high expectations, not disease and pain.

It helped that the Melbourne Model raised the quality of the intake through graduate entry, and hence we could presume that the incoming students had a good grounding in their content domains. We deliberately benchmarked our performance to what we considered the top five programs in the United States and Canada (MSU, UBC, UoW-Madison, Virginia, Toronto) and established a message that our mission was very much creating organizational structures to manage and deliver the highest-quality teacher education program with superb evaluation within a learning-organization structure.

As part of the faculty transformation initiated in 2005, we established a Research Institute to support research, provide research leadership, and establish a research focus (Barry McGaw, ex-Director for Education at the Organization for Economic Co-operation and Development [OECD] was the first director, and John Hattie the second), and all academic staff were formed into clusters or Centers of Research. We sought new forms of revenue (e.g., via professional education, commercialization of curriculum and assessment materials) and had an aggressive internationalization of the faculty (via partnerships, international students).

Yes, we hit many walls: it was an expensive model, it took time for staff to claim ownership of the model and some left, and we had to work with our schools to ensure they welcomed this way of thinking and teaching (and many subsequently worked with the faculty to change their incumbent staff), but in time, there was major support from the faculty. They saw the boldness, the major focus on impacting on our students so they could impact on their students; the reasons for having to modify and improve were understood, and a core group of senior people were fully supportive enough to create the critical mass.

The Master of Teaching (MTeach), the initial teacher education program at the Melbourne Graduate School of Education at the University of Melbourne, was introduced in 2008. It was designed to be a genuine clinical master's degree for graduate students and to produce a new generation of teachers who "are interventionist practitioners, with high-level analytic skills, and capable of using data and evidence to identify and address the learning needs of every student" (Rickards cited in Flesch, 2017, p. 219; McLean Davies et al., 2013). The original design of the MTeach was influenced by the Carnegie Corporation's *teachers for a new era* (2001), most notably in the positioning of teaching as an "academically taught, clinical practice profession."

The MTeach model and structure represented significant shifts from previous initial teacher education offerings, which typically parachuted preservice teachers into two or three placement blocks per year that drew on but were essentially separate from their coursework, much like most traditional teacher preparation (Dinham, 2006; Levine, 2006; Ure, 2010). In his research into initial teacher education, Levine (2006) highlighted the importance of balanced academic and clinical work, 'sustained' placement experiences that facilitate the "immediate application and connection of theory to real classroom situations," and the close connections and collaboration between schools and academic faculties (p. 81). All of these elements were integral to the MTeach design, a design that was heavily influenced by our prior experiences in clinical training. School placements ran alongside coursework from the start of each academic year, assessment tasks required the collection and analysis of evidence from authentic classroom situations, and partnerships were developed that enabled school and university staff to co-teach, provide feedback and mentor preservice teachers collaboratively.

So, a prominent feature of the program from its inception has been the theory and practice nexus in that academic coursework and school practice are integrated and university academic staff and school-based practitioners form strong working partnerships to mentor preservice teachers. This was the key, and the clinical teaching cycle (see chapter 3) underpinned each element of the program, both through University-based subjects and the teaching experience.

This 'unifying' of school and university course components necessitated and enabled the "development of a shared understanding of what excellent teaching and learning look like, the development of a shared metalanguage, and a genuine integration of these across the program" (Kameniar, McLean Davies, Kinsman, Reid, Tyler, & Acquaro, 2017, p. 55).

Since 2008, the MTeach program has implemented a number of initiatives to foster and assess preservice teachers' critical and evaluative thinking and decision-making. Addressing the learning needs of a range of students and using evidence to inform interventions and evaluate practice have been key principles of assessment task design. One such assessment task, and a signature attribute of the program, is the Clinical Praxis Exam (CPE), in which teacher candidates report on the diagnosis, intervention, and evaluation of their practice in relation to specific student learning needs and development (as outlined in the diagram in Chapter 3). This task draws explicitly on and requires the synthesis of theory and content knowledge from core subjects and learning areas or disciplines with evidence from teaching practice, thus enabling meaningful engagement between the coursework site (the university) and the sites of practice (the schools) (Kameniar et al., 2017). Applying the lenses of social and policy theory, educational psychology, literacy theory, and discipline-specific pedagogies challenges the preservice teachers to acknowledge the "complex interplay" of theory and practice (McLean Davies et al., 2013, p. 99). Furthermore, the inclusion of 'praxis' in the task's title drew attention to the "impossibility of our interventions and actions being neutral or inherently benign" (Kameniar et al., 2017, p. 57); in other words, while drawing on existing research and theory about interventionist practice, each preservice teacher needs to consider and reflect on specific contextual factors impacting their focus on students' learning, rather than merely replicating others' interventions.

The evolution of the task in recent years has resulted in an even closer analysis of the key questions in the clinical teaching cycle (as presented in Figure 3.1) in relation to the preservice teacher's own classroom practice. In order to gather the information for the Clinical Praxis Exam, the preservice teacher, during teaching placements, must use classroom evidence and acknowledged research to ascertain what students are ready to learn and what interventions are most appropriate to support students' learning development in the specific learning context. Drawing on the collected evidence, hypotheses need to be formulated as to what the expected impact on learning will be. The preservice teacher implements the interventions and evaluates their impact on the students' learning. Collaboration with academic and school-based staff is essential in the implementation of the interventions, collection of evidence, and preparation of the CPE report.

The Clinical Praxis Exam is presented as an oral examination to panels of staff from both the university and participating placement schools. After the prepared report is delivered, the assessment panel asks questions of the preservice teacher, who has the opportunity to deepen their articulation and defense of their rationale and evaluative thinking processes. In this sense, the CPE is not dissimilar to clinical exams in the health field.

Preservice teachers completing the CPE have found that the oral report format allows them to "directly link theory, research and practice and to try and articulate that in one case," while noting that "the difference [the] intervention made in the learning of [the] focus students' was rewarding" (Kameniar et al., 2017, p. 61). The staff teams, comprised of both university academics and school practitioners, have also commented on the ways in which the Clinical Praxis Exam has "strengthened professional conversations and integrated aspects of coursework with the clinical model in practice" (p. 63).

Reflection on a clinical praxis exam

In order to plan and present the Clinical Praxis Exam, Teacher Candidates were required to use the Clinical Teaching Cycle stages to guide their practice during our recent school placements. This meant that in consultation with my mentor teacher, I needed to identify the learning needs of a student or small group of students and design targeted interventions to support the students to achieve a specific learning goal. With the support of my mentor teacher, I needed to collect evidence of the students' existing skills and knowledge, as well as their home lives, backgrounds, and interests. In planning and implementing my interventions, I was required to draw on evidence-based research and theory from my three coursework subjects, respectively focused on: educational psychology and pedagogy; sociology and policy; and language and literacy across the curriculum. After my interventions were implemented, I evaluated the impact of my approaches on my students' learning using evidence, and reflected on the significance of my interventions for my future teaching.

While my CPE report focused on 'Lucy,' a Year 9 student, my interventions were implemented in a whole-class situation. My series of interventions focused on developing students' use of oral and written language in the Visual Arts classroom.

The school context is a coeducational public secondary school in the suburbs of Melbourne. The school is experiencing a growth in literacy and numeracy development according to national and internal data, and one of the school's current initiatives is encouraging targeted writing across all subjects. This meant that the focus of my interventions aligned with school policy as well as addressed aspects of the Visual Arts curriculum. It is important to note also that about 65% of the students at the school are from language backgrounds other than English (LBOTE), and of these students, about half do not communicate regularly in English at home.

Despite some of the language challenges faced by the students, the school fosters a 'can do' philosophy and has high expectations of the students in terms of academic achievement, mainly to do with each student improving each year.

'Lucy,' a female student, comes from a southeast Asian family background. The evidence I was able to obtain about Lucy—from national testing data, conversations with her classroom teachers, written work samples from different subjects, and my own classroom observations—indicated that she is a conscientious student whose lack of confidence in speaking and writing English in class was inhibiting her development in these areas. Lucy's parents, from all accounts, are very supportive of their daughter and attend parent-teacher nights and other school events. Lucy's family falls into the 65% of the school population from a LBOTE background; however, Lucy, her parents and siblings speak a mixture of English and their original language at home.

In this particular year cohort, the gender balance was skewed towards males. In my Year 10 Visual Arts class, Lucy was one of six girls compared to 13 boys. Four of the girls appeared to be close friends and chose to sit and work together. Lucy sometimes sat away from other students and did not appear to have especially close friends in the class.

Before planning my interventions, there were a number of aspects to consider in relation to Lucy and her position within the class cohort and my specific subject:

- Was her lack of confidence in speaking and writing related to her proficiency in English?
- Did Lucy have an interest in Visual Arts?
- Did the classroom environment, including the positioning of social groupings, impact on Lucy's confidence and self-efficacy?

In order to underpin my planning for teaching, I also needed to consult professional reading and evidence-based research that had been discussed in my coursework. The role of gender in classrooms and learning, LBOTE students' experiences, and specific literacy approaches formed the basis of this reading. Discipline-specific readings and pedagogies associated with Visual Arts teaching were also central to my research.

In order to address my questions about Lucy, I conducted short, informal conversations with each of the students during my first few lessons while students were completing a practical task set by the classroom teacher. I wanted to get to know my students as well and as quickly as possible. Using their completion of their artworks as the starting point for interactions, I was able to channel their discussion of their works into topics around Visual Arts more generally and their own expectations of and attitudes towards the subject. When I spoke with Lucy, she was initially quite shy about talking about her artwork, but I realized that her spoken English was clear and she was able to use, when prompted, some basic but relevant language to describe aspects of her work in relation to color and overall composition. Like most students in the class, she did not spontaneously use language associated with art and design elements. Lucy also demonstrated some enthusiasm for the subject but was unsure whether she would continue with Visual Arts into her senior years.

When the students had completed their artworks, I decided (with the encouragement of the classroom teacher) to ask the students to write a short artist's statement about their works, including details about their inspiration, the materials they used, and what they had learned in the process. My thinking was that this would provide me with written work samples to analyze but would also be an 'authentic' writing task in the subject context. In order to implement this, I wrote a short artist's statement for one of my own works and used it as a model to guide the students. Together we 'deconstructed' my artist's statement, highlighting the use of Visual Arts language, sentence structures, and descriptive vocabulary. For this deconstruction, I was drawing on the Teaching-Learning Cycle (Derewianka & Jones, 2016; Rose & Martin, 2012).

My analysis of Lucy's artist statement revealed that she was able to write in logical sentences and that her spelling was accurate overall. There were some lapses in tense use, but the statement made sense and provided some relevant details about the work's meaning and inspiration. There was room for inclusion of more Visual Arts-specific terminology, such as that modeled through my own artist's statement. Much of Lucy's language was quite generalized. This was by no means particular to Lucy, as many students did not use this type of language in their statements.

I decided that a focus of my teaching, with Lucy and other students in mind, should be the explicit use of Visual Arts language in both oral and written tasks. I also aimed to increase Lucy's confidence in using this language.

Some of the steps of my interventions included:

- Providing Lucy (and other students) with explicit feedback on their artist's statements using the Hattie and Timperley (2007) model and focusing on whole text, sentence, and word levels so that students could identify the specific aspects of their work that needed development, for example, register, syntax, and spelling. For Lucy, I was able to comment positively on many of the technical aspects of her writing; the goal set for her was to use more Visual Arts-specific terminology when describing her work.
- Providing point-of-need scaffolding during students' redrafting of their statements.
- Organizing students into pairs to share their work and provide feedback using a checklist. The pairing of students was strategic. Lucy was paired with one of the 'social' girls. This was done to break down the usual grouping, but also because Lucy and her partner's statements demonstrated different strengths. Lucy's had demonstrated technical competence, whereas her partner had used subject-specific language throughout her piece. I drew on research and professional literature about peer tutoring in my planning for this stage.
- While in their pairs, students were provided with a checklist that I had designed to guide the peer feedback process. I also provided students with sentence stems such as "A strength of your statement is…" and "An area for improvement is…". These sentence stems were intended to provide less confident students such as Lucy with language to guide the feedback and evaluation. During this interaction, I observed Lucy using the sentence starters to comment on her peer's work.

- Asking the students (including Lucy) to read their redrafted artists' statements to a small group of peers while presenting their respective artworks. I hoped that given the feedback from her peer and me and the small group situation, Lucy would feel confident enough to read her work aloud. Lucy read her revised statement aloud and highlighted specific Visual Arts terminology in relation to her artwork.
- Setting a short reflective task in which Lucy and the other students were asked to write a brief paragraph describing 3 ways their learning had developed during the previous lessons. Lucy wrote that she had got to know some students better, had increased her use of Visual Arts language, and had not felt so nervous about speaking in class.

While the impact of my interventions on Lucy's learning development may not have been huge, I believe it was significant in the short time (3 weeks) during which I worked with her. If I were to work with Lucy in the future, I would continue to encourage her 'voice' in the classroom, moving from oral work in pairs, to small groups, to whole-class situations. Judging from my observations of Lucy in her pair and the small group, she was beginning to make stronger social connections with her peers. I would also make the connections between speaking and listening, writing, and making in my classes more explicit to students, including Lucy, so that they understand that using the language to discuss their work and that of others helps them to consolidate their understanding of the artmaking process.

Of significance for my future teaching is my realization that sometimes students are labeled as 'the ESL student,' or the 'quiet girl,' and assumptions about ability and learning may be made based on these. It is important to find ways to 'know' each individual student through collecting a range of evidence, including asking the student about her own learning.

The CPE is just one, albeit critical, example of the ways in which clinical practice and reasoning are assessed in the MTeach. Indeed, it was the CPE that was the greatest change agent of the whole program and created alignment of thinking across the whole program. The dialogue between expert teachers, teacher educators, and preservice teachers is crucial in ascertaining the ways in which clinical reasoning occurs in classroom situation. Evidence of student learning, collected from observations of preservice teachers' classes, forms a tangible basis for this kind of dialogue and mentor feedback (Kriewaldt, Nash, Windsor, Thornton, & Reid, 2018; Kriewaldt & Turnidge, 2013). Collaboration between experts, preservice teachers, and students in the diagnosis, intervention, and evaluation stages of the clinical teaching cycle is analogous to clinical rounds in teaching hospitals during which doctors, medical students, and patients discuss existing conditions and possible interventions. Similarly the adage 'what gets assessed gets valued' applies here, as the message to students is that the program values the ways of thinking of initial teacher education students, asks them to begin the process of becoming an evaluative thinker as outlined in previous chapters, and to know, do, and care about students and demonstrate how they can impact their learning lives. It is not enough to know content, how to teach, how to gain control, how to assess, how to prepare; it is more important to demonstrate that knowing these skills can be translated into impact on students.

Haigh, Ell, and Mackisack (2013) asked 30 mentor teachers and initial teacher education lecturers to devise 20 questions they would ask to the following scenario to judge whether the teacher candidate is ready to teach: "I'd like you to imagine that a colleague has come to you seeking advice about whether their teacher candidate should pass practicum. She is trying to decide if the teacher candidate is ready to teach." Table 7.2 illustrates Haigh et al.'s coding of the 600 (30 × 20) questions.

Not once was the core clinical praxis question asked—"Do the students learn?" The focus was on the 'how' of teaching, on personal attributes, and on control and technique, and this overshadowed whether the teacher has had an impact on any or all students.

Haigh and Ell (2014) presented four vignettes of preservice teachers who were designed as either strong in personal attributes but weak in professional practices, or strong in professional practices but weak in personal attributes. Eighteen mentor teachers were interviewed and asked for their judgements of the preservice teachers in the vignettes. Overall, the mentor teachers rated the preservice teacher in the vignettes as a high pass, pass, low pass, or fail (16). There was remarkable variation in the cues (i.e., which particular part of the scenario) that the mentors used to make these decisions—some argued that certain skills could be learnt when the preservice teachers graduated and went into their own classes, others recalled their own experiences at that stage and weighted this information, and others were

TABLE 7.2 Questions used to assess preservice teachers' readiness to teach.

	Learning as a teacher	Personal qualities	Relationships
Personal attributes	Are they able to act on feedback? Do they reflect critically on their own practice?	Do they have the necessary personal qualities/ dispositions for teaching?	How effective and effective are the their relationships with the children, staff, and parents?
	Knowledge and planning	Enacting teaching and management	Assessment & use of evidence
Professional practices	Do they know the content/pedagogy of the teaching areas?	Are they organized and prepared	Do they gather information about children's progress and use this in their teaching?
	Is their planning appropriately leveled and detailed?	Can they manage the classroom effectively?	

sufficiently concerned to fail a candidate if certain aspects of practice were not well demonstrated during the practicum. For the failed candidate, much time was spent suggesting ways that deficits could be made up and how they might help someone learn the things they do not know or do. The focus was mainly on the personal attributes and the professional attributes, and far too little attention was paid to the impact of teacher candidates on the students. This notion of demonstrating impact, making evaluative judgements about the nature of this impact (the 'what'), the number of students who have been impacted (the 'who'), and the magnitude of the impact (the 'size of the impact') is the core focus of clinical programs.

Some flow-on effects from the MTeach structure, task design, and collaborations have included increasing crossover of school-based staff to teaching roles in university-based coursework subjects, and school–university research collaborations. As such, these close partnerships have informed practice at both sites (Conroy et al., 2013; Grossman, 2010) and have enabled increased understanding of clinical teaching as applicable to initial teacher education and the partnership schools and systems (McLean Davies, Angelico, Hadlow, Kriewaldt, Rickards, Thornton, Tuckerman, & Wright, 2017). As a school-based practitioner in an MTeach partnership school has commented: "The clinical approach and the power of the team have enabled a visible shift in delivery, thinking and reflecting in our classrooms" (McLean Davies et al., 2017). Further to this, participation in the MTeach has impacted on the way in which school staff conceptualize their own practice. At one partnership school, mentoring staff undertaking a clinical teaching certificate aligned to MTeach principles established a praxis group, a collaborative professional development group that uses lesson analysis as a means to improve classroom practice (McLean Davies et al., 2017). This type of initiative has encouraged the use and acceptance of peer feedback among staff and preservice teachers and made stronger the links between research, theory, and practice.

Other course offerings in recent years, including the Master of Clinical Teaching, have drawn on aspects of the MTeach, specifically the clinical teaching cycle and the Clinical Praxis Exam. This degree, offered to qualified teachers, has facilitated a change in thinking and practice for many experienced and mid-career teachers, as they redefine their planning, delivery, assessment, and collaborative practices and act as change agents in their school sites.

After initial teacher education: The development from novice to expert

A challenge for teacher education is the identification of differences between levels of expertise in developing practitioners and implementing suitable strategies to support practitioners at these different levels (Eva, Hatala, LeBlanc, & Brooks, 2007; Rikers & Verkoeijen, 2007). Standards such as those produced by the Australian Institute for Teaching and School Leadership (AITSL)—where teachers move through graduate to proficient to highly accomplished to lead teachers—have attempted to do this for the teaching profession (AITSL, 2015), but more explicit differentiation in relation to clinical practice and judgements needs development. Much depends on the experiences of students in their first two to three years.

Unlike many professions, teachers begin their careers with the same full teaching and legal responsibilities as the most experienced teachers. Main (2009) surveyed about 500 schools and identified high-quality induction programs, welcomed by new teachers and regarded by them as 'making the difference' to the start of their careers. She noted that, in most cases, new teachers were expected to enter into the prevailing beliefs and methods of the school, and if this prevailing view was inconsistent with the methods they brought from their initial teacher education course, and especially if the view was of low standard (as determined by the New Zealand independent inspectorate), then there was a higher likelihood of not staying in the profession. Effective programs (see Figure 7.1) had four components:

- Pedagogical development.
- Socioemotional support.
- Professional agency.
- Structured balance.

Main argued that it "is the act of evaluating, perhaps even more than the results themselves, that makes a critical difference in the induction of beginning teachers (BTs) in low-decile primary schools. In particular, BTs immersed in a culture of collaborative analysis of student data appeared to be experiencing a more effective induction program than beginning teachers that did not engage in collaborative inquiry." Induction was viewed as a selling point in exemplar low-decile schools, where beginning teachers reported low stress levels, a high ethos of care, and more leadership opportunities.

Main concluded that primary schools implementing effective induction programs tended to engage in what Stansbury and Zimmerman (2002) termed a 'high-intensity induction program' containing strong, focused, data-oriented, collaborative plans. However, perhaps owing to their cultural setting (lower socioeconomic schools in New Zealand have a higher proportion of Maori indigenous and Pasifika students), these programs also contained a strong ethic of care.

In 2016, AITSL conducted a survey of stakeholders that included responses from 1,287 school leaders and 2,268 beginning teachers. School leaders are far more likely than early-career teachers to believe that induction is being provided in their school—70% of school leaders reported that they had formal induction in place in their schools, while only 48% of early-career teachers reported receiving a formal induction when they started as a beginning teacher. The lowest focus of these induction programs was teacher well-being (31% of principals and 13% of beginning teachers claimed this was included) and developing professional identity (14% and 7%). It seems it is not the existence of induction programs that is the concern, but the visibility and focus of these programs. AISTL recommends, akin to Main, that the four key areas are: professional practices, professional identity, well-being, and orientation.

Implications for the profession

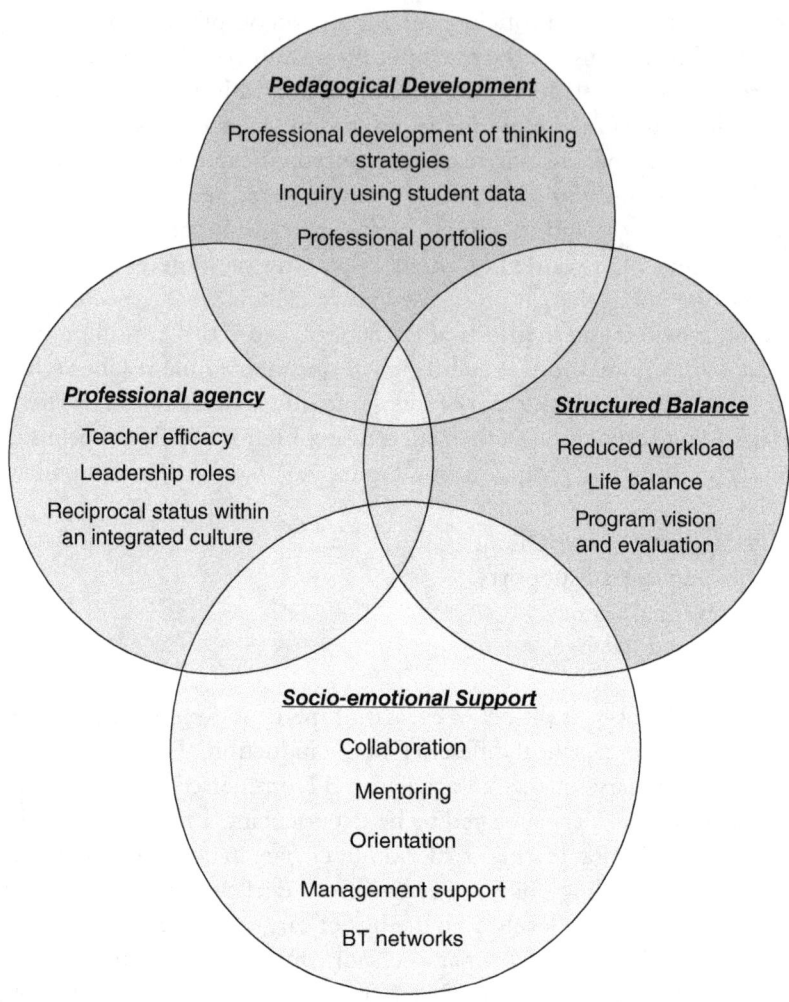

Figure 7.1 The four components of effective programs

Medical education literature highlights the importance of the experience of the practitioners as they progress from novice to expert clinician (Boshuizen & Marambe, 2020; Boshuizen & Schmidt, 2019; Bowen, 2006; Charlin, Boshuizen, Custers, & Feltovich, 2007; Norman, 2005; Schmidt & Rikers, 2007). Medical students, early in their training, tend to focus on isolated signs and symptoms and try to link these to areas of content knowledge they have learned without fully recognizing patterns of symptoms that fit together (Schmidt & Rikers, 2007). Similarly, a novice teacher may take some time to piece together evidence of a child's learning from sources such as work samples, observations, understanding of classroom behaviors, and background factors in order to decide on appropriate interventions. Researchers of medical education also highlight the importance of experience and building knowledge of patterns and incidents; that is, building a repertoire of situations and then using those to inform decision-making. Intermediate-level students of medicine have more information, prior case studies, and experience to draw on than novices and are able to use detailed knowledge from specific sciences (anatomy, physiology, and so on) to articulate the signs and symptoms of the patient. An expert doctor rarely makes these kinds of references; instead they are able to draw on repeated applications of their knowledge and practice in 'packaging' or subsuming of lower-level, detailed concepts (Schmidt & Rikers, 2007; van Mook, de Grave, Wass, O'Sullivan, Zwaveling, Schuwirth, & van der Vleuten, 2009). Using knowledge about contextual factors and enabling conditions is characteristic of expert doctors who are able to rule out diseases and focus on those that are most likely. Schmidt and Rikers use the example of a patient who presents with fever-like symptoms in the midst of an influenza epidemic. Initially, the doctor may diagnose flu; however, after questioning the patient who declares she has recently been in a malaria-infested region, the doctor is able to form different hypotheses and implement interventions accordingly. Schuwirth et al. (2011) comments that an expert does not need more data to solve a problem, but less data and more patterns and higher-order diagnostic and scenario thinking. Again, analogies with teacher education can be drawn. As noted in the previous chapter, the expert teacher will have more experience to draw on and have deeper understanding of the learner, what they know and can do, and how evidence about contextual factors may impact the teacher's choice of interventions. It is also important to understand that there is no single or even optimal approach to intervention (Norman, 2005); a novice teacher or medical professional may seek the solution to a particular scenario, whereas a more proficient or expert practitioner will draw on and evaluate a range of approaches in their selection of interventions.

Integral to the success of initial teacher education and ongoing teacher education reform is systematic collaboration between course providers, school systems, and other community stakeholders. The establishment of partnerships between initial teacher education providers and school networks gives assurance that teacher training meets the needs of employers, schools, and students. And in the case of the University of Melbourne MTeach, it also helps schools think more proactively about their own needs.

A synthesis of 118 meta-analyses of initial teacher education programs showed very large effects when initial teacher education students were actively "engaged in learning different types of teaching and clinical practices," pointing to the need to "acquire the skills needed to engage in specific types of classroom and clinical practices" (Dunst, Hamby, Howse, Wilkie, & Annas, 2020, p. 34). Such interventions included faculty coaching, simulated instruction with deliberate practice, critical-thinking instruction about teaching, modeling teaching practices, and simulated and microteaching opportunities. The lowest effects (<.20) related to the proxy measures of the nature of the degree (undergraduate versus graduate), number of education classes, length of the program, and school-based mentoring programs. These findings reinforce the claims of this chapter, inviting more clinical and evaluative thinking, more opportunity to develop differentiated teaching methods, and high levels of feedback, adjustment, and practice, as well as developing high levels of self-efficacy and high expectations.

In the future, to enhance impact from teacher education programs, selected universities in each jurisdiction may need to take responsibility for moving initial teacher education forward, piloting programs and acting as key sites for transitioning practice and research.

Aligned to enhanced programs is teacher recruitment. To create a strong profession for the future, the selection of candidates into initial teacher education programs needs to be more rigorous; it should not be solely based on academic scores, but also on desirable personal attributes aligned to teaching (see Bowles, Scull, Hattie, Clinton, Larkins, Cicconi, Kumar, & Arnup, 2016). A closer link between the teacher education program and the consequential induction in schools has the potential to be powerful; one notion to support smoother transitions from preservice to classes would be to run a registrar (as per junior doctors in their first year in full practice) system for the last six months to a year of an initial teacher education program. This could be especially beneficial for those who enter into schools that still privatize classrooms and provide minimal induction, and where colleagues do not work together to evaluate and critique their impact on students. One such system is the Teacher Capability Assessment Tool (TCAT) (Figure 7.2), an evidence-based approach to the selection and development of preservice teachers developed at the University of Melbourne, led by Janet Clinton (Clinton & Dawson, 2018).

Teacher capability assessment tool

TCAT takes a life cycle view of teacher development from selection and entry into initial teacher education programs through end-ofprogram readiness to teach (using a parallel exit tool, TXET) into the initial years as a teaching professional. Embedded within the tool are assessments focusing on a range of factors including motivations for teaching, cognitive reasoning skills, and non-cognitive domains.

At selection and entry, the TCAT model comprises two core components (informed self-selection, and cognitive and non-cognitive skill assessment—completed online) and two extended components (structured behavioral interview, and teaching demonstration).

The web-based **informed self-selection** asks for a number of personal attributes and capabilities related to the applicants' experience and readiness to enter preservice training, evidence of their prior cognitive ability (for example, GPA), and their work and professional experience, plus experiences related to teaching and subject area(s) they wish to teach. The free-text responses in this section are assessed against general teacher traits, such as knowing students and how they learn, planning for effective learning, and creating a supportive environment.

The **measures of general cognitive ability** consist of numerical, verbal, and nonverbal reasoning tasks, and the **non-cognitive** section assesses qualities such as disposition, self-regulation and resilience in the face of challenge,

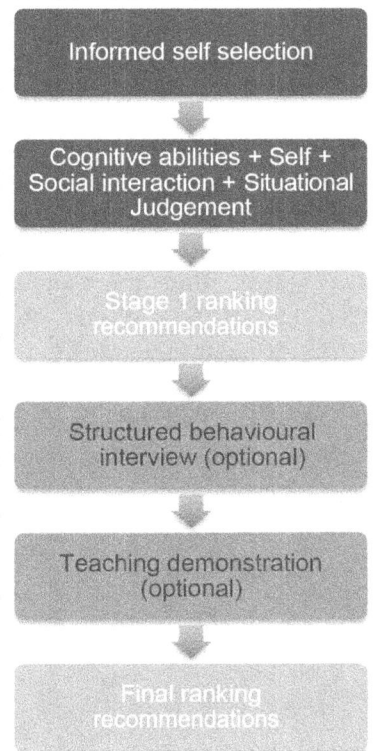

Figure 7.2 The TCAT model of student selection for entry into initial teaching programs

communication style, ability to act fairly, cultural sensitivity, and self-awareness. There is also a set of situational judgment items, which further assess several of the noncognitive factors through a candidate's chosen course of action when faced with common teaching circumstances.

The **interview** component involves a trained panel of interviewers who assess candidates in six key research-supported areas of relevance, including interpersonal skills and behavior, and the **teaching demonstration** component involves candidates being presented with a teaching scenario and asked to prepare a short lesson based on a learning area of their choice, and to present this lesson as a role to a panel of assessors.

Information from TCAT is aggregated and analyzed to provide a profile of the candidate. This profile is used to base selections into the program (each program decides on the optimal weighting of the components) and also assist the preservice teacher to set individual goals relevant to work placement and preparation for teaching practice. When matched with the exit assessment, the progress not only of each student but the impact of the program can be evaluated, leading to identifying strengths and gaps in the program.

Conclusion

The future schooling workforce will need to be prepared for communities that are constantly dynamic, and in turn, schools that will continue to face significant changes. Teachers and other school staff will need to ensure that they are able to collaborate for maximum impact on student learning. In order for the teaching profession to attract and keep highly skilled and well-rounded individuals, career pathways and associated rewards will need to be more aligned. We note, for example, that in some Australian jurisdictions, there is minimum pay raise when a teacher moves from proficient to highly accomplished or lead—instead schools are provided with positions that are highly remunerated and that teachers cannot apply for unless the applicant is certified as highly accomplished or lead. This helps mitigate against these teachers moving to the higher socioeconomic schools that are seen to be easier in which to teach, allows systems to control any perceived blowout of budgets if too many teachers become highly accomplished or lead teachers, and ensures students who most need the best get the best.

CHAPTER 8

A revolution of teaching and schooling

We noted in Chapter 1 that in 1900, 20% of the world's population was literate and numerate. In 2000, 14% of the world's population was illiterate and innumerate. This surely is a stunning transformation—equal if not exceeding the accomplishments of the Renaissance, the enlightenment, the industrial revolution, and the Athenian contributions. With some distance, the dramatic reversal in the world's levels of education could be considered the revolution of the twentieth century. When we ask colleagues why this transformation occurred, the typical answers include the increase in resources, socioeconomic gains, the spread of technology, the policies of governments, and so on. But there is one fundamental reason for this mass literacy and numeracy explosion—because of teachers.

In many senses, we are still basing our fights for improved levels of education on this twentieth-century challenge of improving literacy and numeracy—and indeed, the 14% represent many millions of students, and with every year, a new cohort of billions of students comes to schools to benefit from the teaching of literacy and numeracy. This success must be continued. But in the twenty-first century, schools in the western world are expected to attain much more than improving literacy and numeracy. Schools are asked to take on many more responsibilities, including the social, emotional, and physical well-being of students, and more recently, the development of collaborative learning strategies. Society has upped the ante on what is expected from teachers.

The increasing demands on schools

Richard Elmore (2015) has written that the future of learning in society is virtually unlimited, but the means of transforming information into knowledge through the traditional structures of schooling are limited. We have argued that the purposes of schooling have changed and will continue to broaden; hence, the traditional models of schooling focused on literacy and numeracy primarily are no longer adequate. Rapid developments in technology, communications, and work, as well as worldwide shifts in social demographics, present clear challenges for the schools of the future.

What constitutes excellence in schooling is being redefined. Comparisons between schools, school systems, and nations are frequent, and the information drawn from these comparisons is easily accessible. Increasingly, schools are being called on to address broader outcomes, not only related to student learning, but in relation to well-being, safety, and equity. Societal and economic changes, constantly developing technologies, and research into learning are driving the broadening expectations of schooling (UNESCO, 2013). Student needs are becoming more dynamic, complex, and diverse, such that existing conceptualizations and structuring of schooling may be no longer adequate. Elmore (2015) asserts that the continuing investment of governments in "hard-bound physical structures" and "heavily institutionalized, hierarchical" schooling does not align with the education needs "in an age where learning is moving into mobile, flexible and networked relationships."

Rapid developments in technology, communications, and work, as well as worldwide shifts in social demographics present clear challenges for the schools of the future. Strong social cohesion is related to robust and high-quality education (Hargreaves & Shirley, 2018). Repeated underachievement for minority and low socioeconomic populations leads to social tension in class and ethnicity terms. Increasingly diverse and pluralistic societies require policy settings and educational practices that encourage common citizenship, social cohesion, resilience, and reliance on debate and discussion as problem-solving methods. This book argues that schools that exist in isolation, without collaboration across schools and school sectors, and without systemic integration with other services and institutions such as health, the workforce, and the community, will struggle to address the needs of young people in the twenty-first century. There is a need to increase participation by all in education, training, development, and child health services to ensure every student can reach their potential to become a productive and happy citizen. School completion is important for a young person's health, happiness, and future employment prospects (Oreopoulos, 2007; Productivity Commission, 2012), and these opportunities need to be accessible to all students, including those from demographics with traditionally low school completion rates, those with special needs, and those from disadvantaged backgrounds (Lamb & Rice, 2008). The collaboration of schools and teacher experts with other education-related fields is crucial to the establishment of these goals.

We have highlighted the importance of schools, both present and future, acknowledging the links between social, emotional, physical, and cognitive aspects of child development (Jones & Kahn, 2017). Thirty or forty years ago, dimensions such as well-being and engagement were not necessarily top on the list of schools' priorities. Now, frameworks such as Seligman's *PERMA* (Positive Emotion, Engagement,

Relationships, Meaning, Achievement) (2018) emphasize how important the contributions of schooling and teachers are in the development of the whole child, including cognitive development, emotional development, and academic achievement. Fostering group participation and engagement both within the school and the community will become an even greater focus for schools of the future. While many commentators (including educators) may argue that schools and teachers already have enough to manage with the delivery of ever-expanding curricula, and many of these roles should be the focus of the parents, it makes sense that schools become the key sites or hubs for community engagement and integration with other services (ACER, 2013). After all, most children go to school.

Student outcomes, previously prioritizing academic development, need to also acknowledge overall growth—burgeoning independence and personal responsibility to achieve goals (UNESCO, 1996). Student well-being—emotional, social, and physical—comprises broad elements such as the development of motor skills, understanding of nutrition, self-efficacy, and conflict resolution strategies (UNESCO, 2013), and these elements need to be integrated into school curricula and extracurricular programs. Positive and productive engagement with others is also a fundamental aspect of being part of a school and wider community. In the globalized twenty-first century, young people require far more understanding of the wider world than their twentieth-century counterparts. The starting point for this understanding is school participation in local initiatives and organizations through which young people are encouraged to connect with their communities (West-Bunnham, Farrar, & Otero, 2007) and possible future workplace and vocational opportunities.

The United Nations Sustainability Goals for Education (see https://www.un.org/sustainable) was created to ensure inclusive and equitable quality education and promote lifelong learning opportunities for all. The 2019 report notes that "in 72 countries with recent data, approximately 7 in 10 children aged 3 and 4 were developmentally on track in at least three of the following domains: literacy-numeracy, physical development, social-emotional development and learning," but too many young students were not achieving minimum proficiency levels in reading and mathematics. Of these, about two-thirds were attending school but were not learning in the classroom, or dropped out of school.

From the very start of schooling, the goals of education must address the needs of the whole child and the global citizen, and include the dimensions of cognitive-intellectual, physical, and mental health, including disciplined physical movement, social-emotional development, creativity and innovation including artistic expression, and citizenship and democracy. These dimensions of education overlap, interconnect, and are mutually reinforcing. One reaction, by Arthur (2003), has been the promotion of 'character education,' which, he argues, can be taught and learned, and which he and colleagues argue has been neglected in schools and across the professions. The benefits of character education include the enabling of productive lives and, in turn, more healthy societies. Just as social and emotional learning approaches promote the integration of social and emotional learning approaches in the school context, Arthur argued that the deeply formative experience of schooling provides the opportunity for the modeling of 'virtues' such as self-discipline, compassion, gratitude, justice, humility, creativity, and resilience. The teacher is crucial to the development of students' character education, as core values are consistently fostered in the classroom and the curriculum is examined in relation to ethical and social issues. The school and teachers are in partnership with parents and local institutions and organizations so that the principles are reinforced across a community and 'democratic citizenship' is promoted.

McRae (2019a) emphasizes the importance of these attributes in an age of automation and argues that "teachers will need to help students become engaged citizens who, for their own resilience and society's, [must] embrace those things that cannot be automated" such as creativity, empathy, and fine-motor skills. Crucial to this kind of development is play, which promotes problem-solving strategies, negotiation skills, cooperation, and creativity. McRae argues that "free play is under siege," as play is sacrificed in education contexts for increased standardization and competition (McRae, 2019b; Sahlberg, 2014), and even childcare and kindergarten-age children are expected to engage in more formalized education.

If all of these demands are to be met, what does a perfect schooling system (and beyond the school) look like? Academic outcomes are crucial, particularly in core areas such as language, literacy, mathematics, and numeracy (Ashenden, 2018), and, in their minimalist sense, are the gatekeepers to other forms of knowing, doing, and caring—but the new conceptualization of schools needs to address broader objectives relating to the whole child.

Refocusing schooling

In a major study that created waves of debate, Wilkinson and Pickett (2011) demonstrated the increasing gaps between the affluent and the less affluent across the world, arguing that inequality is behind a wide range of social ills including violence, obesity, imprisonment, and addiction. While the United States has the highest income inequality in the western world, inequality is rising across the English-speaking world, with the top 1% of earners accounting for an increasing share of overall income. Those at the very top of society are advancing at a rapid pace, but the rest are drifting behind.

Schools, and the quality of education they offer, remain a powerful predictor of future earnings and financial stability. A recent Australian report, for example, found that the likelihood of being in the top 10% of all income earners in the country increases dramatically with educational attainment. A major part of the success criteria for education systems needs to be how schools reduce this gap, or at least improve every student's life chances and enjoyment. One of the worries is that this becomes cyclic—those who have higher resources become more likely and powerful enough to demand higher-resourced schools for their students, while those with lower resources miss out on these 'choices'—and thus the inequality gap increases.

While education is a core element in addressing equity issues, schools and teachers cannot do this in isolation. Genuine collaboration and partnerships within schooling systems and with relevant community and industry organizations can be more efficient in terms of spreading expertise, but also socially and economically beneficial (Nous, 2011). Collaboration and partnerships allow access to resources sometimes lacking in so-called 'disadvantaged' schools and those in remote areas (Weldon, 2015), and are important in addressing the education and development of the whole child. This kind of clustering of schools to try to address under-resourcing and equity issues has been implemented in many parts of Ontario, New Zealand and Singapore (Rickards, Toon, & Hattie, 2015).

The disadvantage experienced by low socioeconomic communities generally crosses generational boundaries. Students do not leave poverty at the school gate, and the low expectations some parents have for their children's life chances are hard to ameliorate in the classroom, particularly if the school compounds this situation by also having low expectations. For many of these students, health and nutrition can be paramount to their engagement with school. To break this cycle of intergenerational disadvantage, many of the more successful programs are multidisciplinary. One such framework, the Restacking the Odds project in the Centre for Community Child Health at the Royal Children's Hospital in Melbourne, is investigating the impact of stacking five carefully selected interventions for disadvantaged children and their families in the first eight years across antenatal care, sustained home visiting by a nurse, early-childhood education and care, parenting programs, and support through the first years of school (Molloy, Goldfeld, Harrop, & Perini, 2018).

Addressing disadvantage is not just a health issue, a social service issue, or an educational issue. It requires all services working in unison as a multidisciplinary team. In most models, the interventions are more health-related during the first three years of life, conducted by experts such as maternal-child health nurses and social workers. Opportunities to start addressing educational inequity emerge in early-learning centers, kindergartens, and the first years of schooling. These are vital to ensure as many children as possible start school on an even playing field.

There are many successful examples of services working in unison. For example, multidisciplinary teams have been found to be important for improving youth mental health. Vreeman and Carroll's (2007) meta-analysis of bullying interventions, for example, found programs with multidisciplinary teams of clinicians and educators were more effective than clinician-only or educator-only interventions. A recent report from the Aspen Institute (Berman, Chaffee & Sarmiento, 2018) supports this perspective, arguing that education institutions should adopt a whole-child approach, which caters to students' social, emotional, and academic development both in the classroom and beyond. The report proposes a series of recommendations for embedding a whole-child approach to education in schools, including aligning resources (everything from food assistance to mental health support) and community partners to work with schools and families to support healthy learning and development. While this approach benefits all students, it is particularly valuable for those who have experienced disadvantage, with decades of developmental science research showing that children who have experienced adversity and trauma benefit from specific programs designed to buffer them against excessive stress.

Whether a child's issues are dominated by health, social disadvantage, or educational underachievement, highly skilled professionals are an essential element of meeting the challenges of disadvantage and educational underachievement. This is especially true of the teaching profession. This book focuses on the capabilities and knowledge base required for the new generation of teachers to truly meet the needs of individual learners in complex classrooms. It is essential that the teaching profession is elevated to a true clinical-practice profession where teachers have the evaluative and interventional skills to address the complex and varied needs of students in their class. The skills to work with other experts in both diagnosing and intervening, and to share successes, is one of the core sets of expertise we have identified throughout this book. But what does this look like with real students in real classrooms?

The clinical teacher in action: A multidisciplinary approach

Without a doubt, teachers are juggling a myriad of challenges at any one time. In Australia, about 22% of their students will be developmentally vulnerable on one or more of the domains in the *Australian Early Development Census* (making them less likely to be able to take advantage of the opportunities school offers), and one in seven will have experienced a mental disorder in the previous 12 months, as shown in the 2015 Australian Child and Adolescent Survey of Mental Health and Well-being (which covers four- to 17-year-olds; Laurens et al., 2017).

It is not just the developmentally vulnerable students who need complex and intensive interventions. Evidence suggests that Australia's most gifted and talented young people are not being stretched, with our share of top-performing students declining in science, mathematics, and reading between 2006 and 2018 in the OECD's triennial Program for International Student Assessment (PISA), which assesses the educational performance of 15-year-olds. For the professional clinical teacher to succeed in meeting the needs of individual learners in their classroom across all these academic as well as social and emotional domains, collaborative teams and, in many cases, multidisciplinary teams are required. No one teacher, no matter how expert, can do this on their own, nor should they be expected to.

Multidisciplinary teams are the accepted norm in many other professions, including health, music (for example, groups and orchestras), law, and engineering.

A few decades ago, the solo teacher was the norm: the lone learning facilitator in classrooms with no access to team collaboration nor the internet and the unlimited information we have now. In many ways, successful teachers had to become so privately and learn to work alone. The demands on today's and tomorrow's schools will be too much for most, hence the need to build skills and confidence in working in collaborative teams. The range of professions that interact with young people in their first 18 years must understand the deep knowledge and practice of teachers and, conversely, teachers must use the complementary expertise of the educational psychologists, pediatricians, speech pathologists, social workers, and so on that are supporting the whole family. How to use experts in teams is more critical than being an expert in all these team domains. While the reality is that, of all the professions that may interact with a child, it is the teacher that is observing and interacting with them throughout every day, multidisciplinary involvement privileges all the professionals that have an impact on students with respect to their various perspectives.

Take mental illness as one example. The high incidence of mental illness among children and adolescents is a major challenge (understandably it is more prevalent in adolescence that it is in younger children). Academic learning, social learning, and emotional learning are interdependent, and mental illness breaks that interdependency. Teachers are aware of the prevalence of mental health disorders in young people, but the resources that exist in systems can be disconnected from schools and can be difficult to access. They may notice some of the warning signs, like externalizing behaviors, social isolation, or disengagement, but it is not always clear what they can do to help. If a student does get help from a mental health service, there can be little communication between that service and the school.

In a review in the *Lancet Psychiatry*, Mina Fazel and her colleagues (2014) argued that enhanced basic training for both clinicians and teachers would improve collaboration, so that mental health clinicians are more familiar with school contexts and teachers are better versed in common mental health issues and how to screen for them. Along these lines, the BRIDGE program (Bridging Education and Mental Health in Urban Schools) trains school-based mental health professionals on the classroom context before pairing them with teachers to implement both universal (classroom-wide) and targeted (student-specific) interventions according to the needs of that class. A randomized controlled trial in five urban schools showed the program had a positive effect on observed teacher practices; that all students benefitted from improved relational closeness with teachers, social experiences with peers, and academic self-concepts; and that children with behavioral problems at the start of the year were less likely to be victimized by their peers by the end of the year.

While current systems often treat children's development at school, home, and socially as separate, and this was indeed an expectation in many societies, this is increasingly not the case. Rather, "development and learning are shaped by interactions among the environmental factors, relationships, and learning opportunities they experience, both in and out of school" (Darling-Hammond, Flook, Cook-Harvey, Barron, & Osher, 2020, p. 97), and what happens in one area can often influence what happens in another. If a student is experiencing adversity at home, for example, their ability to learn at school is likely to be impacted.

To improve collaboration across school, home, and health programs, there is a strong argument that the range of services that address students' needs should be colocated within the school. But colocation alone is not a panacea—there can be a wide range of organizational hurdles to overcome to ensure services are successfully delivered. For example, Baweja, Santiago, Vona, Pears, Langley, and Kataoka (2016) looked at the implementation of the Cognitive-Behaviorial Intervention for Trauma in Schools (CBITS) program at eight sites across the United States. The program can be delivered by school staff with training or by onsite mental health clinicians. They found its delivery was hindered when practitioners were faced with competing responsibilities, lack of parent support, lack of logistical support, and a lack of teacher buy-in, but schools that had more organizational structure to deliver the program, particularly those that partnered with mental health agencies (rather than delivering it through school staff), had more success. The opportunity to network with other clinicians delivering the program and the provision of administrative support also contributed to successful delivery.

Colocating services within schools is not a new idea. In Finland, for example, every school has a multi-professional team that usually includes a psychologist, a nurse, a social worker, and a medical doctor. This team is led by the school principal and meets regularly. In the United States, nearly 2,000 schools across the country are home to school-based health centers, typically to provide access to primary health and mental health services for communities that would otherwise have limited access. Walker, Kerns, Lyon, Bruns and Cosgrove (2010) followed a cohort of ninth-grade users and non-users in Seattle over two years and found that using a school-based health center was significantly associated with increases in attendance rates and grade point averages over time for certain students. The number of centers, however, is limited, and they tend to be concentrated in urban areas.

In North Ayrshire, an area of Scotland with significant disadvantage, 'nurture hubs' have been established in early-learning centers and schools for children exhibiting distressed behavior. A partnership between educational psychologists and educators, the program's six nurture principles (which include ensuring the classroom is a safe space and that 'all behavior is communication') are adopted at a whole-school level, not just within the hubs themselves. Students who experience this support are generally more connected and engaged with school, and teachers report feeling more able to support and understand children's behavior behavior (see https://education.gov.scot/improvement/practice-exemplars/nurture-in-north-ayrshire).

In 1999, New Zealand reorganized the professional services under the umbrella notion of resource teachers: learning and behavior (RTLB) who work together with teachers and schools to support the achievement of students in Years 1 to 10 with learning or behavior difficulties, or both. The aim is for the RTLB teams to up-skill teachers to better meet the needs of students within an inclusive education system. There was much resistance, as teachers preferred some of the more challenging students to leave the class and work individually with the RTLBs, and many

RTLBs claimed they could offer better service working individually with the student. But this missed the point, and the evaluations showed that when the RTLBs worked more closely with the teacher, helping them with diagnoses, specific interventions, and the evaluation of those interventions, this enhanced the expertise of the teacher after the exit of the RTLB. The RTLBs left knowledge and best practice tailored to the specific needs of these students and created a stronger team bond, which encouraged teachers to return and seek the added expertise of RTLB specialists (see https://www.ero.govt.nz/publications/resource-teachers-learning-and-behaviour-governing-andmanaging-rtlb-clusters/overview-of-findings/).

Colocating services is not enough on its own. Resources need to be put towards ensuring professionals genuinely work together so there is clear oversight of each child's (or family's) situation illustrated in the case study below. Some schools, which serve highly disadvantaged communities, devote resources to having at least one case manager per school (see Our Place case study p. 136). This person ensures agencies work together and there is clarity on who is responsible for which aspects of a family's care, and for following up on particular issues and ensuring families are getting the services they need.

Case study: Supporting a school-refuser's return to school

Thirteen-year-old Emily has a history of anxiety and, despite being 'bright,' with above-average cognitive abilities, she found the transition from primary to secondary school challenging. She experienced school-based anxiety and started refusing to go to school.

Her school well-being coordinator referred Emily to In2School, an intervention program based in inner Melbourne that uses a wraparound model to help school-refusers.

School refusal is not truancy, but rather when children find themselves unable to attend school for mental health reasons. It is defined as "child motivated refusal to attend school or difficulties remaining in school for an entire day" (Lyon & Cotler, 2009).

In2School uniquely brings teachers and clinicians together for up to six months to assess, plan, and implement needs-based, personalized programs for each young person at home, in the clinic, and in the classroom. They take part in individual therapy, and parent sessions support families to better manage the return-to-school process.

Spread over three phases, a teacher and mental health clinician work with the student and their family at home and in-clinic to conduct initial assessments and build rapport before students attend a transitional classroom for up to 10 weeks. In the classroom, they start building academic, social, and emotional skills while still participating in therapy. Their return to mainstream school is supported and managed carefully.

Emily was diagnosed with autism spectrum disorder and generalized anxiety disorder during the initial assessment phase of In2School. Her exposure to the transitional classroom was graded to help manage her anxiety, and she underwent cognitive behavioral therapy throughout to help challenge some of the unhelpful thinking she was experiencing.

In the classroom, the initial focus was on rebuilding Emily's stamina for learning with games and activities used to introduce the students to one another and to increase their time focusing on learning. Whilst in the classroom, Emily completed individual 'passion' projects, undertook work sent by her secondary school, and joined in literacy, numeracy, and other academic activities with her peers. Emily also had the opportunity to attend 'Out and About' one day each week to reintroduce her to the wider community. During this time, Emily built skills like travelling on public transport, learning photography, and ordering from cafes.

A support plan addressing her academic and emotional needs was developed by the In2School psychologist and teacher in partnership with her mainstream school to support her transition back. She worked up to full-time attendance, first attending preferred subjects until returning full-time after three weeks of transition.

Emily has reported being generally happy back at school, and she says she particularly values the self-regulation skills she learned at In2School ("learning how to calm myself down") and also getting to know other students experiencing similar challenges ("everyone has the same problems").

In2School's unique approach, with educators and clinicians co-located, sees around 80% of its students attending school full-time six months after completing the program. Given many hadn't been at school anywhere from three months to more than one year before attending, its results are significant.

School-based health center referrals in the United States come primarily from teachers, followed by families, and then from the students themselves. As the teacher is the professional who spends the most time with a child, this is perhaps unsurprising. But, as a comparative study of school-based health care provision in Australia, the United States, and Canada showed, placing too much expectation on teachers to pick up the health care needs of students can cause huge strain, particularly where there are limited health resources.

Teachers have a key role to play in triaging students with additional needs, but it is important to stress that they should not be expected to fully diagnose and treat the issue, nor should they be expected to do it alone or be discouraged from seeking a second opinion. The clinical teacher's role is to identify that an issue exists in the first place and flag it for further attention with the appropriate experts. Part of making a case-management approach work is introducing an effective triage system. Just like in emergency medicine, students with the greatest need should receive the most urgent attention. The following case study is an example of this kind of collaboration.

Case study: A team approach to supporting student learning

When Jonathon was 11 years old, he was diagnosed with Benign Rolandic Epilepsy of Childhood (BREC). Jonathon's parents contacted me for learning support when he was in the second term of Year 8. My background is in providing specialist teaching support for students with language-related learning needs. He had experienced a difficult few years after being diagnosed. Medication was required to manage seizures from late in Year 5, and by early high school, this and the disease itself were impacting his concentration and motivation. He was distracted at school, and often too fatigued to complete homework tasks. Jonathon worked hard to appear 'normal' to his friends and teachers, but he found the volume of information he was required to learn across multiple subject areas overwhelming.

While course materials and assessment details were available on the school learning management system, Jonathon found this difficult to navigate. Often teachers would provide many additional resources on these subject sites, and it was not clear to Jonathon how, specifically, these were relevant to assignments or assessment tasks. Utilizing these materials required significant reading capacity and synthesizing abilities, and for Jonathon, this was very labor-intensive. He became dispirited, particularly on receiving feedback on school assessment tasks, and told his parents that the only things he enjoyed at school were lunchtime, where he could talk with his friends, and band, where he could play his saxophone.

Jonathon's neurologist referred him to a clinical pediatric psychologist, who worked in partnership with Jonathon's school and parents to support both his learning and wellbeing. Clinical assessment identified ways in which Jonathon's teachers could support his learning: tasks needed to be broken down and instructions repeated, research assignments should be limited and targeted, and more time given to complete homework and in-school tests. Jonathon's handwriting and fine motor function had been impacted by BREC, and so it was suggested that he use a laptop for all tests and assignments.

Jonathon's psychologist worked directly with the school's well-being team to make it aware of the impacts of his diagnosis and medication on his self-efficacy and mood. The school convened a meeting with Jonathon's year-level coordinator, homeroom teacher, the head of individual learning programs, the head of student well-being, and Jonathon's parents, during which various strategies for implementing the psychologist's recommendations were discussed. Importantly, these were discussed with Jonathon's well-being at the center of the conversation.

Following this, all Jonathon's teachers were briefed on how they might differentiate his learning and support. Teachers discussed the ways in which they would explicitly scaffold his learning and modify assessment with Jonathon and his parents. Modifications were particular to each subject, but broadly supported the high literacy demands of the secondary school curriculum. For example, in science, end-of-unit tests were broken up into subsections to be completed across different days and Jonathon was then given the opportunity to verbally explain his understanding at the end of each component to add to what he had written. In maths, Jonathon used a summary sheet for each test, enabling him to focus on applying rather than remembering theory. In history, research assignments were made more specific. Jonathon was given a defined topic and curated resources to read and synthesize, directing his attention to engaging with new content, rather than spending his homework time trying to identify and source appropriate resources.

As Jonathon was reluctant to draw too much attention to himself in class, he was asked to identify a teacher he could speak to about how he was feeling about school, and he identified his music teacher. This teacher already had a strong relationship with Jonathon and took an active role in checking on his well-being and touching base with the year-level coordinator.

This team approach, where medical experts, the school, and parents work in partnership to support the needs of students with complex health issues, and the needs of these students are considered on a case-by-case basis, is fundamental to a student's overall success. It radically impacted Jonathon's attitude towards school, the success he was able to experience in his academic studies, and his sense of what was possible for himself.

Now in middle adolescence, the ongoing challenge is for Jonathon to be supported but not singled-out at school. As he looks forward to the senior years of school, he needs support in negotiating directly with teachers and taking increased responsibility for his own learning so that he maintains a sense of agency and purpose that will be crucial to his success beyond school. For the many students with specific learning needs, there is the need for constant renewal and adjustment of learning, and for advocates, beyond the family, such as homeroom teachers, to keep an overall perspective on the student's academic progress and well-being.

Where there are adequate resources and a case-management structure, a multi-disciplinary team is able to work together to identify the reasons a student is struggling, ideally in the context of their family, school, and home life, designing an appropriate intervention and evaluation plan, tracking its progress, and making any necessary adjustments as they go. This kind of approach is about bringing experts together to meet the needs of the whole child. It involves the skills of: triaging;

enhancing skills in diagnosing; knowing the best evidence for improving the child from where they are to where the team (collectively) wishes him or her to be; working with families and caregivers as part of the answer; and knowing how to use the best skills available to make the difference.

The schools of the future cannot act as silos. Classrooms can no longer be privatized. Teachers need to develop skills of thinking evaluatively about the use of teams of experts (and this, of course, all requires resources, including time). Addressing equity issues cannot be done within schools in isolation. Genuine collaboration and partnerships within schooling systems and with relevant community and industry organizations can be more efficient in terms of spreading expertise, but also in terms of social and economic benefits (Nous, 2011). After all, children and young people's lives don't exist in silos—school, family, friends, health, and hobbies all interrelate. Health and education are intrinsically intertwined, and acknowledging this gives young people the opportunity to achieve their potential.

Schools working collaboratively with communities

The reconceptualization of schools as part of a network of community organizations with similar goals must be supported by funding and infrastructure (ACER, 2013). The schooling system needs to work closely with families, but also with experts in related fields such as health and social work. The school needs to be the center of a community but requires support from that community. Kania and Kramer (2011) have written about the 'collective impact' a group of community leaders in Cincinnati enabled when they took a collaborative approach to improving student outcomes. These leaders included heads of foundations and private local industries, government officials, representatives from tertiary institutions, and directors of nonprofit groups. As "no single organization, however powerful or innovative, could accomplish this alone" (p. 36), the groups focused the education community on a set of common goals, measured in the same way. Finland allocates blocks of funding and responsibilities to municipalities for both education and social services to reduce issues from independent budgets and priorities between schooling and non-school services related to students (Grubb, Jahr, Neumüller, & Field, 2005). The result of this type of collaboration is "large-scale social change [that] comes from better cross-sector coordination rather than from the isolated intervention of individual organizations" (Kania & Kramer, 2011, p. 38). Once the common agenda is set, schools and teachers, in partnership with families and local organizations, are able to work to reinforce the principles across the community. The following case study presents an example of schools and other services working together to provide early intervention.

Implications for the profession

Case study: The Geelong project – a community of schools and services model of early intervention

The Geelong Project, an exemplar of the Community of Schools and Services model of early intervention (COSS Model), has demonstrated significant achievable social and educational outcomes through early interventions for disadvantaged, at-risk, and homeless young people (see MacKenzie, Hand, Zufferey, McNelis, Spinney, & Tedmanson, 2020).

The COSS Model is a place-based and system reform-oriented approach to youth disadvantage, addressing social and educational outcomes for young people via a youth-focused, family-centered service-delivery approach (MacKenzie, 2018) in collaboration with school welfare staff (MacKenzie & Hand, 2019). In practical terms, the Model represents a raft of innovations to realize a more effective early-intervention system for reducing disengagement from education and early school-leaving, and intervenes to help when family issues are heading towards a crisis and possible homelessness as well as other adverse outcomes (MacKenzie & Hand, 2019).

The COSS Model, set out in Figure 8.1, consists of four foundations: community collaboration; early identification; a flexible practice framework and early intervention support work with families; and robust, embedded longitudinal monitoring and measurement of outcomes. These foundations comprise a significant reform of the local service system of support available for vulnerable young people and their families.

Community collaboration involves forming a collective of schools and community agencies to provide leadership and coordinate the operational work with youth and families. In Australia, COSS Model sites typically call themselves by the name of the community – e.g. The Geelong Project, or The Albury Project in NSW.

Another key innovation in the development of the COSS Model is population-screening for risk, which is undertaken using a series of indicators on the Australian Index of Adolescent Development (AIAD) survey instrument, combined with local knowledge from schools and a brief screening/engagement interview. If data from the indicators and local knowledge (where available) suggests that a young person is vulnerable or at-risk, then support and intervention can be delivered proactively before full-blown crises have developed. This methodology allows risk to be rigorously assessed and a pre-crisis response appropriately delivered.

Third, the practice framework is tiered so that risk and need are rigorously assessed, and young people are provided with the extent of support needed at the time, but no more than needed. If a young person needs help at another time, they can readily access the support. The COSS Model works with youth and families as a cohort over time from Year 7 to Year 12.

A revolution of teaching and schooling

Figure 8.1 The COSS Model

Fourth, the measurement of outcomes is an embedded feature of the model. A range of client data is fed back to practitioners. As such, this is a new way that data is being used in a real-world collective impact model to inform practice and address the social and educational outcomes for vulnerable young people, including the prevention and early intervention of youth homelessness (Hand & MacKenzie, 2019).

The outcomes achieved by The Geelong Project from 2013 to 2017 were a 40% reduction in adolescent homelessness, and at the same time, a 20% reduction in early school-leaving in the pilot schools has shown what a place-based approach is capable of achieving. This has generated interest in Australia and internationally for how educational and social disadvantages might be more effectively addressed (MacKenzie, 2018).

Implications for the profession

A major aim of schooling needs to be increasing the number of students who want to come school prepared to invest in precious knowledge and knowing, and to learn as young people the skills, attitudes, and dispositions to work in a collective and have confidence in the value of working with others. The rebuilding of Doveton College (discussed in the following case study) in a lower socioeconomic area of Melbourne is but another example.

Case study: 'Our Place'—a holistic approach tackling disadvantage

The Our Place model places schools at the center of highly disadvantaged communities to support not just the children attending, but also their families and the wider community.

With the provision of early learning, primary, and early secondary education at its core, the school becomes a hub for the community with wraparound services, including adult education, volunteer opportunities, and allied health services all available from the one site.

The first school to adopt the model was Doveton College in southeast Melbourne, an area with high levels of disadvantage. When the school opened in 2012, 70% of students couldn't read in Grade 5, nearly 47% were starting school with significant developmental vulnerability, and over two-thirds were below the national minimum standard in literacy and numeracy.

While the community continues to face considerable challenges, over the course of eight years Doveton College has become one of the top 50 schools in Australia for growth in NAPLAN (the Australian-wide national assessment of achievement), and students are more engaged and motivated to learn.

In addition, the early-learning service has been rated as exceeding national standards, and the community has embraced opportunities to become involved in programs such as playgroups, adult education, and after-school activities. The coordination of external services (such as social services and child protection) has been highly successful.

The key to Our Place's success lies in its holistic approach; it uses school as the platform to reach the whole family for the simple reason that they go to the school regularly.

Our Place sites have a single entrance, so that no matter the reason for someone's visit—to drop a child at school or attend adult education class, for example—staff can interact with them in a casual and approachable manner.

Families are involved with Our Place early, sometimes from pregnancy. Once a baby is born, their health is monitored, and developmental concerns are identified early. Mothers and fathers are supported to develop important parenting skills like reciprocal communication with their young child.

High-quality early learning is a core element, starting with supportive playgroups for babies from 9 months through to the transition into school. Because school is a familiar place for many Doveton families, starting Prep is much less daunting than in a 'traditional' environment.

Once in school, the focus is on high-quality teaching and learning, with teachers supported to meet the particular needs of students experiencing disadvantage. They take a trauma-informed approach and focus on creating an environment where students from chaotic homes can settle and become ready to learn. Health and well-being support are wrapped around the primary school and into secondary school, with a case-management structure ensuring services like social work, child-protection support, and allied health work together effectively.

Enrichment programs after school support children to develop social skills and community connections, keeping them engaged in meaningful activities. When Doveton College first opened, only 6% of students took part in after-school activities; now 96% of students attend at least two days per week.

The emphasis on adult education differentiates Our Place from other models. With evidence suggesting a mother's education matters when it comes to children's outcomes, and that children do better in homes where at least one adult works, there is a strong argument for supporting adults in the community into education and employment.

A light-touch approach builds relationships with people who may have previously associated school with being place of failure or judgements. Community facilitators focus on chatting to adults in a non-judgmental way about their needs, offering simple opportunities like the chance to have a cup of tea and use a computer to catch up on emails.

This initial engagement can open the door to more involvement, perhaps by volunteering in the garden or by reading with students in the classroom. This gradual process of developing new skills can build adults' self-esteem to the point where they might be ready to start studying themselves. Classes, study groups, and homework clubs are offered to the whole community from within the school, and employment support (down to writing a CV and finding appropriate clothes) is available, too.

Our Place's approach, which is supported by philanthropic funding from the Colman Foundation and the Victorian Department of Education, is person-centered, meeting people where they are at in their own lives. It doesn't fund programs; rather it configures the existing system to deliver what families need at a practical level to help them get their lives back on track. Ultimately, this means parents are able to live more fulfilling lives and better support their children's education and well-being.

The more overarching notion of what it means to have impact is a core notion for developing the clinical teaching role. It applies to the cases above and also to the higher-achieving students. Clinical teachers must diagnose what could support a talented student to accelerate their understanding of a particular concept, chose high-probability interventions, implement them with fidelity, and evaluate the impact of these diagnosis, in the same way they assess all other students.

Case study: A secondary english teacher discusses a gifted student

It is both refreshing and challenging to gain a new, different group of secondary school students each year. Sometimes you are fortunate enough to have taught some of these students in previous years and thus understand their individual differences, but this is not the norm. Secondary school teachers are notorious for not sharing their insights into a student's learning with the receiving teacher, thus pretesting a new group of students is not only good practice, but indeed vital to understanding each student's learning needs. This is most especially the case when one teaches English and English literature, where the diversity in skills and understanding within the student cohort often necessitates a range of different learning needs and approaches.

After pretesting the themes of Shakespeare's Macbeth using a variety of methods, I discovered that Maria's answers to some open-ended questions were far superior to those of her classmates. I included open-ended questions about the main characters' underlying motivations in the pretest to give students the opportunity to demonstrate their higher-order thinking skills. Maria compared Macbeth the character not only to some historical political manipulators, but also to powerful manipulators in the current political climate, which demonstrated her high ability. Armed with this knowledge, I proceeded to 'scaffold' or differentiate Maria's next learning opportunity, while also taking her wider needs into account. Maria was a gifted adolescent female in a coeducational environment, and I was acutely aware that "both the academic and social terrains of school become more rigorous and complicated" (Guthrie, 2020, p. 26) for gifted girls. I did not want Maria to feel that she needed to 'dumb down' or hide her giftedness from her classmates.

I designed the first assessment piece on Macbeth by providing a rubric that included open-ended and closed tasks (later rubrics were designed by the students). Delivering tailored educational rubrics allows for students to choose assessment pieces that appeal both to their preferred mode of learning and provide challenge and depth of the assessment question itself. I also drew on Krathwahl's revision of Bloom's Taxonomy (Krathwahl, 2002) as the model for literal, inferential, analytical, and creative questions. As creativity is deemed a desirable social skill by modern socio-educational systems, it is important that this development holds a prime position in the hierarchy of lesson objectives (Kozbelt, Beghetto, & Runco, 2010) and success criteria. Maria benefited from the stimulation provided by the higher-order level of the question, which in turn negated the boredom of her learning experience. It is important that this gifted student receives different, more extended work, NOT more work. Assessment that provides choice and more advanced-level questions is a must for gifted students.

Krathwald's revised taxonomy is useful for expanding the range and diversity of questions or tasks to include in a rubric. The choice of tasks that allowed for diverse responses from the students was increasingly complex, generating both observable qualitative and qualitative evidence. This allowed Maria the opportunity to demonstrate her learning in a variety of ways. 'One size fits all' should not be the case for any student, and particularly not for gifted students, who may not demonstrate their full potential. Gifted students are an integral part of the Response to Intervention Framework (RTI), as it is not just for the left side of the bell curve. Gifted students require interventions so they do not become bored and disinterested, and underachieve. Maria needed her curriculum differentiated; thus I had to provide more than one way of delivering the instruction.

Beyond clinical teaching: Other important changes

Evolving teaching to a true clinical-practice profession with embedded evaluative thinking and building high-functioning multidisciplinary teams are argued to be necessary steps in preparing young people into the future, but they are not sufficient. There are other important factors that must be in place to lift educational achievement and tackle some of the major challenges facing the education systems today—notably, reducing the widening achievement gap between students from high and low socioeconomic backgrounds, and the high levels of disengagement among upper elementary and secondary students in particular.

The ways in which schools must address the importance of social cohesion and the development of well-rounded young people in a constantly changing world have been emphasized. This book has also advocated for teaching as a clinical-practice profession, in which all practitioners have the training and skills to diagnose their students' learning needs, use evidence effectively, plan and implement interventions, and evaluate the impact of their teaching on their students' learning. Yet all of these goals seem at odds with what Pasi Sahlberg has termed *GERM*— the Global Educational Reform Movement—in which competition (rather than collaboration) between schools and schooling systems, high-stakes testing (and its implications for narrowing of curricula and teaching to the test), and top-down-only approaches to education policy are pervasive (Sahlberg, 2012). Often, these measures inhibit the teacher's ability to engage in deep learning and understanding on a given topic. Is this a cause of the high levels of disengagement seen in many (especially western) countries? His claims, however, are broad-brushed and ignore the many examples of excellent schools that use information from other schools even in an often highly competitive market, who use information from national and international assessment to help diagnose and ask whether the same things are happening in their schools, and who use the positives from the more top-down policies.

For many students in Australia and other western countries, school has become an unappealing place where the students have little say in what they learn, or they feel incompetent, or disconnected, or fail to see the relevance of what they're learning. Or all of the above. In Australia, it is remarkable that 13 years of education are reduced to one number at the end of secondary schooling, used to determine the selection of students into university. Indeed, as we showed earlier with the Jenkin's curve (see Figure 1.2), at best, four to five students per class in upper primary and secondary school want to be there to invest in the learning we ask of them.

Part of this malaise is that students want to be challenged and, especially, challenged appropriately. When we appreciate Nuthall's (2007) finding that about 50% of every class lesson is known already by the students, then the level of challenge is probably not too high; and when Berry (2020) asked teachers what they meant by 'engaging students in learning,' they most commonly claimed that engagement was evident when the students were doing the work—this notion of doing, completing, and handing in often is the antithesis of challenge for young adolescents. In a lot of doing, there can be little challenge and little learning. They are prepared to spend inordinate amounts of time playing video games and watching and being involved in sport or cultural events, as here, learning is dominant, challenge is ever present, and continuous feedback as to how close they are to goals or success criteria are core attributes of these activities. If video games required students to hand in their assignment reflecting on what they did in a video game, parse and detail the pros and cons of every sport or cultural event, and be measured as successful when they have completed and handed in these secondary tasks, then no wonder they would soon be turned off to these activities. Young adolescents want to be challenged; many (not all) are no longer prepared to be compliant to the act of 'doing,' and if we do not challenge them appropriately, they will soon challenge us.

Internationally, curricula are shifting from a primary focus on content to also incorporating deep knowledge, twenty-first century skills (like collaboration, communication, and critical thinking), 'know how' (being able to do something), attitudes, values and beliefs, and the ability to learn independently. It is important that these two aspects of content and deep learning are not seen as competing and independent, and that there are not curricula about deep learning or learning strategies developed separate from the inclusion of within current curricula (Hattie & Donoghue, 2016).

One way to assess more powerfully is to build learner profiles that follow students over time. This allows students and teachers to see the learning progression that the student is taking towards various success criteria rather than prescribing a progression that all must follow. This allows students and teachers to use assessment more as a predictive tool, such as determining the student's current progression, rather than ascertaining what is the next best intervention that others who have followed this progression did next that maximally enhanced progress to the success criteria. It also permits students and teachers to see what students bring to a series of lessons, to together track their progress towards the success criteria of the lessons, to identify missteps, misconceptions, and errors, and to propose what the next steps should be to maximize the speed and success of their learning. These systems exist now, but too often assessment is seen as documentation of what the student has done or not—a look to the past.

One example is Griffin's model developed at the Assessment Research Centre in the University of Melbourne's Graduate School of Education (Griffin, 2018). He has developed scales, from novice to expert, across the various competencies, both academic and personal. Instead of receiving the traditional grade or score at the end of term, which says nothing much about precisely what is known and not known, assessment is made across students' attainments and capabilities in a full learner profile, rather than simply the assigning of a number. This profile shows what they have mastered and where there is room for improvement, covering areas such as content knowledge in academic subjects as well as skills such as communication and collaboration.

Another example is the New Zealand e-asTTle tool (https://easttle.tki.org.nz/), which allows teachers (and students) to set assessments specifically on what they are teaching from the curricula, administer the test immediately (paper, online, or adaptive), and immediately get reports about status, dispositions, best next steps, and trajectories of learning. It is a voluntary system for elementary and high schools, and over 70% of teachers are still using this tool as part of their classroom processes 19 years after it was introduced (see Hattie, Brown, & Keegan, 2005). There are many other examples that are moving away from the notion that assessment is something that teachers do at the end, something that they mark, score, comment on, and hand back with little impact, and that it is a source of induced anxiety and often a waste of time for many students—ask the students to estimate their mark prior to undertaking the test, and in many cases, their prediction is pretty accurate, so not much has been learnt from completing the test work!

These assessments can help teachers (and students) make judgements about where a student is on the progression of learning across a wide range of domains. This requires a shift in how teachers teach, moving away from simply imparting knowledge to focusing more broadly on the intellectual skills required for a particular subject, as well as equipping students to acquire and update the required knowledge. The core notion is that the assessments *help* inform the interpretations that teachers are making, but teachers should not make the decision on assessments alone; they need to include other forms of evidence. Teachers need to make data-based decisions with the data coming from multiple sources. Classroom activities become much more about the application of knowledge rather than just its acquisition, with students learning for themselves and teaching each other, and teachers using a wider repertoire and less didactic teaching methods.

Recalibrating assessment in this way relieves the pressure currently created by the 'drop-dead' end-of-school score that consumes so much energy and many resources in many western school systems. It creates space for teachers and students to do much more than drill content acquisition or teach to the test: it allows room for teachers and students to work together on engaging learning opportunities and for learners to learn about self-assessment, and how assessment can help lead learning rather than always following learning.

Social and emotional skills

This new way of assessing students, described above, reflects an effort to reconnect with the core purpose of schooling—to develop the whole child. Increasingly, research is demonstrating that children's learning and development are influenced by their experiences and relationships both within and outside of school, and that supportive learning environments are most effective when they respond to all aspects of development. Linda Darling-Hammond and her colleagues (Darling-Hammond et al., 2020) have recently outlined in detail what is required to achieve this, covering four areas of practice: supportive environments, productive instructional strategies, social and emotional development, and a system of supports.

Social and emotional learning is an important aspect of developing the whole child. These skills include cooperation, managing conflict, making friends, coping, being resilient, and recognizing and managing one's own feelings. Developing these skills can improve students' connection to school and their sense of belonging, decreases their chances of engaging in problem behavior, and can be a precursor to their investment in the learning that schools ask of them. The premise is relatively simple: if students are experiencing issues with their peers, or feeling depressed or anxious, it is difficult for them to focus on learning. When these barriers are mediated, they are more available to learn. When we feel good about ourselves, we learn better. These coping strategies can, and should, be explicitly taught, but not in isolation—they also need to be integrated throughout the curriculum and the school day.

Seligman's model of well-being, PERMA (2018), which highlights the attributes of positive emotion, engagement, relationships, meaning, and accomplishment as the factors that contribute to well-being, is a useful model to consider in the context of the broader school environment. How many opportunities do students have in their day-to-day learning to develop these attributes? How much is the narrowing of the curriculum undermining their ability to work towards them? These are important questions for school leaders. They are hard to teach, which is reflected in the very low effect-sizes from many of these programs when based in schools, but the aim should be to find more effective interventions (see https://www.visiblelearningmetax.org).

Conclusion

Schools are core social centers of learning. Schools are not only the biggest education intervention systems, but also among the biggest public health intervention systems we have for young people. For a school to be the center of a community, it requires support from that community. The schooling system needs to work closely with families, but also with experts in related fields such as health and social work. The relationship between schools and experts in the health and well-being areas is particularly crucial. The concept that is common to significant place-based interventions is that of 'collective impact,' fed with the evidence of impact.

Teachers and school leaders can be the 'clinical connectors' in the collaboration of various services and experts to support the development of the whole child. We have argued that the professional teacher aspires to put *every* student, no matter where they are on the ability range, on their optimal learning pathway. This requires ensuring that health, education, and community services are aligned and working together. There are many children who learn because of what teachers do, and many who learn in spite of what teachers do, and there are many who have barriers to learning and are not predisposed for many reasons to value or learn from teachers.

CHAPTER

Conclusions

In the mid-1800s, when schools became institutions for the masses, teachers worked out how to be efficient, effective, and ensure students listened, behaved, and learned. Every generation has claimed that schools need to be reinvented, and there has been a litany of failed revolutions. We have employers and politicians saying that this generation is not prepared for the workplace, that they need more basics, or team skills, or more preparation for the job. And they have said this for every generation since mass schooling began. Yet schools go on.

There is so much evidence that the traditional model of schooling has worked for so many that schools ask, why is now the time for major disruption to the traditional model? Yes, there have been tweaks—classes of 40-plus are now rarer, students sit more in groups than straight lines (although they still predominantly work alone when sitting in these groups), and the cane and strap have been abolished, but schools still grade by age, administer oodles of tests to encourage students to focus on learning, value achievement and high scores more than growth and joy of learning, and have loud pleas for more money so we can be left alone to do whatever each teacher considers good teaching and whatever every school principal considers good leading.

As we highlighted in Chapter 1, the industrial model is cracking and the future success and relevance of schooling will hinge on the expertise of teachers and the elevation of teaching to a true 'clinical-practice profession.' Young people must be prepared to live in a constantly changing, globalized world, with all its threats and opportunities, and to be active participants in addressing global issues and problems. Young people have instant access to information; knowledge is increasing exponentially; preparation for lifelong learning is an imperative. This is a challenge, even for the most expert teacher.

Despite substantial increases in spending and many well-intentioned reform efforts, performance in a large number of school systems, including Australia's, has barely improved in decades (Barber & Mourshed, 2007). In the case of Australia, one of the Rudd Government's key proposals in the 2007 election campaign was the implementation of an 'education revolution.' This built on previous national reform initiatives, and other initiatives followed. In terms of national and international indicators, Australia has demonstrated little improvement.

We argue that when schools exist in isolation, without collaboration across schools and school sectors, and without systemic integration with other services and institutions such as health, and without a national vision and leadership prioritizing education as the means of developing each country's most valuable resource, its people, the workforce and the community will struggle to address the needs of young people in the twenty-first century.

A decade ago, Barber and Mourshed (2007) among others highlighted that some school systems reform and perform better than others and that improvement can be fast-tracked according to several key factors. Notable examples were the education systems of Singapore and Finland. At one level was the common focus on recruiting the most suitable candidates to become teachers, the focus on effective teaching for direct student achievement, and the systematic and targeted support provided to ensure that the learning needs of every child can be addressed. This focus on quality teachers and teaching would not have been possible had it not been for placing education at the top of each country's national policy agenda.

In the case of Singapore 50 years ago, when it gained independence, Singapore lacked natural resources and it had a poorly educated population. Through state-led policies that focused on economic development, rule of law, meritocracy, and the formation of human capital, Singapore has achieved extraordinary social and economic progress. The early critical education policy decisions of Singapore, including the language policy, multicultural policies aimed at fostering racial harmony, and the policies to cultivate high-quality teachers have been attributed to the Prime Minister Lee Kuan Yew (Tan, Low, & Hung, 2017). Lee Kuan Yew's top-down visionary leadership was Singapore's turning point.

The transformation in Finland was less straightforward, but education was aligned with its economic development. Changes to education became the main vehicle for social and economic transformation. Political consensus was critical and required long-term vision and commitment. By 1972, a new national curriculum and comprehensive school system began implementation, and for more than 15 years, Finland has been recognized for its educational equity and excellence. Vision and commitment were Finland's turning points (Sahlberg, 2014).

Highly rated school systems are able to thrive due to holding the teaching profession in high esteem and the alignment between goals, strategies, initiatives, and policy so that "the whole system, the way all the parts and pieces fit together" (Tucker, 2014, p. 27) is clear. In Singapore, the alignment and consistency between the Ministry, teacher-training sites, and schools are evidenced in terms of shared goals and understanding of curriculum, assessment, and evaluation (OECD, 2011). Such coherence, not only within the schooling system, but also encompassing other areas such as health, facilitates the enactment of policy that enhances the broad learning and well-being of young people.

Crucial to a turning point in any education system is the positioning of teaching as a profession whose members possess a highly sophisticated set of skills including the abilities to diagnose, intervene, and evaluate the impact of their approaches on student learning.

There are increasing demands on educators, with more students requiring specific help, thus asking teachers to know more about specific attributes of students and optimal methods to enhance all these students' learning. Perhaps the greatest change, however, is coming less in the classroom and more in who is in front of the classroom. There are now more options for choice of vocations, more amateurs and fewer trained (and cheaper) teachers and teacher aides entering our schools, more demands made on teachers, a greater variation of students coming into our schools (ethnicity, country of origin, diagnoses), a continuation of the loneliness or privatization of teaching, more public critique of teachers, and more opportunities for teachers to leave the profession for other ventures (and hard barriers for other professionals to join teaching mid-career)—there are major cracks in the system. Here is why now is a good time for disruption of the traditional model:

Now, the average age of entering teacher education is no longer 17 to 20 (in Australia; it is 27 (https://www.aitsl.edu.au/tools-resources/resource/ite-data-report-2019)—teaching is a second or third vocation (and unlikely to be the last).

Now, with these new teachers having experienced social media, interactions, and collegiality at a level unknown to previous generations, they are less likely to want to be part of a profession that values privacy on the job, that has demanded each teacher develop their own success in the confines of their own classroom, and more likely to engage in the debates about how to teach, curricula, and assessment.

Now, with the salary rates of teachers reasonably flat, they may not stay in teaching beyond 10 years (when the salary flattens out) and may not want to remain in a profession in which experience more than expertise determines their future success. In Australia, starting salaries for teachers rank as the fifth highest of all professions (between $A56,000 to $70,000), but the rise in salary is among the lowest, and most teachers reach close to their maximum by about their tenth year, while their graduate peers are still on the rise (one-third of 40-year-old engineering or commerce graduates earn more than $156,000 a year compared to 2% of teachers), and at that age, those with no degree out-earn teachers (see Goss & Sonnemann, 2016). In these other professions, you rise and rise as a function of expertise. Yes, they all start with valuing experience, but expertise soon dominates.

Now, when it takes an average 25 to 27 more years after beginning as a teacher to become a school leader, many younger teachers may not want to do the 'years on the job,' but prefer to fast track to leadership based on expertise.

Now, when the skills, dispositions, and motivations of those joining the profession are more socially connected via the spread of social media, there is less incentive to be part of a private, lonely, self-educating, and at times 'looked down upon' profession.

Now, with the pressure on teacher education to provide for more students and the demand for higher levels of preparedness for classrooms upon graduation, this is a time to attend to improving the perception and reality of the quality of programs to prepare teachers. In Australia, there are close to 90,000 students in the approximately 400 teacher education programs, with about 7,000 of these students a year gaining full-time employment in a school. In other parts of the world, there are high levels of teacher shortages, not only because fewer are graduating, but also with more moving out of the profession later in their careers (with major barriers to entering mid-career). In Sydney, there are 35,000 registered qualified and experienced teachers looking for employment, but over 90% are not willing to drive more than five kilometers from their home. In 2018, in the Australian state of New South Wales, over 400 new teachers graduated in the creative arts for two positions in schools.

Now, a common finding is that teachers "show the greatest productivity gains during their first few years on the job, after which their performance tends to level off" (Kini & Podolsky, 2016; p. 3). Henry, Bastian, and Fortner (2011) found that across grade levels, teachers' effectiveness increased significantly in their second year of teaching but flattened after three years. The rise in impact is flat after the first two to three years, and the relationship between experience and expertise after the first five years of teaching is close to zero. This flatness of the rate of improving expertise mirrors the salary scales. The slight improvement in impact during the first ten years was most noticeable in schools "led by a strong principal, providing extensive opportunities for collaboration and common planning among teachers, and focused around a shared vision for student achievement" (Kini & Podolsky, 2016, p. 23). Newer teachers thrive and ask for collegiality, whereas older teachers gained their experience in the days when being alone in one's class was the norm, so learning to be successful alone was a critical survival skill. This means many experienced, privatized teachers have little to offer to the new breed of collective teachers.

Now, there are more and more demands on teachers. Chapter 8 outlined the increasing expectations regarding attending to students' social, emotional, and physical well-being and health, the increased percentage of students diagnosed with identifiable (labeled) classifications (more often with at-risk issues), the focus on twenty-first century skills as well as developing precious knowledge, and the increased command for teachers to work in teams (which all cost time, mental resources, and leadership). Teachers often have to deal with these added demands without involvement as a profession in which they agree to the demands in the first place, and often with little prior professional learning about some of the new demands, nor any extra pay or time allowances. There is little recognition from parents, voters, and policymakers that these all come at a cost, and there is little recognition for the expertise needed to deal with these new demands.

What a time to make the move to a collegial profession privileged with high levels of expertise. The expertise has always existed, but it has been subjugated to experience, to the false claim that 'all teachers are equal,' and to the belief that anyone can be (born to be) a teacher. Now is the time for the profession to collectively stand up and proclaim the deep knowledge and understanding it takes to be successful in the profession. It is time to celebrate the major influence that teachers have on the world, on the nation, on everyone. And it is time for the notion of evaluative thinking, perhaps the deepest and highest form of thinking, to be proclaimed as the foundation of the teaching profession.

The stars are aligned

With the increasing need for teachers, with the increasing churn of teachers, with the increasing competition for smart people in other professions, with the increasing demand on teachers to do more and influence students in more ways, now is a time to rediscover the essence of the teaching profession. Expertise, through evaluative thinking and clinical reasoning, could become the rallying cry for a resurgent profession.

This rejuvenation will require deep thinking about the initial education of teacher candidates, their induction into schools, and their development in the first few years of teaching. It will require changes to the career ladder and the privileging of expertise alongside experience. The discussion must focus on the nature and expertise of the leadership required to build collective teams, and shift from how teachers teach to what is the impact of their teaching. It means that there needs to be much education of the parents and voters as to these new priorities and messages about expertise, and it means greater awareness and resource-distribution to develop, upscale, and improve expertise in the profession. Most critically, it demands that the profession embrace, celebrate, and promote the core notion of expertise as its defining feature.

It means that some of the current participants in classrooms would be relegated to support the expert teachers. Instead of, for example, using teacher aides to work with those students most in need of expertise, they may best be used for working with more able students, assisting with marking and commenting (again under guidance, rubrics, and quality-control), and helping the professionals prepare for upcoming lessons. Instead of after-school professional learning sessions with a guest speaker, there would be expert coaches working with teachers to diagnose, evaluate, and maximize their impact. Instead of teachers aiming to be individualistic, alone, and developing their own skills, there would be groups of teachers (not necessarily in the same school) collectively working to support, critique, and share wisdom and expertise. Instead of moving at-risk students out of the class to specialists, the specialists would spend more time with the teacher in the regular classroom, adjusting and enhancing work with at-risk students. Instead of teacher education focusing on control, curriculum, developing resources, and particular teaching methods, it would demand teacher candidates are educated in knowing their impact on their students' learning. The traditional aspects of teacher education would still have a place, but the pendulum needs to swing to the privileging, esteeming, and enhancing of expertise.

The notion of expertise

Of course, expertise has always been the hallmark of the teaching profession. Aristotle claimed that teachers must, at some point, use judgment in deciding a diagnosis and in choosing which strategies to apply, and there was a duty of care in wishing good things for the student, not for the teacher's sake, but for the student's. It is, claimed Aristotle, a deep desire for the well-being of another person, and this often requires meaningful personal interactions, a deep understanding of that person, and compassion and sympathy. This is at the core of the helping professions.

There has been a recurring search for the essence of this expertise among teachers. Royce (1891) questioned "Is there a Science of Education?" (answering 'no'), Dewey (1938) argued he was applying science to education, Lagemann (2000) wrote "The sources of a science of education," and Ericsson, Charness, Feltovich, and Hoffman (2006) edited what they claimed was the first handbook on expertise and expert performance. Early writers (for example, Radosavljevich, 1911) have argued pedagogy means "a science of education." The typical argument against considering teaching a profession or science, however, is that it borrows its facts from other sciences, it has not formulated general principles that are universal, and teaching is mainly concerned with activities and practices. The French Nobel Prize for Literature author Michel Houellebecq (2019) called teaching an "intermediate profession." Is that sufficient?

We would argue that there is knowledge particular to teaching, there is an evidence base to the profession, and there is indeed a "practice of teaching". We would argue that the essence of the profession is not practice and activities, but evaluative thinking by means of deeper reasoning about diagnosis, choice of practice and interventions, fidelity of delivery, and evaluation of the impact of these practices on students.

Recent reviews

Two recent reviews show remarkable synergy with the ideas we are arguing in this book. Darling-Hammond, Flook, Cook-Harvey, Barron, and Osher (2020) reviewed the implications of the science of learning for educational practice. They argue that it is necessary to rethink institutions designed over a century ago based on factory models, and to shift to organizations focused on developmentally supportive relationships and coherent and well-integrated approaches. They argue for well-scaffolded instruction that intentionally supports the development of social, emotional, and academic skills, strategies, and mindsets, and culturally competent, personalized responses to the assets and needs that each individual child presents. Darling-Hammond and colleagues note the increased range of responsibility and outcomes teachers are now responsible for enhancing, and the necessity of access to integrated services and multitiered systems of support to address learning barriers both in and out of the classroom. They also note the need for explicit instruction in social, emotional, and cognitive skills, infusions of opportunities to learn, and the use of educative and restorative approaches to classroom management and discipline. They speak of exploratory inquiry based on explicit instruction, mastery improvement built on motivation mindsets, and feedback informed by appropriately high expectations.

Stigler and Miller (2018) reviewed the recent literature on expertise and expert performance in teaching. They noted that a lot of the expertise claims come from the early study of chess and music, but chess experts do not require the cooperation of the chessboard, and musicians aim to perform a Mozart concerto to the same high standard every time—and this is quite different from the expertise expected from teachers. They noted that everyone has spent over 10,000 hours in classrooms (as students), so surely it is 'common-sense' what it means to be a teacher, although of those 10,000 hours, only a small fraction of the time is spent engaged in learning. They noted that teaching is a cultural activity—teaching practices are more similar within a country than sometimes between countries. For example, in the United States, math classes there include much walking through example problems, then supervising students as they practice solving similar problems with the aim of overlearning these steps to then be used without teacher oversight and completed the steps without errors. Giving feedback is often lost on the students, as students do not know how to listen and engage with this feedback. In Japan, however, math teachers initially present difficult problems and allow students to struggle to solve them on their own. This way, students come up with a variety of solutions—some correct, some incorrect—which they then discuss in class. The aim is for students to deepen connections with core underlying mathematical ideas so they can be adaptive as they confront new problems. Whatever the teaching method, Stigler and Miller (p. 440) argued there were three core and distinct types of learning opportunities: productive struggle (no pain, no gain—students learn more when they are engaged in hard intellectual work), explicit connections (particularly related to what they already know, and an understanding of what success can look like), and deliberate practice (not repetitive, but opportunities that include being taught about alternative strategies and receiving, and being taught to understand informative feedback). Under this model, expert teachers are not defined as those who employ a set of best practices, but instead those who have (1) the ability to assess students' current knowledge both prior to and during instruction, (2) formulate clear learning goals, (3) consider a large number of strategies and routines in their repertoire, (4) make good judgments about which strategies are most appropriate in any given situation, and (5) are able to implement the strategies effectively to create learning opportunities for students.

Stigler and Miller consider developing expertise in analysis as the key to success, although we prefer developing expertise in evaluative thinking. They see expertise as teachers "who can observe and analyse practice in ways that could directly improve their ability to read a classroom situation select an appropriate strategies, and implement the strategy effectively, all while monitoring evidence of students thinking and learning" (p. 447). Specifically, those who can make careful observation and analysis of students' thinking and learning during a lesson can generate cause–effect theories that link the teacher's actions to students' thinking and learning, can generate alternative teaching strategies that can led to improve outcomes for all students, and can use what is working in the classroom to revise one's theory of cause–effect.

Both reviews by Darling-Hammond et al. and Stigler and Miller have much to say about the ways expert teachers 'think,' how they are open to their own biases and misconceptions, and how they, too, are excellent learners with a particular focus on learning more for themselves to maximize their impact on all their students.

The clinical evaluative model

Our major argument is that the teaching profession is based on addressing core questions using evaluative thinking with the aim of enhancing the learning lives of students. Hence, there is a focus on ways of thinking, seeking evidence relating to the core questions with a mission to enhance students' learning and well-being.

The six key educative questions underpinned by evaluative thinking are:

1. What is the student ready to learn and what evidence supports this?
2. What are the possible and preferred evidence-based interventions?
3. What is the expected impact on learning and how will this be evaluated?
4. How will the preferred intervention be resourced and implemented?
5. What happened and how can this be interpreted?
6. How do I collaborate with others (colleagues, students, research) to gain insight about my impact?

There are at least five ways of evaluative thinking:

1. Reasoning and critical thinking about evidence leading to 'where to next' recommendations.
2. Addressing the fidelity of implementation, continually checking for unintended consequences, and allowing for adaptations to maximize the value of outcomes and experiences for students.

3. Investigating potential biases and confounding factors that may lead to false conclusions or decisions.
4. Appreciating that the major aim of teaching is to have desirable, significant, and worthwhile impact on students.
5. Understanding others' points of view leading to judgments of value or worth.

This personifies the teacher as a diagnostician, deliberate intervener, and implementer, a problem-solver and hypothesis tester, a change agent and evaluator of their impact, and a collaborator and seeker of second opinions. The model depends on the centrality of the student and knowing what the students brings to the class through their skills (prior understanding, culture, home), will (dispositions, attitudes to schooling), and their thrill (motivations for learning); it depends on the teacher developing specialized knowledge and skills, appreciation and use of evidence and judgment in practice, accountability to professional standards, and rigorous academic and practical training before and during their learning lives as a teacher.

This clinical approach is not clinical in any cold, dispassionate sense, but rather a focus on evaluative judgments dependent on knowledge, relationships, and criteria of success, making the classroom an inviting place for students to come and engage in the challenge and joy of learning. It is a focus on a deep understanding of the students, as well as the surface, deep, and transfer outcomes from any series of lessons. It is the interplay of evidence from classrooms and research with judgment about the consequential impact of choosing high-probability interventions. It is more clinical reasoning (problem-solving, decision-making, judgment, openness to experience and evidence) than any kind of automatic processing or dependence on tests, robots, or impersonal information.

This clinical evaluative model has profound implications for the preservice education of students, who must develop a sufficiently deep knowledge base, develop the evaluative thinking skills, and learn how to collaborate with others about their thinking and impact. If this is mirrored in the tasks preservice teachers are asked to undertake, such as the clinical praxis assessments, then preservice students will quickly appreciate what instructors actually value. As critical is teaching initial teacher education students how to work in teams, how to have confidence in the investment of working in teams, and how to see the impact they are having through the eyes of the students.

The messaging for those considering teaching as a career, as well as for parents, policymakers, and the press, needs to be about enhancing the esteem of the profession—there is expertise, many teachers have it, and there are skills and knowledge needed to become and move through the profession; experience matters, but expertise trumps experience over time. Instead of seeking failure and using this as an excuse for one's own pet theories to improve schools, the focus should be on seeking and esteeming success. Nearly every report (and there are so many) usually includes a first chapter bemoaning how bad schools are, how the world is changing but schools are not, and noting that teaching is the same 'assembly line' model that has existed for the past 150 years. Instead, there needs to be a recognition that there are pockets (in some places, vast pockets) of excellence in our schools, and we should start by recognizing this excellence and expertise—the major question then becomes how to upscale this expertise.

There is also a need to consider ways to strengthen the career structure, professional standards, and pay of teachers (for example, advertise for teachers who can demonstrate evidence of impact, higher levels of evaluative thinking, and skills to coach and work in teams). Moreover, we need to consider mechanisms that facilitate teachers to work collaboratively across transdisciplinary professions to ensure that every child has the opportunity to grow and maximize their learning.

Teaching is a profession defined by the skills of evaluative reasoning focused on maximizing impact on the learning lives of students. This bar is high, but it is attainable and is already attained by many: it should be the rallying cry for all those who want to improve the quality and lives of teachers and who want to improve the quality and learning lives of students.

References

Abbott, A. A. (1988). *Professional choices: Values at work*. National Association of Social Workers Press.

ACARA. (n.d.). *The Australian Curriculum*. Retrieved from www.acara.edu.au/curriculum

ACER. (2013). *Partnerships for school improvement: Case studies of school-community partnerships in Australia*. Melbourne: Australian Council for Education Research. Retrieved from http://research.acer.edu.au/policy_analysis_misc/21/

Alter, J., & Coggshall, J. G. (2009). *Teaching as a clinical practice profession: Implications for teacher preparation and state policy*. New York: National Comprehensive Centre for Teacher Quality. Retrieved from https://eric.ed.gov/?id=ED543819

Anderson, L. M., Evertson, C. M., & Brophy, J. E. (1979). An experimental study of effective teaching in first-grade reading groups. *The Elementary School Journal, 79(4)*, 193–223.

Aronson, E., & Patnoe, S. (2010). *Cooperation in the classroom: The jigsaw method*. Pinter & Martin.

Arthur, J. (2003). Character education in British education policy. *Journal of Character Education, 1(1)*, 45–58.

Ashenden, D. (2018, 4 May). *An end to the industrial model of schooling?. Inside Story*. Retrieved at: https://insidestory.org.au/an-end-to-the-industrial-model-of-schooling/.

Atash, M. N., & Dawson, G. O. (1986). Some effects of the ISCS program: A meta-analysis. *Journal of Research in Science Teaching, 23(5)*, 377–385.

Atkinson, C., and Maleska, E. T. (1962). *The Story of Education*. Philadelphia: Chilton Books.

Atteberry, A., Loeb, S., & Wyckoff, J. (2013). *Do first impressions matter? Improvement in early career teacher effectiveness* (No. w19096). National Bureau of Economic Research.

Australian Institute of Teaching and School Leadership (AITSL). (2015). *National Professional Standards for Teachers*. Melbourne: Australian Institute for Teaching and School Leadership Limited.

Bangert, R. L., Kulik, J. A., & Kulik, C. L. C. (1983). Individualized systems of instruction in secondary schools. *Review of Educational Research, 53(2),* 143–158.

Barber, M., & Mourshed, M. (2007). *How the world's best-performing schools systems come out on top.* New York: McKinsey & Company. Retrieved from https://mckinsey.com/industries/public-and-social-sector/our-insights/how-the-worlds-best-performing-school-systems-come-out-on-top#.

Barnes, H. (1989). Structuring knowledge for beginning teaching. Knowledge base for the beginning teacher. In M.C. Reynolds and American Association of Colleges for teacher Education (Ed.), *Knowledge base for the beginning teachers* (pp. 13–22). New York: Pergamon Press.

Baweja, S., Santiago, C. D., Vona, P., Pears, G., Langley, A., & Kataoka, S. (2016). Improving implementation of a school-based program for traumatized students: Identifying factors that promote teacher support and collaboration. *School Mental Health, 8(1),* 120–131.

Berliner, D. C. (1992). The nature of expertise in teaching. In F.K. Oser, A. Dick, & J.L. Patry (Eds.) *Effective and responsible teaching: The new synthesis* (pp. 227–248). San Francisco: Jossey-Bass.

Berliner, D. C. (1994). Expertise: The wonders of exemplary performance. In J. N. Mangieri and C. Collins Block (Eds.), *Creating powerful thinking in teachers and students* (pp. 141–186). Ft. Worth, TX: Holt, Rinehart and Winston.

Berliner, D.C. (2004). Describing the behavior and documenting the accomplishments of expert teachers. *Bulletin of Science, Technology & Society, 24(3),* 200–212.

Berman, S., with Chaffee, S. & Sarmiento, J. (2018). *The practice base for how we learn: supporting students' social, emotional, and academic development-consensus statements of practice from the Council of Distinguished Educators.* Washington, DC: The Aspen Institute.

Berry, A.E. (2020). *Engaging students in classroom learning: Exploring upper primary teachers' perspectives on student engagement.* Unpublished doctoral dissertation, University of Melbourne, Australia.

Best, J. R., Miller, P. H., & Naglieri, J. A. (2011). Relations between executive function and academic achievement from ages 5 to 17 in a large, representative national sample. *Learning and individual differences, 21(4),* 327–336.

Biesta, G. (2007). Why "what works" won't work: Evidence-based practice and the democratic deficit in educational research. *Educational Theory, 57(1),* 1–22.

Blair, J.A. (1995). Informal logic and reasoning in evaluation. *New Directions for Evaluation, 68,* 71–80.

Blatchford, P., Kutnick, P., Baines, E., & Galton, M. (2003). Toward a social pedagogy of classroom group work. *International Journal of Educational Research, 39(1–2),* 153–172.

Blatchford, P., Pellegrini, A. D., & Baines, E. (2015). *The child at school: Interactions with peers and teachers.* Routledge.

Blatchford, P. & Russell, A. (2021). *Rethinking class size: The complex story of impact on teaching and learning.* London: UCL Press.

References

Blatchford, P., Russell, A., Bassett, P., Brown, P., & Martin, C. (2007). The role and effects of teaching assistants in English primary schools (Years 4 to 6) 2000–2003. Results from the Class Size and Pupil—Adult Ratios (CSPAR) KS2 Project. *British Educational Research Journal, 33*(1), 5–26.

Bolton, S., & Hattie, J.A.C. (2018). Cognitive and brain development: Executive function, Piaget, and the prefrontal cortex. *Archives of Psychology, 1(3),* 1–16.

Boshuizen, H. P. A., & Marambe, K. N. (2020). Misconceptions in medicine, their origin and development in education and working life. *International Journal of Educational Research, 100,* 101536.

Boshuizen, H. P. A., & Schmidt, H. G. (2019). The development of clinical reasoning expertise. In J. Higgs, G. M. Jensen, S. Loftus, & N. Christensen (Eds.). *Clinical reasoning in the health professions* (pp. 57–65). (4th edition). Edinburg UK: Elsevier.

Bowen, J. L. (2006). Educational strategies to promote clinical diagnostic reasoning. *New England Journal of Medicine, 355*(21), 2217–2225.

Bowles, T., Scull, J., Hattie, J., Clinton, J., Larkins, G., Cicconi, V., Kumar, D. & Arnup, J. L. (2016). Conducting psychological assessments in schools: Adapting for converging skills and expanding knowledge. *Issues in Educational Research, 26(1),* 10–28.

Breakspear, S. (2017). Embracing agile leadership for learning-how leaders can create impact despite growing complexity. *Australian Educational Leader, 39(3),* 68.

Broudy, H. S. (1956, January). Teaching—Craft or profession? *The Educational Forum 20*(2), 175–184.

Bryk, A., & Schneider, B. (2002). *Trust in schools: A core resource for improvement.* Russell Sage Foundation.

Buckley, J., Archibald, T., Hargraves, M., & Trochim, W. M. (2015). Defining and teaching evaluative thinking: Insights from research on critical thinking. *American Journal of Evaluation, 36(3),* 375–388.

Burn, K., & Mutton, T. (2013). *Review of 'research-informed clinical practice' in initial teacher education.* British Education Research Association (BERA). Retrieved from https://www.bera.ac.uk/wp-content/uploads/2014/02/BERA-Paper-4-Research-informed-clinical-practice.pdf.

Caplan, B. (2018). *The case against education: Why the education system is a waste of time and money.* Princeton University Press.

Carnegie Corporation of New York (2001). *Teachers for a new era: A national initiative to improve the quality of teaching.*

Carroll, A., Houghton, S., & Lynn, S. (2013). Friendship in school. In J. Hattie & E. Anderman (Eds.), *International Guide to Student Achievement* (pp. 70–73). Routledge.

Carter, K., Cushing, K., Sabers, D., Stein, P., & Berliner, D. (1988). Expert-novice differences in perceiving and processing visual classroom information. *Journal of Teacher Education, 39(3),* 25–31.

CCSSO Task Force on Teacher Preparation and Entry into the Profession (2012). *Our responsibility, our promise: Transforming teacher preparation and entry into the profession.* Washington DC: Council of Chief State School Officers.

Charlin, B., Boshuizen, H. P., Custers, E. J., & Feltovich, P. J. (2007). Scripts and clinical reasoning. *Medical Education*, *41(12)*, 1178–1184.

Chase, W. G., & Simon, H. A. (1973). The mind's eye in chess. In W.G. Chase (Ed.), *Visual information processing* (pp. 215–281). Academic Press.

Chi, M. T., Feltovich, P. J., & Glaser, R. (1981). Categorization and representation of physics problems by experts and novices. *Cognitive Science*, *5(2)*, 121–152.

Christie, F., & Derewianka, B. (2010). *School discourse: Learning to write across the years of schooling*. A&C Black.

City, E. A., Elmore, R. F., Fiarman, S. E., & Teitel, L. (2009). *Instructional rounds in education*. Cambridge, MA: Harvard Education Press.

Claxton, G. (2013). *What's the point of school?: Rediscovering the heart of education*. Oneworld Publications.

Clinton, J., Cairns, K., McLaren, P., & Simpson, S. (2014). *Evaluation of the Victorian deaf education institute real-time captioning pilot program 2013: Executive summary*. Commissioned by the Victorian Deaf Education Institute. Melbourne, Australia: Centre for Program Evaluation.

Clinton, J., & Dawson, G. (2018). Enfranchising the profession through evaluation: a story from Australia. *Teachers and Teaching*, *24*(3), 312–327.

Clinton, J., Dinham, S., Savage, G., Aston, R., Dabrowski, A., Gullickson, A., Calnin, G., & Arbour, G. (2015). *Evaluation of the implementation of the Australian professional standards for teachers*. Melbourne: AITSL.

Clinton, J.M., & Hattie, J.A.C. (2014). Teachers as evaluators – An empowerment evaluation approach. In Fetterman, D., Kaftarian, S., & Wandersman, A. (Eds.). *Empowerment evaluation: Knowledge and tools for self-assessment, evaluation capacity building, and accountability*. Thousand Oaks, CA: Sage.

Cochrane, A.L. with Blythe, M. (1989). *One man's medicine: an autobiography of Professor Archie Cochrane*. London: BMJ Books.

Cochran-Smith, M., & Boston College Evidence Team. (2009). "Re-culturing" teacher education: Inquiry, evidence, and action. *Journal of Teacher Education*, *60*(5), 458–468.

Condliffe L.E. (2000). *An elusive science: The troubling history of education research*. The University of Chicago.

Conroy, J., Hulme, M., & Menter, I. (2013). Developing a 'clinical' model for teacher education. *Journal of Education for Teaching*, *39(5)*, 557–573.

Cronbach, L. J., & Snow, R. E. (1977). *Aptitudes and instructional methods: A handbook for research on interactions*. Irvington.

Csikszentmihalyi, M. (2020). *Finding flow: The psychology of engagement with everyday life*. Hachette UK.

Cuban, L. (1993). *How teachers taught: Constancy and change in American classrooms, 1890–1990*. Teachers College Press.

Cuban, L. (2003). *Why is it so hard to get good schools?*. Teachers College Press.

Cuban, L. (2013). *Inside the black box of classroom practice: Change without reform in American education*. Harvard Education Press.

Darling-Hammond, L. (2000). How teacher education matters. *Journal of teacher education, 51*(3), 166–173.

Darling-Hammond, L., & Bransford, J. (2012). *Preparing teachers for a changing world: What teachers should learn and be able to do.* New York: Wiley.

Darling-Hammond, L., Flook, L., Cook-Harvey, C., Barron, B., & Osher, D. (2020). Implications for educational practice of the science of learning and development. *Applied Developmental Science, 24(2),* 97–140.

Darling-Hammond, L., & Lieberman, A. (eds.) (2012). *Teacher education around the world: Changing policies and practices.* New York: Routledge.

De Groot, A.D. (1946). *Het denken vanden schaker.* Amsterdam: Noord Holland.

DEECD. (2013). *Strategic plan 2013–2017.* Melbourne: Victorian Department of Education and Early Childhood Development. Retrieved from https://www.education.vic.gov.au/about/department/Pages/stratplan.aspx.

Derewianka, B., & Jones, P. (2016). *Teaching language in context.* New York, NY: Oxford University Press.

Dewey, J. (1938). *Experience and education.* New York: First Touchstone Edition, 64–67.

Dewey, J., & Bentley, A. F. (1960). *Knowing and the known* (No. 111). Boston: Beacon Press.

DeWitt, P. M. (2016). *Collaborative leadership: Six influences that matter most.* Corwin Press.

DeWitt, P. M. (2017). *School climate: Leading with collective efficacy.* Corwin Press.

Dickens, C. (1854). *Hard times.* London: Bradbury & Evans.

Dinham, S. (2006). *Teaching and teacher education: Some observations, reflections and possible solutions.* ED Ventures, Paper No. 2 (May), 3–20.

Dinham, S. (2016). *Leading learning and teaching.* ACER Press.

Dinham, S., Ingvarson, L., & Kleinhenz, E. (2008). *How can we raise the quality of school education so that every student benefits?* Melbourne: Business Council of Australia.

Dockterman, D. (2018). *Insights from 200+ years of personalized learning. NPJ Science of Learning, 3*(1), 1–6.

Donohoo, J. (2016). *Collective efficacy: How educators' beliefs impact student learning.* Corwin Press.

Dunst, C. J., Hamby, D. W., Howse, R. B., Wilkie, H., & Annas, K. (2020). Research synthesis of meta-analyses of preservice teacher preparation practices in higher education. *Higher Education, 10*(1), 29–47.

Elliott, E. (1996). What performance-based standards mean for teacher preparation. *Improving Professional Practice, 53*(6), 57–58.

Elmore, R.F. (2005). Accountable leadership. *Education Forum, 69*(2), 134-142

Elmore, R. F. (2006). International perspectives on school leadership for systemic improvement. In *OECD Activity on Improving School Leadership: International conference* (pp. 1–28).

Elmore, R. F. (2008). Leadership as the practice of improvement. In B. Pont, D. Nusche & D. Hopkins (Eds.). *Improving School Leadership Volume 2: Case Studies on System Leadership.* OECD.

Elmore, R. F. (2015). The future is learning, but what about schooling? *Inside Higher Ed*. Retrieved from https://www.insidehighered.com/blogs/higher-edgamma/future-learning-what-about-schooling

Elmore, R. F. (2019). The future of learning and the future of assessment. *ECNU Review of Education, 2(3)*, 328–341.

Elmore, R., & City, E. (2007). The road to school improvement: It's hard, it's bumpy, and it takes as long as it takes. *Harvard Education Letter, 23(3)*, 1–3.

Emler, N. (1990). A social psychology of reputation. *European Review of Social Psychology, 1*, 171–193.

Ericsson, K. A. (2014). *The road to excellence: The acquisition of expert performance in the arts and sciences, sports, and games*. Psychology Press.

Ericsson, K. A., Charness, N., Feltovich, P. J., & Hoffman, R. R. (2006). *The Cambridge handbook of expertise and expert performance*. New York.

Eva, K. W., Hatala, R. M., LeBlanc, V. R., & Brooks, L. R. (2007). Teaching from the clinical reasoning literature: combined reasoning strategies help novice diagnosticians overcome misleading information. *Medical Education, 41(12)*, 1152–1158.

Facione, N. C., & Facione, P. A. (2008). Critical thinking and clinical judgement. In *Critical thinking and clinical reasoning in the health sciences: A teaching anthology*, San Francisco, Academic Press.

Fazel, M., Hoagwood, K., Stephan, S., & Ford, T. (2014). Mental health interventions in schools in high-income countries. *The Lancet Psychiatry, 1(5)*, 377–387.

Fisher, A., & Scriven, M. (1997). *Critical thinking its definition and assessment. Centre for research in critical thinking*. CA, USA/Centre For Research In Critical Thinking: Edgepress.

Flesch, J. (2017). *Committed to learning – A history of education at the University of Melbourne*. The Miegunyah Press.

Folger, J. K., & Nam, C. B. (1967). *Education of the American population* (Vol. 3). US Department of Commerce, Bureau of the Census.

Forzani, F. M. (2014). Understanding "core practices" and "practice-based" teacher education: Learning from the past. *Journal of Teacher Education, 65(4)*, 357–368.

Gage, N. L. (1978). *The scientific basis of the art of teaching*. Teachers College Press.

Gamble, J. (2010). *Teacher professionalism: A literature review*. Johannesburg: JET Educational Services.

Glazerman, S., Mayer, D., & Decker, P. (2006). Alternative routes to teaching: The impacts of Teach for America on student achievement and other outcomes. *Journal of Policy Analysis and Management, 25(1)*, 75–96.

Goldfeld, S., O'Connor, M., Sayers, M., Moore, T., & Oberklaid, F. (2012). Prevalence and correlates of special health care needs in a population cohort of Australian children at school entry. *Journal of Developmental & Behavioral Pediatrics, 33(4)*, 319–327.

González, N., Moll, L. C., & Amanti, C. (Eds.). (2006). *Funds of knowledge: Theorizing practices in households, communities, and classrooms*. Routledge.

Goss, P., & Sonnemann, J. (2016). *Widening gaps: What NAPLAN tells us about student progress*. , Melbourne: Grattan Institute.

Gray, S., Romaniuk, H., & Daraganova, G. (2016). *Adolescents' relationships with their peers*. Retrieved at: https://growingupinaustralia.gov.au/research-findings/annual-statistical-reports/adolescents-relationships-their-peers

Griffin, P. (ed.) (2014). *Assessment for teaching*. Cambridge University Press.

Griffin, P. (ed.) (2018). *Assessment for teaching* (2nd edition). Cambridge University Press.

Grossman, P. (2008). Responding to our critics: From crisis to opportunity in research on teacher education. *Journal of Teacher Education, 59(1),* 10–23.

Grossman, P. (2010). *Learning to practice: The design of clinical experience in teacher preparation*. Washington DC: American Association of Colleges for Teacher Education & National Education Association.

Grossman, P. L., Valencia, S. W., Evans, K., Thompson, C., Martin, S., & Place, N. (2000). Transitions into teaching: Learning to teach writing in teacher education and beyond. *Journal of Literacy Research, 32(4),* 631–662.

Grubb, N., Jahr, H., Neumüller, J., & Field, S. (2005). *Equity in education thematic review: Finland country note:* OECD. Retrieved from http://www.oecd.org/education/innovation-education/36376641.pdf.

Guthrie, K.H., (2020). The weight of expectations: A themed narrative of gifted adolescent girls' reflections of being gifted. *Roeper Review, 42*(1), 25–37

Habermas, J. (1989). *The structural transformation of the public sphere*, trans. Thomas Burger. Cambridge: MIT Press.

Haigh, M., & Ell, F. (2014). Consensus and dissensus in mentor teachers' judgements of readiness to teach. *Teaching and Teacher Education, 40,* 10–21.

Haigh, M., Ell, F., & Mackisack, V. (2013). Judging teacher candidates' readiness to teach. *Teaching and Teacher Education, 34,* 1–11.

Hand, T. & MacKenzie, D. (2019). Data matters: Using data in a collective impact research and development project and the backbone role of Upstream Australia, *Parity, 32(6),* 16–17.

Hargreaves, A., & Shirley, D. (2018). What's wrong with well-being? *Educational Leadership, 76(2),* 58–63.

Hartley, S. S. (1977). *Meta-analysis of the effects of individually paced instruction in mathematics*. Unpublished doctoral dissertation, University of Colorado at Boulder.

Hattie, J.A.C. (1997). *From standards to accreditation via performance assessments: Some psychometric considerations relating to the NCATE "new" accreditation process.* Washington, DC.: National Council for Accreditation of Teacher Education.

Hattie, J.A.C. (2007). The paradox of reducing class size and improved learning outcomes. *International Journal of Education, 42,* 387–425.

Hattie, J.A.C. (2009). *Visible learning: A synthesis of over 800 meta-analyses relating to achievement*. London: Routledge.

Hattie, J.A.C., (2015a). *What does work in education: The politics of collaborative action*. Open Ideas at Pearsons. Retrieved from https://www.visiblelearning.com/groups/politics-collaborative-expertise

Hattie, J.A.C., (2015b). *What doesn't work in education: The politics of distraction*. Open Ideas at Pearsons. Retrieved from https://www.visiblelearning.com/groups/politics-distraction.

Hattie, J.A.C. (2015c). The applicability of visible learning to higher education. *Scholarship of Teaching and Learning in Psychology*, 1(1), 79-91.

Hattie, J.A.C., (2017). *Time for a reboot*. In T. Bentley & G. Savage (Eds.), *Status of Australian schools*. Melbourne University Press.

Hattie, J.A.C., Anderson, M., Clinton, J., & Rickards, F. (2015). Developing an evidence base model for the effects of teacher education programs on teacher candidates. In T.O. Seng & W.C. Liu (Eds.). *Teacher Effectiveness: Capacity building in a complex learning era*. Singapore: Cengage Learning Asia.

Hattie, J.A.C., Brown, G.T., & Keegan, P. (2005). A national teacher-managed, curriculum-based assessment system: Assessment Tools for Teaching & Learning (asTTle). *International Journal of Learning*, 10, 770–778. http://tinyurl.com/2gqhg8

Hattie, J.A.C., & Clarke, S. (2019). *Visible Learning: Feedback,*. Oxford, UK: Routledge

Hattie, J.A.C., & Donoghue, G. (2016). Learning strategies: A synthesis and conceptual model. *Nature: Science of Learning*, 1. doi:10.1038/npjscilearn.2016.13.

Hattie, J.A.C. & Hamilton, A. (2018). *Cargo Cults Must Die*. Released September, 2018. https://us.corwin.com/sites/default/files/cargo_cult_white_paper_john_hattie_final.pdf

Hattie, J.A.C., & Larsen, S.L. (2021). *The purposes of education*. Routledge.

Hattie, J.A.C., & Timperley, H. (2007). The power of feedback. *Review of Educational Research*, 77(1), 81–112.

Hayes, A., & Hegarty, P. (2002). Why teaching is not a profession—and how it might become one: A brief report of the findings of the APPLE project and some thoughts on the professionalisation of teaching. *Education*, 30(1), 30–35.

Henry, G.T., Bastian, K. C., & Fortner, C. K. (2011). Stayers and leavers: Early-career teacher effectiveness and attrition. *Educational Researcher*, 40(6), 271–280.

Hill, C.L. & Ridley, C.R. (2001). Diagnostic decision making: Do counsellors delay final judgements? *Journal of Counseling and Development*, 79, 98–104.

Holliday, T.W., Gautney, J. R., Friedl, L., Bailey, S., Harvati, K., Hublin, J. J., Smith, F.H., Stringer, C., Trinkaus, E., Wolpoff, M.H., & Zilhão, J. (2014). Right for the wrong reasons: Reflections on modern human origins in the post-Neanderthal genome era. *Current Anthropology*, 55(6), 696–724.

Holyoak, K. J. (1991). Symbolic connectionism: toward third-generation theories of expertise. In K.A. Erickson, & J. Smith (Eds.). *Towards a general theory of expertise: Prospects and Limits*. Cambridge University Press.

Horak, V. M. (1981). A meta-analysis of research findings on individualized instruction in mathematics. *The Journal of Educational Research*, 74(4), 249–253.

Houellebecq, M. (2019). *Serotonin*. London: William Heinemann.

House, E. R. (1995). Putting things together coherently: Logic and justice. *New Directions for Evaluation*, 1995(68), 33–48.

House, E. R. (2014). *Evaluating: Values, biases, and practical wisdom*. IAP.

Ingersoll, R. M., & Merrill, E. (2011). The status of teaching as a profession. In J. Ballantine & J. Spade (Eds.), *Schools and society: A sociological approach to education* (4th ed., pp. 185–189). CA: Pine Forge Press: Sage Publications.

Ingvarson, L., Beavis, A., & Kleinhenz, E. (2007). Factors affecting the impact of teacher education programmes on teacher preparedness: implications for accreditation policy. *European Journal of Teacher Education, 30*(4), 351–381.

Ingvarson, L., & Hattie, J. (Eds.). (2008). *Assessing teachers for professional certification: The first decade of the National Board for Professional Teaching Standards*. JAI/Elsevier.

Jenkins, L. (2015). *Optimize your school: It's all about the strategy*. Corwin Press.

Jensen, B. (2012). *Catching up: Learning from the best school systems in East Asia. Summary report*. Grattan Institute.

Jones, S. M., & Kahn, J. (2017). *The evidence base for how we learn: Supporting students' social, emotional, and academic development*. Mathematica Policy Research.

Jun, S. W., Ramirez, G., & Cumming, A. (2010). Tutoring adolescents in literacy: A meta-analysis. *McGill Journal of Education/Revue des sciences de l'éducation de McGill, 45*(2). 219–238

Kahneman, D. (2011). *Thinking, fast and slow*. Macmillan.

Kameniar, B., McLean Davies, L., Kinsman, J., Reid, C., Tyler, D., & Acquaro, D. (2017). Clinical Praxis Exams: Linking academic study with professional practice knowledge. In *A companion to research in teacher education* (pp. 53–67). Singapore: Springer.

Kania, J., & Kramer, M. (2011). *Collective impact* (pp. 36–41). FSG.

Katz, M. B. (1971). *Class, bureaucracy, and schools: The illusion of educational change in America*. New York: Praeger.

Kaufman, D. M., & Mann, K. V. (2014). Teaching and learning in medical education: how theory can inform practice. *Understanding Medical Education: Evidence, theory and practice, 2*, 7–29.

Kelley, P., & Camilli, G. (2007). *The impact of teacher education on outcomes in center-based early childhood education programs: A meta-analysis*. New Brunswick, NJ: National Institute for Early Education Research, Rutgers University.

Kennedy, M. (2016). Parsing the practice of teaching. *Journal of Teacher Education, 67*(1), 6–17.

Kini, T., & Podolsky, A. (2016). *Does teaching experience increase teacher effectiveness? A review of the research*. Palo Alto: Learning Policy Institute. Retrieved from https://learningpolicyinstitute.org/product/does-teaching-experience-increaseteacher-effectiveness-review-research

Kozbelt, A., Beghetto, R.A., & Runco, M.A. (2010). Theories of creativity. In R.J. Sternberg and J.C Kaufman (Eds.), *The Cambridge handbook of creativity*. Cambridge, UK: Cambridge University Press.

Krathwahl, D.R. (2002). A revision of Bloom's taxonomy: An overview. *Theory into Practice, 41*(4), 212–218.

Kriewaldt, J., McLean Davies, L., Rice, S., Rickards, F., & Acquaro, D. (2017). Clinical practice in education: Towards a conceptual framework. In *A companion to research in teacher education* (pp. 153–166). Singapore: Springer.

Kriewaldt, J., Nash, M., Windsor, S., Thornton, J., & Reid, C. (2018). Fostering professional learning through evidence-informed mentoring dialogues in school settings. In *Educating Future Teachers: Innovative Perspectives in Professional Experience* (pp. 157–172). Singapore: Springer.

Kriewaldt, J., & Turnidge, D. (2013). Conceptualising an approach to clinical reasoning in the education profession. *Australian Journal of Teacher Education, 38*(6), 7.

Kutnick, P., & Blatchford, P. (2014). *Effective group work in primary school classrooms*. Dordrecht: Springer.

Lagemann, E.C. (2000). *An elusive science: The troubling history of education research*. Chicago: University of Chicago Press

Lamb, S., & Rice, S. (2008). *Effective strategies to increase school completion report: Report to the Victorian Department of Education and Early Childhood Development*. Melbourne: DEECD. Retrieved from http://www.curriculum.edu.au/leader/effective_strategies_to_increase_school_completion.27002.html? issueID=11745

Larkin, J., McDermott, J., Simon, D. P., & Simon, H. A. (1980). Expert and novice performance in solving physics problems. *Science, 208*(4450), 1335–1342.

Laurens, K. R., Tzoumakis, S., Dean, K., Brinkman, S. A., Bore, M., Lenroot, R. K., Smith, M., Holbrook, A., Robinson, K.M., Stevens, R. & Harris, F. (2017). The 2015 Middle Childhood Survey (MCS) of mental health and well-being at age 11 years in an Australian population cohort. *BMJ Open, 7(6),* e016244.

Levin, H. (1988). Cost-effectiveness and educational policy. *Educational Evaluation and Policy Analysis, 10*(1), 51–69.

Levine, A. (2006). *Educating school teachers. Executive summary*. Education Schools Project.

Ling, D. (1988). *Foundations of spoken language for hearing-impaired children*. Alexander Graham Bell Association for the Deaf. Washington DC: Alexander Graham Bell Association for Deaf.

Loomis, A.K. (1939). The over-crowded curriculum. *The Journal of Educational Research, 32(6),* 457–459.

Lopez, O. S. (1995). *Classroom diversification: An alternative paradigm for research in educational productivity*. Unpublished doctoral dissertation, University of Texas, Austin.

Lortie, D. C. (2002). *Schoolteacher: A sociological study*. University of Chicago Press.

Louden, W. (2008). 101 damnations: The persistence of criticism and the absence of evidence about teacher education in Australia. *Teachers and Teaching: theory and practice, 14*(4), 357–368.

Louden, W., Heldsinger, S., House, H., Humphry, S., & Fitzgerald, D. (2010). Learning from teacher education: The impact of teacher education on knowledge of literacy and mathematics teaching. *Study of effective teacher education: Progress report*, 2.

References

Lupton, R., & Thomson, S. (2015). Socioeconomic inequalities in English schooling under the Coalition Government 2010–15. *London Review of Education*, *13*(2), 4–20.

Lyon, A. R., & Cotler, S. (2009). Multi-systemic intervention for school refusal behavior: Integrating approaches across disciplines. *Advances in School Mental Health Promotion*, *2*(1), 20–34.

MacKenzie, D. (2018). *Interim report: The Geelong project 2016–2017*. Melbourne: Swinburne University and Barwon Child Youth and Family Services, retrieved from https://apo.org.au/node/133006

MacKenzie, D. & Hand, T. (2019). Place Matters… Place-based 'collective impact': A new service delivery paradigm, *Parity*, *32*(2), 4–5.

MacKenzie, D., Hand, T., Zufferey, C., McNelis, S., Spinney, A. & Tedmanson, D. (2020). *Redesign of a homelessness service system for young people,* AHURI Final Report 327, Australian Housing and Urban Research Institute Limited, Melbourne, retrieved from http://www.ahuri.edu.au/research/final-reports/327

Main, S. (2009). Balanced development: a Māori model for beginning teacher support. *Asia Pacific Journal of Education*, *29*(1), 101–117.

Mann, H. (1867). *Life and works of Horace Mann*. Vol. 2. Walker, Fuller.

Masters, G. (2014). *Is school reform working?* Australian Council for Educational Research.

Mayer, D. (2006). The changing face of the Australian teaching profession: New generations and new ways of working and learning. *Asia-Pacific Journal of Teacher Education*, *34*(1), 57–71.

Mayer, D. (2014). Forty years of teacher education in Australia: 1974–2014. *Journal of education for teaching*, *40*(5), 461–473.

McCandless, T. (2017). *Schooled into place: A mixed methods social semiotic analysis of school marketing materials.* Unpublished doctoral dissertation, Deakin University, Australia.

McKenzie, P., Weldon, P. R., Rowley, G., Murphy, M., & McMillan, J. (2014). *Staff in Australia's schools. 2013: Main report on the survey*. Melbourne, ACER.

McLean Davies, L., Anderson, M., Deans, J., Dinham, S., Griffin, P., Kameniar, B., Page, J., Reid, C., Rickards, F., Tayler, C. & Tyler, D. (2013). Masterly preparation: embedding clinical practice in a graduate preservice teacher education programme. *Journal of Education for Teaching*, *39*(1), 93–106.

McLean Davies, L., Angelico, T., Hadlow, B., Kriewaldt, J., Rickards, F., Thornton, J., & Wright, P. (2017). Supporting the development of the profession: The impact of a clinical approach to teacher education. in T., Bentley & G.C Savage, (eds.). *Educating Australia: Challenges for the decade ahead* (pp. 209–226) Melbourne Univ. Publishing.

McLean Davies, L., Dickson, B., Rickards, F., Dinham, S., Conroy, J., & Davis, R. (2015). Teaching as a clinical profession: translational practices in initial teacher education–an international perspective. *Journal of Education for Teaching*, *41*(5), 514–528.

McMahon, J. A., & Thompson, M. (2014). Health and physical education and the online tertiary environment at two universities: Preservice teachers' perceived' readiness' to teach HPE. *Australian Journal of Teacher Education (Online)*, *39*(3), 120.

McRae, P.A. (2019a). *(Un)intended consequences: Artificial intelligence, automation and the future of public education*. Public lecture with Dominic Barton and Phillip McRae, retrieved from https://www.philmcrae.com/presentations.html

McRae, P.A. (2019b). *Think exponentially, act incrementally*. Alberta School Councils Association keynote, Edmonton, retrieved from http://philmcrae.com/presentations.html

Mitchell, M.L.W. (1987). *A comparison of the effectiveness of innovative instructional methods utilized in lower division mathematics as measured by student achievement: A meta-analysis of the findings.* Unpublished doctoral dissertation, University of Arizona.

Miyake, A., Friedman, N.P., Emerson, M.J., Witzki, A.H., Howerter, A., & Wager, T.D. (2000). The unity and diversity of executive functions and their contributions to complex 'frontal lobe' tasks: A latent variable analysis. *Cognitive Psychology*, *41*, 49-100.

Molloy C., Goldfeld S., Harrop C., Perini N. (2018). *Restacking the odds: Antenatal care: An evidence-based review of the relevant measures to assess quality, quantity, and participation*. Melbourne, Australia.

Mourshed, M., Chijioke, C., & Barber, M. (2010). *How the world's most improved school systems keep getting better*. New York: McKinsey & Company. Retrieved from https://mckinsey.com/industries/public-and-social-sector/our-insights/how-the-worlds-most-improved-school-systems-keep-getting-better

Murphy, S. C., Barlow, F. K., & von Hippel, W. (2018). A longitudinal test of three theories of overconfidence. *Social Psychological and Personality Science*, *9*(3), 353–363.

Nelson, E. E., Jarcho, J. M., & Guyer, A. E. (2016). Social re-orientation and brain development: An expanded and updated view. *Developmental Cognitive Neuroscience*, *17*, 118–127.

Nguyen, T. D., Pham, L., Springer, M. G., & Crouch, M. (2019). *The Factors of Teacher Attrition and Retention: An Updated and Expanded Meta-Analysis of the Literature*. Working paper.

Nias, J. (1997). Would schools improve if teachers cared less? *Education 3-13*, *25*(3), 11–22.

Nickerson, R. S., Perkins, D. N., & Smith, E. E. (2014). *The teaching of thinking*. Routledge.

Nietzsche, F. (2009/1889). *Twilight of the Idols, or, How to Philosophize with a Hammer* (Götzendämmerung, oder, Wie man mit dem Hammer philosophiert). Oxford: Oxford University Press.

Norman, G. (2005). Research in clinical reasoning: past history and current trends. *Medical Education*, *39*(4), 418–427.

Nous. (2011). *Schooling challenges and opportunities: A report for the review of funding school panel*. Melbourne: Nous Group. Retrieved from http://www.nousgroup.com/au/about-us/news/gonski-review-of-funding-for-schooling-released.

Nuthall, G. (2007). *The hidden lives of learners*. Wellington: NZCER Press.

OECD. (2011). *Strong performers and successful reformers in education: Lessons from PISA for the United States*: OECD Publishing. Retrieved from http://www.oecd.org/pisa/46623978.pdf

OECD. (2012). *Preparing teachers and developing school leaders for the 21st century: lessons from around the world*. Paris: OECD Publishing. Retrieved from http://www.oecd.org/site/eduistp2012/49850576.pdf

OECD. (2015). *Education policy outlook*. Paris: OECD Publishing. Retrieved from http://www.oecd.org/education/education-policyoutlook-2015-9789264225442-en.htm

Oreopoulos, P. (2007). Do dropouts drop out too soon? Wealth, health and happiness from compulsory schooling. *Journal of Public Economics, 91*, 2213–2229.

Parsons, S. A., Vaughn, M., Scales, R. Q., Gallagher, M. A., Parsons, A. W., Davis, S. G., ... & Allen, M. (2018). Teachers' instructional adaptations: A research synthesis. *Review of Educational Research, 88*(2), 205–242.

Patton, M. Q. (2005). Qualitative research. *Encyclopedia of statistics in behavioral science*. John Wiley & Sons.

Pearson, P. D., & Gallagher, G. (1983). The gradual release of responsibility model of instruction. *Contemporary Educational Psychology, 8*(3), 112–123.

Pham, L.D., Nguyen, T.D., & Springer, M.G. (2020). Teacher merit pay: A meta-analysis *American Educational Research Journal*, Advance online publication: https://doi:10.3102/0002831220905580

Pfost, M., Hattie, J., Dörfler, T., & Artelt, C. (2014). Individual differences in reading development: A review of 25 years of empirical research on Matthew effects in reading. *Review of Educational Research, 84*(2), 203–244.

Piaget, J., & Inhelder, B. (1969). *The psychology of the child*. Trans. Helen Weaver. New York: Basic Books.

Piaget, J., & Inhelder, B. (1973). *Memory and intelligence*. New York: Basic Books.

Popper, K. (1995). *Karl Popper: philosophy and problems* (Vol. *39*). Cambridge University Press.

Posner, M. I. (2008). Measuring alertness. *Annals of the New York Academy of Sciences, 1129*(1), 193–199.

Preskill, H., & Boyle, S. (2008). Insights into evaluation capacity building: Motivations, strategies, outcomes, and lessons learned. *The Canadian Journal of Program Evaluation, 23*(3), 147.

Productivity Commission. (2012). *Schools workforce*. Canberra: The Productivity Commission.

Qu, Y., & Becker, B. J. (2003, April). *Does traditional teacher certification imply quality? A meta-analysis*. Paper presented at the Annual Meeting of the American Educational Research Association, Chicago, IL.

Radosavljevich, P. R. (1911). Pedagogy as a science. *The Pedagogical Seminary*, *18*(4), 551–558.

Rickards, F., Toon, D. & Hattie, J. (2015). *Future school workforce: Requirements report produced for Price Waterhouse Coopers*. Melbourne, Australia.

Rikers, R. M., & Verkoeijen, P. P. (2007). Clinical expertise research: A history lesson from those who wrote it. *Medical Education*, *41*(12), 1115–1116

Rose, D., & Martin, J. R. (2012). *Learning to write, reading to learn: Genre, knowledge and pedagogy in the Sydney School*. Sheffield: Equinox.

Roser, M., & Ortiz-Ospina, E. (2016). Literacy. *Our world in data*. Published online at OurWorldInData.org. Retrieved from: https://ourworldindata.org/literacy.

Rowe, L. (2020). *Exploring collective intelligence in human groups*. Unpublished doctoral dissertation, University of Melbourne.

Royce, J. (1891). Is there a science of education? *Educational Review*, *1*(1), 23–24.

Rubie-Davies, C. M. (2010). Teacher expectations and perceptions of student attributes: Is there a relationship?. *British Journal of Educational Psychology*, *80*(1), 121–135.

Ryan, D. (2007). *Teachers told to take control*. Retrieved from https://www.theage.com.au/education/teachers-told-to-take-control-20070917ge5tvg.html.

Ryle, G. (1945, January). Knowing how and knowing that: The presidential address. In *Proceedings of the Aristotelian Society* (Vol. 46, pp. 1–16). Aristotelian Society, Wiley.

Sackett, D. L., Rosenberg, W. M., Gray, J. M., Haynes, R. B., & Richardson, W. S. (1996). Evidence based medicine. *BMJ: British Medical Journal*, *313*(7050), 170.

Sahlberg, P. (2012). A model lesson: Finland shows us what equal opportunity looks like. *American Educator*, *36*(1), 20–27.

Sahlberg, P. (2014). *Finnish lessons 2.0: What can the world learn from educational change in Finland?* Teachers College Press.

Schleicher, A. (2016). *Colombia should improve equity and quality of education*, retrieved from http://www.oecd.org/education/colombia-shouldimprove-equity-and-quality-of-education.htm.

Schmidt, H. G., & Rikers, R. M. (2007). How expertise develops in medicine: knowledge encapsulation and illness script formation. *Medical Education*, *41*(12), 1133–1139.

Schmidt, W. H., Cogan, L., & Houang, R. (2011). The role of opportunity to learn in teacher preparation: An international context. *Journal of Teacher Education*, *62*(2), 138–153.

Shulman, L. S. (1986). Those who understand: Knowledge growth in teaching. *Educational Researcher*, *15*(2), 4-14.

Schuwirth, L. W., Verheggen, M. M., Van der Vleuten, C. P. M., Boshuizen, H. P. A., & Dinant, G. J. (2001). Do short cases elicit different thinking processes than factual knowledge questions do?. *Medical Education*, *35*(4), 348–356.

Schwandt, T. A. (2018). Evaluative thinking as a collaborative social practice: The case of boundary judgement making. *New Directions for Evaluation*, *2018*(158), 125–137.

Sclafani, S. (2008). *Rethinking human capital in education: Singapore as a model for teacher development*. Queenstown, MD: The Aspen Institute. Retrieved from https://assets.aspeninstitute.org/content/uploads/files/content/docs/education/SingaporeEDU.pdf.

Scriven, M. (1967). The methodology of evaluation. *AERA Monograph Series on Curriculum Evaluation, 1, Perspectives of Curriculum Evaluation*.

Scriven, M. (1979). Newer perspectives in the evaluation of school improvement programs: Goal-free evaluation, school improvement profile. In P. Hood (Ed.), *New perspectives on planning, management, and evaluation in school evaluation* (pp. 48–56). Far West Laboratory.

Scriven, M. (1981). *The logic of evaluation*. California: USE: Edgepress.

Scriven, M. (1991). Pros and cons about goal-free evaluation. *Evaluation Practice, 12*(1), 55–62.

Scriven, M. (1994). Duties of the teacher. *Journal of Personnel Evaluation in Education, 8*(2), 151–184.

Scriven, M., & Paul, R. (1987). Critical thinking. In *The 8th Annual International Conference on Critical Thinking and Education Reform*, CA.

Seligman, M. (2018). PERMA and the building blocks of well-being. *The Journal of Positive Psychology, 13*(4), 333–335.

Shanteau, J. (1992). Competence in experts: The role of task characteristics. *Organizational Behavior and Human Decision Processes, 53*(2), 252–266

Sharratt, L., & Planche, B. (2016). *Leading collaborative learning: Empowering excellence*. Corwin Press.

Shulman, L. S. (2015). PCK: Its genesis and exodus. In A. Berry, P. Friedrichsen, & J. Loughran (Eds.), *Re-examining pedagogical content knowledge in science education* (pp. 13–23). Routledge.

Slavin, R. E., Lake, C., Davis, S., & Madden, N.A. (2011). Effective programs for struggling readers: A best-evidence synthesis. *Educational Research Review, 6(1)*, 1–26.

Smith, T.W., Baker, W.K., Hattie, J.A., & Bond, L. (2008). A validity study of the certification system of the National Board for Professional Teaching Standards. In L. Ingvarson & J.A.C. Hattie (Eds.), *Assessing teachers for professional certification: The first decade of the National Board for Professional Teaching Standards* (pp. 345–380). Advances in Program Evaluation Series #11. Oxford, Elsevier.

Snook, I (2003). *The ethical teacher*. Dunsmore: Palmerston North.

Spellman, B.A., & Schauer, F. (2012). Legal reasoning. *Virginia Public Law and Legal Theory Research Paper*, (2012-09).

Stansbury, K., & Zimmerman, J. (2002). Smart induction programs become lifelines for the beginning teacher. *Journal of Staff Development, 23*(4), 10–17.

Stigler, J.W., & Miller, K. F. (2018). Expertise and expert performance in teaching. In K.A. Ericsson, R.R. Hoffman, A. Kozbelt, & A.M. Williams (Eds.), *The Cambridge handbook of expertise and expert performance* (pp. 431–452).

Stojiljković, S., Djigić, G., & Zlatković, B. (2012). Empathy and teachers' roles. *Procedia-Social and Behavioral Sciences, 69*, 960–966.

Swanson, H. L., & Alloway, T. P. (2012). Working memory, learning, and academic achievement. In K. R. Harris, S. Graham, T. Urdan, C. B. McCormick, G. M. Sinatra, & J. Sweller (Eds.), *APA handbooks in psychology. APA educational psychology handbook, Vol. 1. Theories, constructs, and critical issues* (p. 327–366). American Psychological Association.

Tan, O. S., Low, E. L., & Hung, D. (Eds.). (2017). *Lee Kuan Yew's educational legacy: The challenges of success*. Springer.

Teacher Education Ministerial Advisory Group (TEMAG). (2014). *Action now: classroom ready teachers report*. Canberra: Department of Education Retrieved from https://docs.education.gov.au/action-now-classroom-ready-teachers-report

Timperley, H. (2010). Using evidence in the classroom for professional learning. *Presented to the Ontario Education Research Symposium*. Retrieved from https://www.educationalleaders.govt.nz/Leading-learning/Professional-learning/Using-evidence-in-the-classroom-for-professional-learning.

Timperley, H., & Alton-Lee, A. (2008). Reframing teacher professional learning: An alternative policy approach to strengthening valued outcomes for diverse learners. *Review of Research in Education, 32*(1), 328–369.

Tomlinson, C. A. (2005). Grading and differentiation: Paradox or good practice?. *Theory into Practice, 44*(3), 262–269.

Tucker, M. S. (ed.) (2014). Chinese lessons: Shanghai's rise to the top of the PISA League tables. *National Center on Education and the Economy*. Retrieved from https://eric.ed.gov/?id=ED556320

Tyack, D. B., & Cuban, L. (1995). *Tinkering toward utopia*. Harvard, University Press.

UNESCO. (1996). *Treasure Within: Report to UNESCO of the International Commission on education for the twenty-first century*. Paris: UNESCO Publishing. Retrieved from https://unesdoc.unesco.org/ark:/48223/pf0000109590.

UNESCO. (2013). *Towards universal learning: What every child should learn: Learning Metrics Task Force Report 1:* UNESCO Institute for Statistics and the Center for Universal Education at the Brookings Institution. Retrieved from https://www.brookings.edu/product/learning-metrics-task-force/

Ure, C. L. (2010). Reforming teacher education through a professionally applied study of teaching. *Journal of Education for Teaching, 36*(4), 461–475.

van Mook, W. N., de Grave, W. S., Wass, V., O'Sullivan, H., Zwaveling, J. H., Schuwirth, L. W., & van der Vleuten, C. P. (2009). Professionalism: evolution of the concept. *European Journal of Internal Medicine, 20*(4), e81–e84.

Victorian Competition and Efficiency Commission. (2013). *Making the grade: Autonomy and accountability in Victorian schools*. Melbourne:Victorian Competition and Efficiency.

Victorian Curriculum and Assessment Authority (n.d.). *Victorian Curriculum*. Retrieved from https://victoriancurriculum.vcaa.vic.edu.au/

Vo, A. T. (2013). Visualizing context through theory deconstruction: A content analysis of three bodies of evaluation theory literature. *Evaluation and Program Planning, 38*, 44–52.

References

Vo, A. T., & Archibald, T. (2018). New directions for evaluative thinking. *New Directions for Evaluation, 2018*(158), 139–147.

Vreeman, R. C., & Carroll, A. E. (2007). A systematic review of school-based interventions to prevent bullying. *Archives of Pediatrics & Adolescent Medicine, 161*(1), 78–88.

Walker, S. C., Kerns, S. E. U., Lyon, A. R., Bruns, E. J., & Cosgrove, T. J. (2010). Impact of school-based health center use on academic outcomes. *Journal of Adolescent Health, 46*(3), 251–257.

Ward, J., & Thomas, G. (2013). *National Standards: School sample monitoring and evaluation project, 2010–2012*. Report to the Ministry of Education. Ministry of Education.

Waxman, H. C., Wang, M. C., Anderson, K. A., Walberg, H. J., & Waxman, C. (1985). Adaptive education and student outcomes: A quantitative synthesis. *The Journal of Educational Research*, 228–236.

Weiss, C. H. (1998). *Evaluation: Methods for studying programs and policies*. Pearson College Division.

Weldon, P. (2015, March). *The teacher workforce in Australia: Supply, demand and data issues, Policy Insights 2*. Retrieved from http://research.acer.edu.au/policyinsights/2/

West, E. G. (1965). *Education and the State*. London: Institute for Economic Affairs.

West-Burnham, J., Farrar, M., & Otero, G. G. (2007). *Schools and communities: working together to transform children's lives*. Stafford: Network Continuum Education.

Whitehead, A. N. (1929). *The function of reason*. Boston: Beacon Press.

Widen, M., Mayer-Smith, J., & Moon, B. (1998). A critical analysis of the research on learning to teach: Making the case for an ecological perspective on inquiry. *Review of Educational Research, 68*(2), 130–178.

Wilkinson, G. (2005). Workforce remodelling and formal knowledge: The erosion of teachers' professional jurisdiction in English schools. *School Leadership and Management, 25*(5), 421–439.

Wilkinson, R., & Pickett, K. (2011). *The spirit level: Why greater equality makes societies stronger*. Bloomsbury Publishing USA.

Willett, J. B., Yamashita, J. J., & Anderson, R. D. (1983). A meta-analysis of instructional systems applied in science teaching. *Journal of Research in Science Teaching, 20*(5), 405–417.

Young, M., Lambert, D., Roberts, C., & Roberts, M. (2014). *Knowledge and the future school: Curriculum and social justice*. Bloomsbury Publishing.

Zeichner, K., Payne, K. A., & Brayko, K. (2015). Democratizing teacher education. *Journal of Teacher Education, 66*(2), 122–135.

Zhang, L., Basham, J. D., & Yang, S. (2020). *Understanding the implementation of personal learning: A research synthesis*. Educational Research Review, 100339.

Index

Page numbers in *italics* refer to figures, those in **bold** indicate tables.

'abstract knowledge' 80
ACER 123, 133
adaptation 70
adolescence 29
Alter, J. and Coggshall, J.G. 80, 99–100
anchoring bias 71
Anderson, L.M. et al. 93
anecdotal fallacy 73
Aristotle 23, 149
Arthur, J. 123–124
Aspen Institute 125–126
assessments 140–142; developmental continuum 35–36; formative 47; PISA 7–8, 126; preservice teachers **113**; student teacher selection (TCAT) 118–119; Teacher Candidates: Clinical Praxis Exam (CPE) xiv, 107–112; teacher performance (TPA) 103
Atteberry, A. et al. 97
audiology and hearing-impairment viii–x, 12, 82
Australian Child and Adolescent Survey of Mental Health and Well-being 126
Australian Early Development Census 11, 126
Australian Institute for Teachers and School Leaders (AITSL) xii, 87, 102, 103, 114–115
autonomy 85, 86–87, 89; forms of 20–21

Barber, M. & Mourshed, M. 84, 144, 145
Baweja, S. et al. 128
Bell and Lancaster monitorial model of schooling 17
Berliner, D.C. 56, 57, 71, 84, 89; et al. 55–56
Berman, S. 125–126

Berry, A.E. 140
biases, potential 71, 73–74
Blair, J.A. 73
Blatchford, P. et al. 86
Bolton, S. & Hattie, J.A.C. 27, 28
Bowen, J.L. 100
Breakspear, S. 70
BRIDGE program 127
Broudy, H.S. 84
Bryk, A. & Schneider, B. 27
Buckley, J. et al. 73, 74

Caplan, B. 6–7
Carnegie Corporation 52, 98
Carroll, A. et al. 29
case-management approach 130–133
CBITS program 128
centrality of the student 25, 32, 66–67, 72, 95, 152
challenge and engagement 140
character education 123–124
Charlin, B. et al. 100–101
Chase, W.G. & Simon, H.A. 53
Chi, M.T. et al. 55
child development phases 27–29
chunking 53, 55
City, E.A. et al. 48
class sizes 24
clinical evaluative model 151–153
clinical practice: multidisciplinary approach 126–133; six questions 32–33, 52; teaching role 138; *see also* teacher education (ITE) for clinical profession

Index

Clinical Praxis Exam (CPE) xiv, 107–112
Clinton, J. et al. 25, 102
Cochran-Smith, M. & Boston College Evidence Team 38, 41, 96
codeveloping success criteria 43–44
cognitive biases 71, 73
Cognitive–Behavioral Intervention for Trauma in Schools (CBITS) program 128
collaboration/partnerships 11; evidence-based teaching cycle 42, 44, 48, 50, 51–52; multidisciplinary approach 126–133; professional practice 83–84; schools and other services 122, 125, 143; schools–communities 133–139; teacher education (ITE), xiv, 107, 108, 114, 112, 115, 117
collaborator, teacher as 75
collegial observation 48–49
collegial sharing 37
colocating services 128–129
communities–school collaboration 133–139
compulsory schooling and professional autonomy 19–21
confirmation bias 71, 73
Conroy, J. et al. 99
COVID-19 pandemic vii
craft, teaching as 86–87
critical thinking 74; and reasoning 66–69
Csikszentmihalyi, M. 53–54
Cuban, L. 21, 70; Tyack, D.B. & 3–4
curricula: debates 21–22; developmental continuum 35; international shift 140; knowledge vs. practice approaches 93–94

Darling-Hammond, L. 96; & Lieberman, A. 92–93; et al. 127–128, 142, 149–150, 151
De Groot, A.D. 53
decision-making: and adaptation 70; medical education 101; stages of evidence-based teaching cycle 34–52; teaching as profession 79, 80, 85–86
deep and surface learning 60, 61
deep knowledge base *see* expertise of teachers; knowledge/knowledge base
deliberate practice 54, 55
'democratic citizenship' 124
developmentally vulnerable students 11, 126
Dewey, J. 149; & Bentley, A.F. 75
Diagnosis, Intervention, Implementation, Evaluation (DIIE) 62, 70–72, 75, 82, 83, 89–90
Dickens, C. 21
Dinham, S. 100; et al 85

disability 11–12; team approach to support student learning (case study) 131–132
disadvantage: case studies 134, *135*, 136–137; inequality and 124–126
Dunst, C.J. et al. 117
duties of teachers 30

early childhood teacher (example) 36
early intervention, COSS Model of (case study) 134, *135*
early primary teacher (example) 44–45
e–asTTle tool 141
EdReports 42
effect sizes: performance-based pay 85, 88; personalized learning 18, **19**; teacher education 96; teaching methods 39; Visible Learning research 59
Elmore, R.F. x, 84–85, 87, 89, 121, 122
empathy 75
engagement and assessment 139–142
engineering profession 81, 83
English language-center teacher (example) 50
enthusiasm for learning (Jenkins curve) 9–10, 140
Ericsson, K.A. 54, 55, 57; et al. 149
evaluative thinking 55, 59, 61, 63–66, 89–90, 99; and characteristics of professions 80–84; clinical evaluative model 151–153; critical thinking and reasoning 66–69; maximizing impact on student learning 72; others' points of view 74–75; potential biases and confounding factors 71, 73–74; and six key questions **64**
evidence-based teaching 11–12; model 32–33; stages of cycle 34–52
evidence, defining 33–34
executive functioning 27–228
expected impact of learning and evaluation 43–45
experienced and expert teachers, compared 57–59
expertise of teachers 11–12; development 114–118; knowledge and practices 31–32; learning strategies 72; need for recognition 5–6; notion of 149; proposed reforms 148–149; research 55–59, 150–151
experts, characteristics of 53–55

Facione, N.C. & Facione, P.A. 101
fallibilism 74
falsifiable evidence/falsification 73, 74
Fazel, M. et al. 127

Finland 85, 128, 133, 145
flexibility 70
formative assessment 47

Geelong Project–COSS Model of early intervention (case study) 134, *135*
gifted students 11, 126; secondary English teacher (case study) 138–139
Glass, G. xii
Glazerman, S. et al. 96
Global Education Reform Movement (GERM) 139–140
goal-free model of evaluation 70–71
Goldfeld, S. et al. 11
government and private schools, compared 8–9
Gray, S. et al. 29
Griffin, P. 49, 141
Grossman, P. 95; et al. 96–97
groups 25–27

Habermas, J. 74
Haigh, M. & Ell, F. 113–114; et al. 113
halo effect 73
Hattie, J.A.C. xi–xii, 6, 7, 8, 18, 24, 61, 70; & Bolton, S. 27, 28; & Clark, S. 43; & Donoghue, G. 23, 39, 140; et al. 94–95; & Hamilton, A. 3; Ingvarson, L. 87; and Larsen, S. 74; & Timperley, H. 111
Hayes, A. & Hegarty, P. 89
health centers, school-based 128, 130–133
hearing-impairment viii–x, 12, 82
Henry, G.T. et al. 147
highly accomplished and lead teachers (HALTs) 87–88
Houellebecq, M. 149
House, E.R. 63–65, 73
hypothesis tester, teacher as 74

impact on learning: collaboration to evaluate 51–52; expected 43–45; maximizing 72; teacher education (ITE) 94–97
implementation: evaluative thinking 69–72; monitoring and measuring *46*
income and educational attainment 124–125
individualism 24–25
individualized instruction 17–18, **19**, 24
induction programs for newly qualified teachers 115, *116*, 118
inequality and disadvantage 124–126
Ingvarson, L. & Hattie, J. 87; et al. 88
initial teacher education (ITE) *see* teacher education (ITE) for clinical profession

interpretation 49–50; potential biases 71, 73–74
intervenor, teacher as 71–72
interventions: possible and preferred 38–43; resourcing and implementing 45–49

Jenkins curve: enthusiasm for learning 9– 10, 140
Jigsaw method 39, 60
judgments of value 74–75
junior secondary teacher (example) 40–41

Kahneman, D. 71
Kameniar, B. xiv
Kania, J. & Kramer, M. 133
Kaufmann, D.M. & Mann, K.V. 101
Kennedy, M. 93–94, 96
Kini, T. & Podolsky, A. 147
knowledge/knowledge base 88–89; 'abstract knowledge' 80; importance in teacher educator 100–101; and knowing 22–24; vs practice approaches 93–94; and practices of expert teachers 31–32
Kriewaldt, J. et al. 49, 97, 112
Kutnick, P. & Blatchford, P. 25–26

Lancet Psychiatry 127
Larkin, J. et al. 53
Larsen, S. 74
learner profiles 140–141
learning expert, teacher as 72
legal profession 80–81
Levin, B. 7
Ling, D. x, 12
literacy and illiteracy rates 3, *4*, 121
longitudinal studies of teacher education 96–97
Louden, W. 102; et al. 96
Lupton, R. & Thomson, S. 9

McCandless, T. 8–9
McDonald, R. xi
McLean Davies, L. et al. 114
McMahon, J.A. & Thompson, M. 98
McRae, P.A. 124
Main, S. 115
Mann, H. 20
maximizing impact on student learning 72
Mayer, D. 95, 102
medical education 99–101, 116–117
medical profession 81–82, 83
Melbourne Graduate School of Education (MGSE) 103; Assessment Research Centre 141; Clinical Praxis Exam (CPE) xiv, 107–112; MTeach model x, 104–107

mental health 125–126, 127, 128
metacognition 35
mind frames model 61–62
Mourshed, M. & Barber, M. 84, 144, 145; et al. 88
multidisciplinary approach 126–133
music profession 81

Nationally Consistent Collection of Data for School Students with Disability 11
Nelson, E.E. et al. 29
Nguyen, T.D. et al. 85
Nickerson, R.S. et al. 23
Norman, G. 101, 117
'not invented here' effect 73
novice and expert teachers: compared 55–56, 59, 71; development 114–118
numeracy and innumeracy rates 3, 121
'nurture hubs' 128
Nuthall, G. 100, 140

OECD 6; PISA 7–8, 126
online programs for teacher education 97, 98
ostrich effect 73
others' points of view, understanding 74–75
Our Place model: holistic approach to tackling disadvantage (case study) 136–137
overeducation claim 6–7
overlearning 53, 54, 55

Parsons, S.A. et al. 70
partnerships *see* collaboration/partnerships
pattern recognition 53, 55
Patton, M.Q. 65
pay/remuneration 85, 86, 88, 120, 146
peer relations in adolescence 29
performance-based pay 85, 88
PERMA framework 122–123, 142
personal attributes and professional practices of preservice teachers 113–114
personalized learning 18, **19**, 24
Piaget, J. and Indhelder, B. 27–28
PISA 7–8, 126
Popper, K. 73, 74
post-compulsory schooling 29
Preskill, H. & Boyle, S. 65
private and government schools, compared 8–9
problem-solver, teacher as 74
professional autonomy *see* autonomy
professional practice 80, 83–84, 89

profession(s): definition of 79–80; evaluative thinking and characteristics of 80–84; knowledge base of teaching 88–89; teacher education and rise of standards 87–88; teaching as 84–86; vs teaching as craft 86–87

Qu, Y. et al. 96

random-controlled studies of teacher education 96
readiness: to learn 34–37; to teach **113**
Reid, C. xii–xvi
relational trust 26–27
remuneration/pay 85, 86, 88, 120, 146
reputation in adolescence 29
research and evaluation, compared 65
resources 42
resource teachers: learning and behavior (RTLBs) 128–129
Restacking the Odds project 125
Rickards, F. viii–x
Roser, M. & Oritz-Ospina, E. 3, *4*
Royce, J. 149
rubrics 35
Ryle, G. 23

Sackett, D.L. et al. 98
Sahlberg, P. 139
salaries *see* remuneration/pay
Schmidt, H.G. & Rikers, R.M. 117
school model vii; experience of students 9–10; history of successes and limitations 3–5; need for new 5–7, 146–148; reforms 144–145; time for a reboot 7–8
schooling: broadening outcomes of 21–24; refocusing 124–126
school-refuser, supporting return to school (case study) 129–130
schools: increasing demands on 121–124; as social settings 25–27
Schuwirth, L.W. et al. 117
Schwandt, T.A. 74
science of education/learning 149–150
Scriven, M. 30, 65, 70–71, 73
self-fulfilling prophecy 73
Seligman, M. 122–123, 142
senior secondary teacher (example) 37
Shanteau, J. 90
Shulman, L.S. 88–89
Singapore 88, 145
Smith, T.W. et al. 57

social and emotional skills 142
social relations 25–27
Stansbury, K. & Zimmerman, J. 115
Stigler, J.W. and Miller, K.F. 150–151
Stryker, E. 74
students: centrality of 25, 32, 66–67, 72, 95, 152; experience of 9–10
success criteria 43–44
supportive relationships 26
surface and deep learning 60, 61

Teacher Capability Assessment Tool (TCAT) for student teacher selection 118–119
teacher education (ITE) for clinical profession 92–94; and clinical practice 98–100; evidence of impact 94–97; importance of educator knowledge 100–101; novice to expert development 114–119; prospective teachers 97–98; recent claims for reform 101–114
Teacher Education Ministerial Advisory Group (TEMAG) 102–103
teacher education and rise of standards 87–88
teacher recruitment 118–119
Teachers for a New Era (Carnegie Corporation) 52, 98
teaching assistants/aides 86
teaching performance assessment (TPA) 103

'thinking aloud' method 53
Timperley, H. 51
& Alton-Lee, A. 87; & Hattie, J.A.C. 111
'twenty-first century' skills 22–23
Tyack, D.B. & Cuban, L. 3–4

UNESCO 122, 123
United Nations Sustainability Goals for Education 123
upper primary teacher (example) 47–48

video games 140
Visible Learning xii, 59–62
Vo, A.T. 65–66
Vreeman, R.C. & Carroll, A.E. 125

Walker, S. et al. 128
Weiss, C.H. 65
whole-child approach 125–126, 132–133
Wilkinson, R. & Pickett, K. 124
working backwards 53–54

'young adulthood' 29
Young, M. et al. 22

Zeichner, K. et al. 100
Zhang, L. & Basham, J.D. 18, 24

For Product Safety Concerns and Information please contact our EU representative GPSR@taylorandfrancis.com
Taylor & Francis Verlag GmbH, Kaufingerstraße 24, 80331 München, Germany

www.ingramcontent.com/pod-product-compliance
Lightning Source LLC
Chambersburg PA
CBHW081842230426
43669CB00018B/2788